Marriage
Matters

Marriage Matters

Perspectives on the Private and
Public Importance of Marriage

Janice Shaw Crouse

Transaction Publishers
New Brunswick (U.S.A.) and London (U.K.)

This book is printed on acid-free paper that meets the American National Standard for Permanence of Paper for Printed Library Materials.

Library of Congress Catalog Number: 2011022101
ISBN: 978-1-4128-4607-3
Printed in the United States of America

Library of Congress Cataloging-in-Publication Data
Crouse, Janice Shaw.
    Marriage matters : perspectives on the private and public importance of marriage / Janice Shaw Crouse.
        p. cm.
    Includes index.
    ISBN 978-1-4128-4607-3
    1. Marriage. 2. Marriage—Social aspects. I. Title.
        HQ519.C76 2012
        173—dc23
                2011022101

This book is dedicated to
Gilbert L. Crouse Sr.
my husband—the love of my life.

Together we have forged a strong and happy marriage
that matters...to us and to our children:
Jack and Charmaine Crouse Yoest
and
Gilbert Jr. and Naomi Liles Crouse
and to our grandchildren:
Hannah, John, Helena, Sarah, and James Yoest
Gilbert Lewis Crouse III (Lewis) and Charles

Contents

Acknowledgments   ix

1.   Introduction   1

Part I: The Groundwork for Strong Marriages   15

2.   Preserving Love and Romance   17

3.   Bring Back Dating   39

Part II: Marriage: Safe Haven for Sexuality   63

4.   Centrality of Sex   65

5.   Why Casual Sex Causes Harm   89

Part III: Marriage: The Impact on the Private Sector   113

6.   Marriage Benefits for Individuals   115

7.   The Benefits of Marriage for Children   139

Part IV: Marriage: The Impact on the Public Sector   159

8.   The Ramifications of Same-Sex "Marriage"   161

9.   Legislative and Public Policy Challenges to the
     Institution of Marriage   183

10. Conclusion   209

Appendix   221

Index   227

Acknowledgments

I want to express my deep appreciation to my mother, the Reverend Ruth Baird Shaw, who modeled the sacredness of marriage, the sacrificial love of a parent, the generous spirit of service and exemplifies what it means to be a lady—accomplished, well-educated, wise, warm, and gracious. At eighty-eight, mother's award-winning blog is read by thousands; her latest book comes out the summer of 2012.

I also want to express appreciation to the memory of my father, the Reverend Charles C. Shaw, who loved me unconditionally, would have given his life for me, believed in me, supported my every effort and taught me to recognize and respect integrity and authenticity in a man. A veteran of WWII, he was truly a member of the "Greatest Generation" and to his seven children he was a great daddy!

I want to thank my associates at Concerned Women for America who provided their skills, talents, and insights to enrich the messages of this book—Brenda Zurita, Lauren Levy, Hannah Swanson, Rebekah Tooley, and Kristin Dowd.

I especially want to thank my husband, Gilbert L. Crouse Sr. whose editing and insights contributed some magical lines in this book.

1

Introduction

Two pure souls fused into one by an impassioned love—friends, counselors—a mutual support and inspiration to each other amid life's struggles, must know the highest human happiness;—this is marriage, and this is the only cornerstone of an enduring home.
　　　　　　　　　　　　—Elizabeth Cady Stanton (1815–1902)

The July 13, 2009 *Time* magazine cover story[1] surveyed the matrimonial landscape and offered this summary of the ramifications of marital decline and deterioration: hardship, misery, and devastation to women and children, especially among the nation's underclass. The author, Caitlin Flanagan, asked the question that is the basis for this book: "How much does [marriage] matter?" She answers her own question with a succinct sentence: "More than words can say." Then, she continues with this assertion: "There is no other single force causing as much measurable hardship and human misery in this country as the collapse of marriage. It hurts children, it reduces mothers' financial security, and it has landed with particular devastation on those who can bear it least: the nation's underclass."

On Valentine's Day 2011, CNN began airing a "freedom to marry" campaign; this $10 million public education effort is designed to "explain" why "marriage matters." The advertisements focus on concepts that are deliberately left nebulous—love, commitment, and family—but the unions it celebrates span the whole spectrum of possible couples. The end result, of course, is that when the possible arrangements included within the definition of marriage are expanded to include everything, it ends up meaning nothing. That is the very reason this book became necessary—at the same time that whole segments of society are dismissing marriage as unnecessary, other segments are campaigning to expand the definition of marriage. While determined special interest advocacy groups are trying to redefine marriage in ways that will make it that much less relevant, the media treats the public to a succession of high-profile infidelity scandals by public officials and celebrities.

Serious scholars and researchers face a tough task in trying to repair the damage to marriage, and counselors are left trying to restore the wrecked lives of women and children from the fallout in personal lives and in society as marriage has been undermined and declared unnecessary, irrelevant, and/or impossible. The result is a whirlpool of controversy surrounding the role and significance of "marriage"—so much so that many people are left wondering who to believe in the cascade of opinions aired by a myriad of commentators and pundits. Whether denigrating marriage, trying to redefine it or working to strengthen marriage as an institution of civil society, the issue of marriage is still capable of becoming the cover story or making the headline above the fold.

Social science research has convinced the majority of them that marriage matters; demographic data makes the case that marriage matters. Common sense, accumulated wisdom, and shared experience agree: Marriage has far more impact on adults than most people acknowledge. Researchers indicate that married people have better health, longer and more productive lives, greater general happiness and better mental health than nonmarried individuals. Further, they also agree that marriage performs a critical function for society. Nothing harms children quite the way that not having married parents does. Flanagan summarizes, "On every single significant outcome related to short-term well-being and long-term success, children from intact, two-parent families outperform those from single-parent households." She adds, "Few things hamper a child as much as not having a father at home."

Marriage, then, is important because the family is the context within which the next generation establishes lifelong habits, and develops character. The child will learn—to the degree that the child's family has the desirable characteristics and the child's family life prepares him or her—to become a well-adjusted, productive adult who will contribute to the community and nation as a law-abiding and involved citizen. In this context, jurist Joseph Story wrote, "Marriage is treated by all civilized societies as a peculiar and favored contract. It is in its origin a contract of natural law."[2]

In spite of the overwhelming evidence that marriage matters for individuals as well as society, the overwhelming message for young people today is that marriage can wait; your twenties are for establishing your career, having fun, traveling, finding yourself and sowing your "wild oats," not for settling down "prematurely" into marriage and establishing a family. As a result, the median age for first marriages in the United States has gone up to around age twenty-six for women and twenty-eight for men—that is the highest age since the Census Bureau began keeping track of such information.

The fact that they are deferring marriage does not mean those young people are not forming relationships and having sex. In fact, according to the National Longitudinal Study of Adolescent Health, more than 93 percent of adults eighteen to twenty-three years old who are in a romantic relationship are having sex; even among those active in conservative churches, it is almost 80 percent. So, the bottom line for today's young people is that it is okay to "hook up" [have multiple casual sex relationships and numerous recreational sex experiences] or to cohabit [move in together as a couple], but they are "too young for marriage," "can't afford to get married," "can't afford a wedding," or should "make sure this is the right person before getting married."

Even the word "marriage" is loaded today; pressures come to bear on the personal, philosophical, and political dimensions of marriage. People argue about the appropriate role of the government in promoting marriage and whether defending traditional marriage is discriminatory of singles, those who are divorced, and those who struggle with same-sex attractions. Others worry that marriage is too closely aligned with religious and moral views about sexuality and argue that promoting marriage violates the "separation of church and state." Still others think that marriage is nothing but a legal contract that can be altered to suit the whims of current thinking.

This book endorses the principles laid out by the Witherspoon Institute[3]: Marriage matters in profound ways to a free society, "which depends upon citizens to govern their private lives and rear their children responsibly, so as to limit the scope, size, and power of the state. The nation's retreat from marriage has been particularly consequential for our society's most vulnerable communities; minorities and the poor pay a disproportionately heavy price when marriage declines in their communities."[4] Throughout this book, there is evidence that marriage "advances the public interest" and is an institution that "society should endorse and support." In addition, we advocate support for those "laws and public policies that will reinforce and support" marriage rather than undermine it, and we call upon the nation's leaders to "support public policies that strengthen marriage as a social institution."[5]

Social scientists agree that traditional marriage is a "tough sell" for contemporary youths who are prolonging their adolescent stage far into their twenties. In 1960, two-thirds of twenty somethings were married; in 2008, only 26 percent were.[6] The sexual revolution of the 1960s ushered in a new way of thinking about sex that completely separated it from the context of marriage and the family. Magazines like *Playboy*, Broadway plays like *Hair*, and college campuses that abandoned policies of *in loco parentis* created an "anything goes" environment that made marriage seem old-fashioned and portrayed "family values" as prudish and the object of derision. The fact of the matter, however, is that the hoopla in the media about the "joys of casual sex" illustrated by the promiscuous lifestyles of glamorous Hollywood celebrities was foolishly embellished propaganda; even the earliest legitimate research revealed that the media portrayals of sex bore little resemblance to the reality.[7] Those early studies showed the same result as later, more sophisticated ones: married sex produces the best orgasms and the most frequent as well as most satisfying sex.

In addition to providing the best relationship for the couple—the husband and wife—there is general agreement among marriage scholars that, compared to all other household arrangements, marriage is by far the very best place to raise children; further, it is the best place for the well-being and health of adults. Indeed, most social scientists agree that marriage also has very important positive social consequences for communities and nations. The traditional married-couple family is the most effective training ground for building citizens who contribute to the common good, especially in the minority communities. Marriage conveys numerous economic, educational, health, and safety benefits that establish a foundation from which communities and nations thrive. Marriage has been called the "social glue" for the way that it binds fathers to their children and unites couples while helping to strengthen the bonds between people and their nation.[8]

Marriage is virtually a universal societal institution; cultures around the globe consider marriage the link that unites parents with their children and families to their communities. While marriage is a critical institution in civil society, researchers agree that it is endangered and, currently, is in a "fragile" state. Some even call the situation a "crisis" in that there is heated public debate (based on unfounded assertions of antifamily ideologues) as to whether a married couple—mom and dad—family is the most stable and nurturing environment for couples and their children. After forty years of distorted data and misrepresentation about the questions related to family structure, there are, literally, thousands of studies that agree that the best family structure for children's well-being is the married couple—mom and dad—family.

They also agree on the social costs of family disintegration. American taxpayers pay an enormous price for family fragmentation: divorce, unwed childbearing, crime, drug abuse, education dropouts, domestic violence, chronic illness, poverty, foster care, etc. This tremendous body of research, however, does not deter those who have a vested interest in seeing the current negative trends continue and seeing the institutions of marriage and family—as they have traditionally been composed—disintegrate beyond functionality.

Gone are the days of Brady Brunch families and June Cleaver-style households; they have morphed into ABC's "Modern Family"—a show promoted as "redefining what family means," and portrayed as "one big straight-gay, multicultural, traditional, happy family."[9] According to Brian Powell, a sociology professor at Indiana University, 60 percent of Americans in 2010 believe, "If you consider yourself to be a family, then you [are] one."[10] Pew Center research finds that Americans are "sharply divided" over the changing definitions surrounding the family and the various ways that has affected society, but they agree that "women raising children without a male partner is bad for society."[11]

Without strong marriages, there cannot be strong democracies because democracy depends on an informed, mature citizenry of good character. My friend, Robert W. Patterson, spells out the inextricable link between marriage and the markets in Adam Smith's *The Wealth of Nations* and points out that Gary Becker makes the same connection in his *Treatise on the Family* because the "division of labor maximizes production in the market and in the home." Preserving and strengthening marriage are essential, not just for the well-being of individual citizens, but also for American exceptionalism. Our future as a free nation rests on our ability to reproduce productive and upright citizens who will contribute to the nation's strength and stability. The breakdown of marriage and family threaten America's ability to produce the caliber of citizens who will be capable of sustaining our heritage of self-governance. The present trajectory of our society, however, is not promising. Paul Amato, Distinguished Professor of Sociology and Demography at Pennsylvania State University, wrote that the "...changes in American marriage and family structure since the 1960s have decreased the mean level of child well-being in the population, lowered the well-being of many adults, increased child poverty, and placed a large financial burden on our society."[12]

Currently, married couple households are a little less than half of households in the United States.[13] This stands in stark comparison to 1950 when 78.2 percent of households were married couples; by 1970 that percentage had dropped 7.6 points to 70.6 percent of all households. From 1970 to 1990, the percentage dropped another 14.6 points to 56.0 percent. Then, from 1990 to 2010, there was another drop of 6.3 percentage points to the current 49.7 percent. Having married-couple families constitute less than half of American households is a situation that undermines the "law of the land" as established by the American Congress. Public Law 104-193—Personal Responsibility and Work Opportunity Reconciliation Act of 1996—clearly states Congressional "findings": (1) Marriage is the foundation of a successful society, (2) Marriage is an essential institution of a successful society which promotes the interests of children, and (3) Promotion of responsible fatherhood and motherhood is integral to successful child rearing and the well-being of children.

Matthew Spalding of the Heritage Foundation has written a book, *We Still Hold These Truths: Rediscovering Our Principles, Reclaiming our Future*,[14] that defends "the family, centered on marriage…as the natural or pre-political institution of a free society." The family, Spalding argues, is "deeply embedded in Western civilization and the worldview of the American founders." In his review of Spalding's book, Peter Lawler[15] points out that the founding fathers were more likely to be influenced by John Locke than by "natural and divine principles," and that the Lockean emphasis on "individualistic principles" are inadequate to explain "who we are as political, social, familial, and communal beings who lovingly assume personal responsibility for the duties we have been given."[16] Lawler's thesis is that the founders were more likely to believe in an "incoherent mixture of classically republican, Christian and Lockean elements."[17] He continues by arguing that neither a "founder's view" nor a Lockean view gives us the "whole truth about who we are as social and relational persons created in the image of God."[18] While the founders did not completely buy into Lockean individualism, they lacked what Lawler called a "coherent alternative."[19] As a result, they did not completely understand "why the family and religion are good for their own sakes as the core of who we are"; thus, Lawler holds, we cannot learn from the founders "the whole truth about who we are as social and relational persons created in the image of God."[20]

There is a strange dichotomy in Locke's ideas—while his views about liberty and individual rights were built into the Declaration of Independence, they are also encapsulated in today's radical individualism. The enormous difference between then and now is that the founders balanced personal liberty with Judeo-Christian moral traditions, and they understood fully and stated forcefully the indispensable role of morality and religion in the maintenance of a self-governing society (see the oft-quoted statement of John Adams[21]). With the two in balance, an individual's freedom was not considered an excuse for immorality as it is today, nor was it considered tolerable to rationalize irresponsible behavior that impinged on the common good. Our nation's founders recognized, as do all rational human beings, that anyone acting without moral constraints threatens the social order, whether that person is in a position of power that influences huge segments of the populace or is merely a lone individual terrorizing innocent bystanders.

Yet from the early 1900s until now, the individualistic conception of marriage has increasingly prevailed. Couples were able to set the terms for unions, whether to have a legal ceremony and determine the parameters of their marriage contract, or merely "live together" without legal or even casual bonds. Even the marriage contract can now be terminated at the will of only one of the parties in the marriage, making it not a very binding contract. Thus, marriage has gone from a sacred covenant with a legally binding contract that protected those entering the agreement (as well as any children produced by the union) to a "contract" that is more easily terminated without any liability for damages than most other contracts. Even the "social institution" aspects of marriage have weakened as parenting has been disassociated from marriage—though, ironically, the push toward same-sex "marriage" has given new impetus to the idea that marriage is a social institution as a new group wants the sanction of marriage. Further, high-profile, die-hard feminists—Gloria Steinem and Helen Gurley Brown—who formerly repudiated marriage are now married and publicly embrace marriage as an institution. Steinem confessed that she used to see marriage as "limiting," but that she now sees "having someone in your corner for life" as "limitless."

If the populace views marriage as nothing more than an individual's choice among many equally valid options for making individuals "happy," we might as well (as Flanagan points out in the *Time* cover story) "hold the wake" for marriage. But, rightly understood, marriage has a higher purpose and more noble function. One of the prime reasons that marriage has lasted, virtually unchanged, throughout most of history is that it has at its heart the responsibility for raising up the next generation "to protect and teach it, to instill in it the habits of conduct and character that will ensure the generation's safe passage into adulthood." We do not have to look far to see the consequences of failure in that function: it means a culture where kids run wild and look for opportunities to vent their emotions in violence—as happened in April 2011, in another of a long series of shocking public instances of violence and trashing in fast-food restaurants, when a teenage girl in a McDonald's restaurant thought another girl was "looking at her man." She and a friend brutally attacked and savagely beat the girl until she went into convulsions. Onlookers filmed the carnage and warned the attackers to leave after someone alerted the police. Such incidents no longer shock; they appall us, but they are frequent enough that the shock has worn off.

Daniel Patrick Moynihan, in his 1993 report, "Defining Deviancy Down," wrote about the ways society has gradually tolerated more deviant behavior so that criminal behavior is now accepted as "normal" in ways that previously would have been considered abnormal by any standard. Even Moynihan would be appalled to see how his predictions have been realized. The McDonald's assault is not an isolated incident; the phenomenon has its own name—restaurant rage. In a Maryland suburb on March 18, 2011, a restaurant manager suffered broken ribs and a collapsed lung after a patron at Outriggers objected to his high bill and attacked the manager. In Florida, a man dining at Olive Garden became so irritated by the noise of an autistic four-year-old at the next table that he choked the boy's father. In Toledo, Ohio, a woman at a McDonald's drive-through window became enraged when told that Chicken McNuggets were unavailable.[22] These are visible results of societal turmoil and the far-reaching impact of family breakdown as people's rage and lack of self-control erupts in ways that threaten others going about their everyday business.

Bullying has become so widespread that President Obama convened a White House conference to discuss the issue. In all the news coverage about that event, no one mentioned a CDC study in 2009, the Massachusetts Youth Health Survey (MYHS), that found bullies and their victims are more likely than peers to have experienced violence within their families. The MYHS interviews with 6,000 students discovered that those involved in bullying were five times more likely to have been hurt physically by a family member—an event that occurs at much higher frequency in families where one of the adults is only a partner rather than a biological parent—than those who had never been a victim or perpetrator of bullying. A story in the *Boston Globe* added that perpetrators of bullying are more likely to have witnessed violence against other family members.

In the absence of real-life daddies, the government is becoming the father in the family—though not a very effective one. A report in *USA Today*[23] indicates that Americans "depended more on government assistance in 2010 than at any other time in the nation's history." A record 18.3 percent of the nation's personal income was a payment from the government, in the form of Social Security, Medicare, food stamps, unemployment benefits, and other federal programs. Personal wages, at 51 percent in 2010 and 50.5 percent in February 2011 accounted for the lowest share of income since the government began tracking the data in 1929.

One of the oldest axioms about marriage is the claim that "two can live more cheaply than one," which is not really that far off the mark. Many financial advantages accrue to a couple when they "merge" their separate "businesses" into one. Married couples save more and are more cautious spenders than unmarried people. David Popenoe, codirector of the National Marriage Project at Rutgers University, argues, "Married people work harder, they advance further in their job, they save more money, and maybe invest more wisely. That is because, one can speculate, they are now working for something larger than themselves. They are working for a family."[24]

No wonder many in our nation are coming to the defense of marriage. The website for Prop. 8 in California put it so well:

> Traditional marriage is the foundation of society and has served [us] well for centuries. [Marriage] exists to strengthen society, encourage monogamous and loving marriages and to provide the optimal environment to ensure the well-being of children. Thirty-one other states, including California have voted on this issue and every single one decided [to uphold] traditional marriage.[25]

It is important to note, however, that the marriage movement is not merely a "right-wing religious backlash" against the distortions of marriage and the trend toward more secular views of marriage. Instead, though there is a large number of faith-based and conservative leaders at the forefront of the marriage movement, there are also leaders of many different faiths, many different nations, and many different political, social, and ideological persuasions. The uniting principle that binds the academic, political, and faith-based activists in the movement is that each sees the damage to children and adults, to communities, to our entire society, and even the worldwide ramifications of declining rates of marriage and the negative trends resulting from the breakdown of the family. Many leaders in the pro-marriage and pro-family movement are part of the World Congress of Families,[26] which periodically sponsors celebrations of marriage and family at major cities (Prague, Geneva, Mexico City, Warsaw, Amsterdam, Moscow, and Madrid) to share research and build networks among those who are concerned about the future of marriage and the family and are working to provide leadership in shaping the marriage and family movement.

No wonder family researchers and historians are concerned. Gary Becker, Nobel Laureate author of *A Treatise on the Family*,[27] describes the family in the Western world as "radically altered" by events over the last three decades. Glenn T. Stanton, author of *Why Marriage Matters: Reasons to Believe in Marriage in Postmodern Society*, describes the decline in marriage and the breakdown of the family as the "common denominator driving other social ills."[28] While associated social ills mount, too many Americans remain oblivious to the implications for our children and the future of our nation. The situation unfolding before us is unprecedented in history. According to the Census Bureau, of the 8,750,000 additional households since 1970, one-parent homes accounted for 8,420,000 of the total (96 percent) while, at the same time, the number of two-parent families increased by only 330,000.[29]

At this point in American history, the confusion, ambivalence, and controversy over marriage are at a tipping point where the outcome is uncertain and the stakes enormous. This book is meant to help tip the scales toward marriage—to bring in experience, common sense, and research data that will make a compelling case that marriage matters. The reams of research data and the common experiences of teachers, social workers, and law enforcement officers who see the outcomes of family breakdown on a day-to-day basis need to break through the media fog to reach the minds of the public to change attitudes and convince young people that marriage matters for each of them and that it matters for all of us.

Part I of *Marriage Matters* discusses the groundwork for strong marriages: How do couples build a relationship that will last in a throw-away culture? The nondating fad and the lack of romance in the hook-up trend are given an in-depth exploration.

Part II focuses on sex as a central aspect of marriage and the harms that are inherent in casual, recreational sex.

Part III looks at the ways that marriage matters to individuals in general and to children in particular. This section of *Marriage Matters* looks at the human dimension of marriage and how the institution of marriage affects the private sector.

Part IV moves to the public policy arena and how ideologically driven activists' long-term and determined push for same-sex "marriage" is a serious attack on one of the nation's foundation stones. Part IV also briefly explores several of the marriage and family public policy issues confronting legislators.

This book represents much of what I have learned about the marriage issue in close to twenty years of research, writing, and working in the public policy arena in the nation's capital. Over the past decade, I have headed the research arm of the nation's largest public policy women's organization, Concerned Women for America. I serve on the boards of the Howard Center and the Institute on Religion and Democracy—two nongovernment think-tank organizations that also care deeply about the marriage and family crisis and work to repair the damage done to marriage, which has resulted from forty years of social experimentation. In my professional experience, I have seen a mountain of studies, papers, and reports that agree—across ideological and partisan divides—that marriage matters. It matters in very profound ways for women and children.

As America struggles to figure ways out of the 2011 fiscal crisis, I am very aware that marriage also matters profoundly to the whole of society. The public costs of the social disintegration and crime related to family breakdown is incalculable, but all experts agree that the financial costs are exorbitant. The cost in human capital is even higher. We have treated marriage as optional when it is a foundation stone for all of society. We have arrogantly assumed that our generation was smart enough to fashion a new view of social institutions that was more modern and "hip" and that there would be no consequences. What we have learned, to our sorrow, is that the consequences of the decline in marriage and the breakdown of the family have been disastrous, not just for the thousands of lives destroyed and people who have been negatively affected, but the consequences for marriage and family as social institutions have been devastating to the cultural environment and to the stability of the nation. Many of those who thought that "sexual freedom" would be liberating have found, too late and to their regret, that the dregs of "Fortune's cup" are bitter indeed.[30]

To summarize:

> Decades of social-science research have confirmed the deepest intuitions of the human heart: As frightening, exhilarating, and improbable as this wild vow of constancy may seem, there is no substitute. When love seeks permanence, a safe home for children who long for both parents, when men and women look for someone they can count on, there are no substitutes. The word for what we want is marriage.[31]

Notes

1. Caitlin Flanagan, "Is There Hope for the American Marriage?" *Time Magazine*, July 2, 2009, http://www.time.com/time/covers/0,16641,20090713,00. html (accessed September 29, 2011).
2. As quoted in Chuck Donovan, "Marriage, Parentage, and the Constitution of the Family," *WebMemo No. 2783*, The Heritage Foundation, January 27, 2010, http://www.heritage.org/Research/Reports/2010/01/Marriage-Parentage-and-the-Constitution-of-the-Family (accessed September 29, 2011).
3. "Marriage and the Public Good: Ten Principles," The Witherspoon Institute, June 2006, http://www.protectmarriage.com/files/WitherspoonReporton-Marriage.pdf (accessed October 11, 2011).
4. Ibid., 5.
5. Ibid., 5–8.
6. Suzanne Venker, "Why Marriage Matters: Part 1 or 3," *Conservatism, Email, Feature, in the Family Way*, November 23, 2010, http://www.newsrealblog.com/2010/11/27/why-marriage-matters-part-1-of-3/ (accessed September 29, 2011).
7. The most "authoritative" and arguably the most "truly scientific" of the early studies (1994) was the National Health and Social Life Survey (NHSLS) at the University of Chicago. More than 200 interviewers interviewed close to 3,500 respondents and found that married couples are the happiest and most satisfied sexually.
8. David Popenoe and Barbara Dafoe Whitehead, *The State of Our Unions: The Social Health of Marriage in America, 2003* (Rutgers University: The National Marriage Project, 2003), 4, http://www.virginia.edu/marriage-project/pdfs/SOOU2003.pdf (accessed October 11, 2011).
9. Brian O'Keefe and Lauren Sher, "The Modern Family Phenomenon," *ABC News*, February 18, 2011, http://abcnews.go.com/Entertainment/ModernFamily/modern-family-phenomenon-scenes-secrets-sitcom/story?id=12948560&page=1 (accessed September 29, 2011).
10. John Berman and Enjoli Francis, "What Makes a Family? Children, Say Many Americans," *ABC News*, September 15, 2010, http://abcnews.go.com/WN/defines-family-children-americans-survey/story?id=11644693&page=2 (accessed September 30, 2011).
11. Rich Morin, "The Public Renders a Split Verdict on Changes in Family Structure," Pew Research Center, February 16, 2011, http://pewsocialtrends.org/2011/02/16/the-public-renders-a-split-verdict-on-changes-in-family-structure/1/ (accessed September 30, 2011).

12. Paul R. Amato, "Recent Changes in Family Structure, Implications for Children, Adults, and Society, National Health and Medical Research Council (NHMRC)," *NHMRC Brief*, April 2008, http://healthymarriageinfo. org/resource-detail/index.aspx?rid=3372(accessed October 5, 2011).

13. Janice Shaw Crouse, "Can Marriage Recover from the Assault of Radical Individualism," Graph for the Day, *American Thinker*, November 17, 2010, http://www.americanthinker.com/blog/2010/11/graph_for_the_day_for_ november_2.html (accessed September 30, 2011).

14. Matthew Spalding, *We Still Hold These Truths: Rediscovering Our Principles, Reclaiming our Future* (Wilmington, DE: Intercollegiate Studies Institute, ISI Books, 2010), 232.

15. Peter Augustine Lawler, "The Limits of the American Founding: What Our Political Fathers didn't Teach Us," *The Family in America* (Summer 2010): 295–309.

16. Ibid., 296.

17. Ibid.

18. Ibid.

19. Ibid., 297.

20. Ibid., 296.

21. "We have no government armed with power capable of contending with human passions unbridled by morality and religion...Our Constitution was made only for a moral and religious people. It is wholly inadequate to the government of any other." President John Adams, 1798.

22. Mary Elizabeth Williams, "When Customers Attack: America's Restaurant Rage," *Salon.Com*, August 11, 2010, http://www.salon.com/life/feature/2010/08/11/restaurant_rage/ (accessed October 5, 2011).

23. Dennis Cauchon, "Reliance on Uncle Sam Hits a Record," *USA Today*, April 25, 2011, http://www.usatoday.com/news/nation/2011-04-26-government-payments-economy-medicare.htm (accessed October 5, 2011).

24. As quoted in Tim Lanigan, "Looking for Long-Term Dividends? Try Marriage," *For Your Marriage.org*, http://foryourmarriage.org/looking-for-long-term-dividends-try-marriage/ (accessed October 5, 2011).

25. "Why Marriage Matters," *Yes on 8, Protect Marriage*, http://www.protect-marriage.com/why-marriage-matters (accessed October 5, 2011).

26. The website for the World Congress of Families is: http://www.worldcongress.org/ (accessed October 5, 2011).

27. Gary S. Becker, *A Treatise on the Family* (Cambridge: Harvard University Press, 1991), 1.

28. Glenn T. Stanton, *Why Marriage Matters: Reasons to Believe in Marriage in Postmodern Society* (Colorado Springs, CO: NavPress, 1997), 18.

29. U.S. Bureau of the Census, *Income, Poverty, and Health Insurance Coverage in the United States: 2009* (P60-238), Table 4. Poverty Status of Families, by Type of Family, Presence of Related Children, Race, and Hispanic Origin: 1959 to 2009, http://www.census.gov/hhes/www/poverty/data/historical/families.html (accessed October 5, 2011).

30. From Homer—"The bitter dregs of Fortune's cup to drain."

31. Linda Waite and Maggie Gallagher, *The Case for Marriage: Why Married People are Happier, Healthier and Better off Financially* (New York: Doubleday, 2000), 203.

Part I

The Groundwork for Strong Marriages

2

Preserving Love and Romance

'Twas my one Glory
Let it be Remembered,
I was owned of Thee.

—Emily Dickenson, #1028

My husband and I had just returned from a vacation at places favored by couples—some on weekend getaways, others honeymooning. We enjoy seeing couples holding hands and stealing kisses. But sadly, growing numbers of couples on getaways together have nothing adorning their ring fingers. These couples no doubt think that their love can survive without promises and commitment, but love requires exclusivity. Love is not love if it does not insist, "I am yours; you are mine."

Songwriters used to give us lyrics like "love and marriage/ go together like a horse and carriage/ ...you can't have one without the other." But secularists of various stripes have tried to loosen the connection between love and marriage. Television has brought Hollywood values and dysfunctional relationships into our living rooms and mainstreamed once-bohemian ideas that the commitment of marriage is a barrier to personal fulfillment, an unwanted restriction of independence, and a loss of freedom. As a result of buying into those foolish nostrums, a large percentage of the population is accumulating crippling emotional baggage in their attempts to "score" love and sex outside the bonds of marriage.

Love introduces enormous complexity into our lives. On the positive side, the emotion of love brings joy and the hope of a lasting bond. That, however, is not the end of the matter. If we were purely rational beings, there would not so often be a gap between our professed beliefs and our behavior.

Love is often paired with other strong emotions and desires—fear, anger, pride, envy, greed, and/or lust. Sometimes we have feelings that we are not even fully conscious of, feelings that spring from suppressed hurts; these can flare up and override our normally rational decision-making processes and produce destructive reactive responses that conflict with the moral standards of our professed beliefs.

If our beliefs are to determine our behavior, they must be grounded in truth and govern the emotions and needs that drive us. Only then will the moral principles to which we give lip service become strong convictions that serve to impose boundaries on our behavior so that we develop real character. Otherwise, even the promises of marriage will be little more than "till death do us part...or not."

Love and sex unleash the strongest of our feelings and passions. While love and sex without promises are part of the foolish unrealistic imaginings of the postmodern mind, truth has a way of coming to the fore in the least expected places. Never was this more evident than in the movie *Vanilla Sky*. In a poignant scene, Cameron Diaz's character frantically tells Tom Cruise's character that he made promises to her. When he declared that he had made no promises, she replied—with the strength of absolute certainty—that the intimacy of their intercourse the night before had constituted a promise. Sadly, though she uttered truth, the movie presented her as a psychopath.

Promises count only when reinforced by commitments, and they are only meaningful and effective when the person making them develops strong character. Even then, being the fallible creatures that we are, we need all the assistance we can get to make good on our promises. It helps to have the reinforcement of a ceremony, of a public declaration before God and assembled family and friends that raises expectations of others whose opinions we value, in whose eyes we wish to be esteemed, and whom we do not wish to disappoint. Plus, there can be great value in having milestones, a moment in time delineating one stage from another.

As much as I enjoy watching couples in love, it is bittersweet to see those who settle merely for strong feelings, that "half a loaf" of mere physical desire. Theirs is such a flawed start that often does not lead to fulfillment. The odds of a dead end are high. The many emotions they will have to contend with can be overwhelming; love's passion is volatile and unpredictable.

I should know. It was such a shock when some of my younger siblings expressed surprise that our marriage had lasted. My first reaction upon hearing this was bewilderment; how could they doubt the passionate love my husband and I shared?

With time and reflection, I understand their misinterpretation of the explosive intensity of our strong personalities. It is no simple matter to contain such a volatile combination of two hard-driving individuals. Certainly, without commitment, it could not have lasted. Enduring love and sex without promises? No way! Without the sacred covenant of marriage? Impossible.

The marriage ceremony includes the promise to love and to cherish "for better or for worse, for richer or for poorer, in sickness and in health." Many couples have found their solid financial circumstances gone; others have ended up caring for an incapacitated mate. None of us knows the challenges we might face in the future. The life of Joni Eareckson Tada is inspirational because even though she became a quadriplegic as a teenager and has spent the last thirty-seven years of her life in a wheelchair, her life radiates joy and happiness. She even found romance and is happily married. Former CNN star interviewer, Larry King, clearly found her puzzling and, perhaps, even a bit intimidating.[1]

The idea of embracing difficulties is alien in a world of drive-through dinners, year-round climate control, and whirlpool baths. But Joni lives out the Scripture that explains: whenever we face trials, we are to "consider it pure joy." Joni Eareckson Tada, as an ambassador from an alien world, told Larry King that she thanks God for her wheelchair, which she calls her "passport to joy" because "there are more important things in life than walking."

King brought the conversation around to Joni's marriage with prurient curiosity. How, he wondered, could they have a marriage when they could not "have an intimate physical life?" Joni responded graciously that they could be intimate "just like any other couple."

King, clearly skeptical, responded, "Except you don't have feeling, right, below the neck?"

Joni again patiently tutored King in the things that do not come easy. "But there is more to romance," she replied, "than what happens below the neck, Larry."

She enumerated the results of a hard-won relationship: "And I think that the joy and the commitment and the love and the affection and the respect and the honor and the duty and the devotion that flows between my husband and me is more precious and, perhaps, it is more unique in this society than maybe many marriages."

Larry King, now at age seventy-two in his seventh marriage, moved on. He, with all his capacities intact, has the "feeling," but she, the one in her wheelchair, has had a happily "intact" marriage for twenty-two years.

Ironically, the romantic ideal today is still—in spite of the decline in marriage and cynicism about marriage among many today—that a man and a woman will fall in love, get married, have a family, and grow old together.

What is more delightful than seeing the growing oneness of a married couple learning to connect with each other in a dozen different ways? Sometimes it shows up in their humorous exchanges; other times simply in the way they glance at each other. One thing I especially enjoy seeing is when a couple manages to coordinate things despite little being said—a little like dancers or skaters who know each other's moves by heart. Whether married five years or twenty, the telltale signs of connectedness sparkle as they share the joys of life or glow warmly in the way they support one another in the hard places. Also, it is gratifying to see the ever-growing sureness of one another as couples deepen in their understanding, affection, and acceptance of each other.

In "Tall Trees in Georgia," the late Eva Cassidy laments having chosen independence ahead of love with these words:

> The sweetest love I ever had/ I left aside/ because I did not want to be/ any man's bride

Now older, alone and pining to be married, she advises:

> Control your mind/ my girl/ and give your heart to one/ for if you love all men/ you'll surely be left with none

From this brief, poignant account, we catch a glimpse of the near-universal yearnings of the heart for a life's mate—not merely a fleeting desire for some semicommitted "significant other."

In contrast to the almost universal longing for marriage, the late-night stand-up comedians offer a variety of disparaging takes on marriage. The better ones make us chuckle—even laugh uproariously, by highlighting the absurd miscues, mistakes, miscalculations and, yes, mule-headedness in our familial relationships, all evidence of the foibles inherent in our human frailty. Another brand of comics provoke pinched laughs from us as they snarl and bark out their crude, cutting, hate-laced, anger-drenched diatribes about married life; they use their bawdy, blistering humor to lacerate us for our defects, failures, and the sins we commit as we struggle with the challenges of life as husband and wife, parent and child. These cynical, pitiless critics—unlike God who remembers that we are made of dust—portray the shortfalls and weaknesses of our efforts to love and denounce the whole enterprise of marriage as a miserable fraud deserving only searing comedic contempt.

Seen through their bitter, anger-warped lenses, marital sex gets little but sarcasm and ridicule. They are not alone in their disparaging comments. Sex in marriage, when spoken of at all—and usually by those whose relationship no one would want to emulate—is nearly always belittled as dull, boring, or ludicrous. It is pictured—on the supposedly rare occasions it is actually attempted—as a pale excuse for the alleged excitement of promiscuous "fooling around." Regular folks with normal, happy marriages (and thus who know better) can only wonder what sort of experience lies behind this deluge of derogatory bile that is the staple of TV sitcoms and comedic monologues. Why even expend the energy to ridicule marriage if it is as pointless and unpalatable as it is portrayed? Even more to the point, if marriage were "as advertised," why would anyone ever want to be married? It seems likely that the subtle (and not so subtle) putdowns of marriage go hand-in-hand with the decline in marriage rates.

In addition to the media's mistreatment of marriage, there are all the worn-out jokes at weddings about the guy getting a ring both for his finger and one for his nose (like some prize bull?), or worse, the old saw about getting a millstone tied round his neck. Also, there are all the jokes about how you can tell that the honeymoon is over. Altogether, there is a constant stream of would-be comedians spouting comments that make solitary confinement sound preferable to marriage.

Again, if this is the whole truth or even half the truth, why marry? Just what kind of foolish delusions are being pursued by those who marry?

In Scripture, we find the Creator's pronouncement, "It is not good for man to live alone." (In St. Ambrose's interpretation, this is God's counsel, i.e., the wisdom of God, as opposed to a commandment.) But if anyone should know what is and is not good, certainly it is the Creator, since He understands exactly how He infused the need for marriage into the very fabric of our humanity—in our need for communication, our need to know and be known, to love and be loved. He is the architect; He wrote the blueprint. So clearly, the needs that are met through marriage spring from the very essence of our humanity.

As to our yearning for communication, note that the account of creation reports that God "spoke," addressing the fact of man's inadequacy as a solitary being. Compare that to instances where we describe our response to some circumstance as, "I said to myself," or "I told myself." Self-talk can be an important indicator of attitudes, values, or emotional state, but it is incomplete communication. It is only a start. The very fact that we learn of someone's self-talk reveals that they needed to go further by verbalizing to someone else what they said to themselves. Our need for communication is clearly part of the *Image Deo*.

By publicly exchanging vows of fidelity and promises of love, those who marry begin a work of building something larger than they know. If and when both husband and wife lay aside their resentments when they do not get their own way, learn to appreciate their differences, and thus achieve a deeper understanding of one another than the mere romantic attraction that brought them together initially, their affection for each other can steadily deepen until the relationship they create turns out to be "something really special." Remarkably, such an example becomes an influence on the lives of everyone who chances to witness the love they share.

As we are all too painfully aware, many of these efforts fail in large and sometimes dramatic ways, but even those marriages which fall short of their full potential in small ways can still be something magnificent. Such is the case any time a marriage nurtures, shelters, and protects, when it is a stage where scenes of love and joyful celebration are played out again and again—along with huge helpings of "I'm sorry, forgive me; I blew it." Certainly the children that come from marriage are vital to the future of society, but the contributions of these good marriages do not end there. By building good marriages, these couples create virtue. In some immeasurable way, the goodness they create— simply by living in conformity to the natural order designed by the Creator—is of benefit not just to the couple; their success contributes vitality to the whole community with whom they interact.

Inasmuch as the sun holds the planets in their orbits, providing light and energy, these good marriages are little anchor points both within the local community and reaching out across the entire society. Though it is not their conscious intent, the way married couples live generates something akin to a magnetic field that helps to hold a community together. Their vital presence helps to stabilize the whole.

A good marriage generates life and energy in such a marvelous way that it radiates outward, nourishing all in its path. In short, to marry is to start another branch on the tree of life with all of its bountiful potential, large and small.

Humans are never perfect; hence, all marriages, despite our early romantic illusions, will have imperfections. But by continuing to strive toward the ideal, even through their imperfections, the marriage builders keep the ideal alive. Their efforts serve to encourage us all, and as their love endures, even though flawed, it points to the validity of the potential that exists. Ultimately, the commitment to build a marriage persisting through "sickness and health" produces something larger than the mere sum of the parts.

By themselves, pieces of cardboard are flimsy and weak, but cut the pieces carefully, crease and bend them, staple them and, finally, tape them together so as to form a box, and you can produce something strong enough to protect fragile crystal goblets or carry a heavy load of canned goods. Just so, when two become one, they forge a strength that is not otherwise attainable.

Is this fulfillment? For some, yes. They find the burdens and constraints of married life—the responsibility, the give and take, the need to forgive and ask forgiveness—a fair price to pay for the abundant joys and compensations of marriage. Others may choose—or be forced to accept—the independence, the lack of encumbrance and accountability of a single life. Many have done so, saints and sinners alike, but the solitary, single life—though it be as brilliant as a supernovae, powerful as a gamma ray burst or dramatic as a shooting star—can never fulfill the function in a community that marriages do, regardless of singles' numbers or gifts.

Without the energizing presence and wealth of relational networks that marriages foster, community life can never achieve full development. An army platoon, a ball team, a symphony orchestra—all can produce coordinated, organized activity, wonderful camaraderie, even strong bonds of friendship and affection. Yet they do not have the life-generating capacity of a community comprised of couples engaged in the elemental business of building marriages, raising and educating children, gathering together to worship and give thanks, and uniting in the sharing of communal meals of celebration. Nothing else comes close to generating the array of connections as do families living in communities. Such connection is the end product of couples working at the essential, irreplaceable task of building marriages and families.

Why is the tradition of the visit to grandmother's house for holiday celebrations such an enduring, iconic image? Why are we so drawn to it, whether or not it is a part of our own personal experience? What makes it tug so at our hearts? Undoubtedly, it is because the event—whether in wistful imagination or actual reality, smooth and warm or rough and gritty—represents a particular fulfillment of our very humanity, the realization of some of our deepest needs, hopes and dreams. In particular, it embodies a connection to something larger than ourselves, of belonging to a whole which includes those no longer present but who, by their own marriages, started new branches from which we have grown.

Those who have been blessed to have this experience first hand know well how fortunate we are to have the opportunity to so celebrate our place in the family tree. We have abundant reason to give thanks for our ancestors who embraced the bonds of matrimony and commenced to build something that blessed not just themselves but all who would be touched—directly and indirectly—by their lives.

On a recent airplane flight, I sat beside a college student named Jason who initiated a conversation. When he found out that I studied the data about marriage, he said to me, "I don't believe in true love anymore." I said, "Oh, Jason, that makes me really sad. Why would you say that?" He replied that his sister had lived with her boyfriend for about five years, got married, and was divorced about a year later. "I was so shocked," he said. "You know, Jason," I responded, "that doesn't shock me at all because the data bears this out. Most cohabiting relationships no longer lead to marriage, and those that do have a very high rate of divorce. Contrary to what is generally thought, they don't lead to a happy marriage." He replied, "Well, I can tell you this. I am not ever going to get married. My parents are divorced, now my sister is, and I don't know anybody who is happily married."

Jason is not alone. More and more young adults, because they have seen too much divorce and too many miserable marriages, do not believe in love—or in marriage. For them, marriage does not matter. For them, marriage is irrelevant to love and romance; in fact, they see marriage as an outdated institution that squelches love and romance. Dr. Neil Clark Warren interviewed five hundred individuals asking them to tell him about the marriage they most admired. Nearly half could not recommend even one single healthy exemplary marriage.[2] How sad is that?

Separating Love and Romance from Marriage

Marriage used to be the only socially acceptable household structure for couples and the inevitable next step when a couple "fell in love." Today, however, critics rush to debunk marriage and to promote the idea that love and romance thrive best in uncommitted relationships, while marriage, according to the prevailing cultural messages sent to young people, stifles individuality, closes the door to freedom, and limits a couple's spontaneity and affection. How ironic, then, that marriage is very important to most Americans and around 90 percent of Americans will marry during their lifetime.[3] Yet, at the same time that most people hold those views, the pendulum is swinging in the opposite direction. The contemporary marriage rate is less than half the level in 1969; fewer people are getting married, and they are waiting longer to get married.[4] The divorce rate today is more than 60 percent higher than it was in 1960[5] and remains high in spite of increased efforts to strengthen marriage as a social and cultural institution.

As I noted, popular songs used to have lyrics like Frank Sinatra's "love and marriage/ go together like a horse and carriage/ ...you can't have one without the other."[6] Disagreeing that marriage is "an institute you can't disparage,"[7] "progressives" and the pop culture have been remarkably successful in unlinking the connection between love and marriage. The decline in marriage rates should surprise no one.

But reality intrudes with a vengeance. Love—once typically cherished and nourished within a marriage relationship—is now crude beyond belief in much of pop music. In her book, *Prude: How the Sex-Obsessed Culture Damages Girls*, Carol Platt Liebau wrote, "A significant portion of the 'hottest' songs and acts in America routinely purvey the tawdriest, most unwholesome messages both about sex and about male-female relationships."[8] Liebau cites one study of the top ten CDs since 1999. Of the 159 songs studied, 42 percent contained either general sexual content (23 percent) or an explicit description of sexual intercourse (19 percent). In 68 percent of the songs, it was not clear whether the sexual encounter was inside or outside an existing relationship, and in 18 percent of the songs, sound effects accompanied the sexual content.[9]

All the crude vulgarity, inevitably, desensitizes the emotions and, as a consequence, love is often associated in our popular culture more with pure physicality (including violence) than with romance. Shockingly, the Billboard #1 hit for some time during 2010 was "Love the Way You Lie" by Eminem, featuring Rihanna.[10] It sent a message that "wrong" can "feel" right: "As long as the wrong feels right/ it's like I'm in flight/ high off of love." Never mind that the lyrics portray an extremely abusive relationship based on lies:

> You swore you've never hit 'em/ never do nothing to hurt 'em/ now
> you're in each other's face/ spewing venom/ and these words/ when

you spit 'em/ you push/ pull each other's hair/ scratch, claw, bit 'em/ throw 'em down/...but you promised her/ next time you'll show restraint/...but you lied again...[11]

Experience shows that love introduces an enormous amount of conflicting feelings into couples' lives—and at least doubly so outside the bonds of marriage. Love is often paired with other strong emotions and desires—fear, anger, pride, envy, greed, and/or lust. Sometimes we have feelings that we are not even fully conscious of, feelings that spring from suppressed hurts; these can flare up and override our normally rational decision-making processes and produce destructive reactive responses that conflict with the moral standards of our professed beliefs (as illustrated by Eminem's song).

Sex as a Promise

Love and sex unleash passionate feelings—think of the memorable love matches in history—Jacob and Rachel, Romeo and Juliet, Robert and Elizabeth Barrett Browning. Those intense emotions are more safely expressed within a marriage relationship, where they are protected by vows before a couple's friends and family and where the relationship, being more clearly defined, is that much more secure. Beyond the relationship dimensions and benefits, though, marriage conveys public acknowledgment of a couples' union and brings to bear community pressures that help to protect the wife.

The protection of marriage does not have to be onerous (one of the many false claims of feminist ideology); this is so beautifully attested to by the three brief lines of Emily Dickenson's poem #1028: *'Twas my one Glory—Let it be Remembered—I was owned of Thee.* Dickenson's words convey a relationship of deep emotions, something soul stirring. Those words also speak of total surrender, of an all-consuming passion, and, I am confident that those lines convey the hunger of many women's souls. Her sentiments cause something to stir in many, both male and female. The poet captures the idea that to be known, to be understood and completely accepted, is an integral part of being loved, of belonging. What are the odds that those deep sentiments will be fulfilled outside of marriage, where passion and belonging are not bound together?

Yet there is another dimension, "ownership," that carries with it a huge obligation and enormous responsibility. It is not about domination or control, but it is about as territorial as you can get. It demands complete fidelity and total faithfulness. Lovers, inevitably, demand exclusive rights. "You are mine," they say. Monogamy is essential to their mutual need, and nothing is more painful to lovers, even among those who were formerly promiscuous, than infidelity. In marriage, that connectedness that was initially based on mutual attractiveness moves deeper to ultimately be based on the meaning to be had in meeting each other's needs, the apex of belongingness.

Marriage under Imperfect Circumstances

Generations of men and women in this country have made their marriages succeed, often under what we would consider today as impossible circumstances. Many of the stories include women who chose to follow their men into very uncertain and even dangerous situations; yet, the accounts of their marriages are filled with love and romance. There is such a story in the Bible. A messenger arrives bearing expensive gifts. He had been sent back to his homeland to find a wife for a wealthy relative's unmarried son. The host receives the messenger warmly and is willing to send a beautiful young virgin to be wedded to the relative's son. There is only one condition. The messenger must delay his return for ten days. The messenger insists that he must return immediately. The host replies that the young lady must agree to the arrangement. When she is consulted, she decides to go with the messenger. They return to the homeland; she marries the son and they eventually have twin boys.

The young woman's name was Rebekah, and you can find an account of her life as Isaac's wife in the book of Genesis. What stirs my imagination, more than the problems they faced as husband and wife, is the amazing way she chose—as a young girl, probably no more than fifteen or sixteen—an unknown future in an unfamiliar land cut off from everyone she knew. She could only have dimly perceived the full reality of her choice to embark on this adventure. Likewise, the mysterious, rich young man in Rebekah's imagination probably bore little resemblance to the real person she met at the end of her journey.

Most of us can guess what her dreams were like.

Her early years had probably been happy and sheltered. We are told she was a beautiful virgin with a kind and generous disposition. So it seems likely that her optimism was uncontaminated by bitter experiences. No doubt she had the audacious hopes of youth, the unquenchable thirst for life that comes with blind assurance of great possibilities. Adventure beckoned her. A wealthy Prince Charming waited. Coupled with her hopes and dreams was likely a primal drive to find love, to mate, and have children—whether she was aware of it yet or not. In short, she was a young girl eager to become a woman.

This ancient story shares basic similarities with more modern ones.

Near the end of the 2003 movie *A Painted House*, based on a John Grisham novel, a pretty girl stands at a proverbial crossroads in life. A brute of a young man has just accosted her when a second young man aptly named Cowboy arrives on the scene. In a testosterone-fueled battle between the two men, the brutish one is killed. Cowboy, an outsider who knows that a plea of self-defense will be no defense at all in the local court, realizes that he will have to leave or end up being hung. No one is surprised that Cowboy has won the pretty girl's heart. She makes an immediate choice to go with him into an uncertain future, knowing only that she wants to be with him. She hardly knows him, but she will go where he goes.

Such are the mysterious ways of a girl and guy.

Some view love—illustrated in both the Biblical and the modern story—as powerful as an outgoing tide. Others see it as nebulous and transient as the fog. Whether strong or ephemeral, the inner force of womanhood has made generations of women follow their men into the unknown.

It staggers the imagination to think about the uncertainty facing the first European settlers on this continent, or the pioneers who blazed trails through mountains and forests to tame the American West. Generations of women left secure homes to go west with a husband who could not guarantee shelter, safety, or sustenance. Those women realized that they would likely have their babies with little to no medical care. They knew there was a high probability of death in childbirth and, if they did indeed survive, they would bury some of their babies.

Nevertheless, brave pioneer women followed their men; some did not live through the hazardous trip, and others were buried without ever seeing their dreams realized. Most early cemeteries have family plots showing men buried alongside a beloved young wife who died in childbirth and, often, several babies who died in infancy. Still these pioneers could not be stopped. They conquered the wilderness and filled it with children.

Their choices and the consequences of their world appall many progressives today. To follow some man, to belong to him, is inconceivable to them. But the feminists' view of patriarchy is not quite the way earlier women lived it. Biblical characters like Sarah, Rebekah, Rachael, Tamar, Rahab, and Ruth were not passive women. They acted decisively—within the constraints of their environments—to shape their future and the future of their children.

In these women's stories, I see far more partnership—even in the bad old days of patriarchy—than do today's critics. The patriarch Abraham loved his wife, Sarah, and acceded to her wishes during her conflict with Hagar. Rebekah and Isaac betrayed the subterfuge of their claim to be brother and sister by acting like the sweethearts they were, unaware that the king was watching them from his window. Jacob loved Rachael so much that he was willing to work for seven years, and then another seven years, to earn her as his bride. His love for her was so great that her death in childbirth with their second son was very much on his mind even as he lay dying decades later. In fact, before his death, he wanted to settle one last matter with his son Joseph, Rachael's firstborn. All those many years later, Jacob was still troubled that he had been unable to bury Rachael in the family tomb next to where he was to be buried. And he was driven to try to make Joseph understand.

How do these stories of romance, love, and marriage from long ago compare with the stories of today? What messages do they send for this contemporary era?

There is a track of innumerable young women today who are not so very different than I was as a girl. I certainly had a burning desire to have a career and "be somebody," but there was this guy. Oh, I had seen the struggles of my parents and I had no illusions as to the difficulties of merging two individuals into harmonious married life. But there was this guy who met all the requirements for marriage, including personal integrity and strong character. We were drawn together with the boundless hope of youth and the power of young love, I followed my heart, heedless of all the uncertainties. I wanted to belong to him, and like millions of women before me, being with him and wanting to build a life with him trumped all my reservations about getting married.

There is another track of women—those with predispositions and experiences vastly different from mine. For them, freedom is so free it has become license. They have no desire to belong to someone completely, exclusively, and permanently. I can understand and have a measure of sympathy for those who have not met a worthy guy who completely steals their heart. What I cannot relate to is the idea of someone who falls in love with Mr. Right, who is suitable for marriage in every way, yet does not wish to be his, totally and completely—and permanently.

Perhaps a parent's bad marriage or a divorce is so crippling that fear or cynicism overcomes such couples. Perhaps promiscuity has robbed other couples of the mysterious power that fuses two persons' hearts. Whatever the case, it is a terribly sad loss to be stripped of the capacity to be "foolish" enough to make a lifetime commitment to the love of one's life.

Sadly, one central factor influencing those in this second track has to be celebrity role models. To gauge their influence, look at the covers of magazines filling rack after rack along the checkout lanes in the supermarket. In an earlier time, the tabloids fed our curiosity with features about Hollywood *marriages,* and then the focus spiraled downward to feed us stories about Hollywood *couples,* complete with the adorable babies that are born out-of-wedlock. Now, the tabloids offer accounts of Hollywood *hookups*—relationships that often are over by the time the magazines hit the newsstands.

Fulfilling the Promise of Love and Romance

Think back to earlier generations' relationships forged on the anvil of common dreams, mutual commitment, and shared sacrifice. Think of the weeks, and sometimes months, when couples had only each other's company and each other to depend upon. Think of all those couples who lived out their pledge to be together "until death do us part." Can you imagine today's temporarily famous couples wanting to be buried side-by-side like their early American ancestors?

Additionally, while many young people still talk longingly about the idea of "growing old together" with the love of their life, most do not believe that it is a realistic dream because "young love" does not often see examples today of what "old love" can be.

In a 2005 interview with Larry King, Billy Graham said of his wife Ruth,[12] "... I love her so much. And I love her more now—interestingly, I love her more now, and we have more romance now than we did when we were young."

Love and romance—in old age? Young people snicker at the thought. At best, they write it off as the childish sentimentality and clouded memory of doddering old age.

But what if they are wrong? What if a couple married for so long really does experience romance that is strong, that stirs the blood?

My friend, Frederica Mathewes-Green, described Ruth and Billy's relationship as having "all the lamps still blazing." Many young people find that description puzzling; they find old couples amusing and cannot picture them with their "lamps still blazing." Speaking of their retirement years, Billy once said, "It's a wonderful period of life for both of us. We've never had a love like we have now—we feel each other's hearts."[13]

How can young people comprehend "old love" when their only experience is "new love" that is framed by romance, flirtation, excitement, and pleasure? Youths experience the heights of soaring passion but often do not quite know how to cope with the aftermath when their emotions plunge into deep valleys where they question the validity and transient euphoria of sexual intercourse. In the absence of a marriage commitment, they have good reason to fear—and to feel exploited. After the intense and volatile emotions that are unleashed in the early explorations of new love, feelings can rebound from a crest of great excitement and exuberance to an undertow of emptiness or isolation. Tears of happiness can suddenly turn into a seeming desert of loneliness. These realities of our emotional makeup speak to the need for the security of vows of commitment "till death do us part."

New love is about a couple learning to cope with what it means to be naked, not merely physically but also emotionally. This is especially true when they have said by their words and actions not just "I desire you" or "you excite me," but "I need you." Often, the more intense and complete their intimacy, the more exposed they feel afterward. And there is something in our nature—particularly in youth—that rebels at the experience of being vulnerable, that feels angry at feeling as though self-sufficiency and independence have eroded. Lovers can be, and usually are, intensely territorial, responding with anger and outrage at any hint of infidelity by their mates or encroachment by a flirtatious interloper. At the same time, they feel unease as they realize that being a couple increasingly diminishes their autonomy. Add to this confusing mixture of needs the fact that freedom-loving young sweethearts are driven to one another's embrace, not merely by physical desire alone, but also by a deep—though often unrecognized—emotional need to belong. Surely, in the face of these conflicting desires, we are driven to mate because God hardwired us to do so.

Both poets and comedians have chronicled the irony and hilarity of all this pushing and pulling. It is hard to say which is more often thought: "The path of true love never did run smooth"[14] or "Lord, what fools these mortals be!"[15]

Old love has a better understanding than new love of the dual dimension of intimacy. In youth, the fireworks of physical passion—the God-designed motivating force that initially drives us to mate—can obscure the quieter but equally critical process of bonding that is occurring with every tender touch and embrace. This process of cementing the two together is seen only indirectly through its mysterious consequences, something that the Scriptures refer to when it speaks of "the two becoming one." The observable physical union of the couple—with its potential to create new life—is important and consequential. However, the unseen emotional bonding that accompanies sexual intimacy—if properly nourished within the bonds of marriage—can unite couples for life, thus equipping them to nourish any new life with which God blesses them.

But youth, caught up in the tumult and excitement of new love, has a limited awareness of how the intimacy of physical contact, or even mere eye contact, is at work to knit couples together with emotional bonds of connectedness, to produce an ever-stronger sense of wholeness, of completeness, of oneness. The life stories of Ruth and Billy Graham dramatically illustrate one of love's great paradoxes—the surrender of their autonomy in marriage did not diminish them (as many today fear), but the process of becoming husband and wife produced an expanding fulfillment of each of their personhoods, just the opposite of what might be expected.

God made the business of establishing and maintaining a couple's unity compelling by making sexual intimacy—between a man and a woman who love each other deeply and tenderly—one of the greatest pleasures of which humans are capable. We see a parallel process in nature when an oyster produces a pearl. Each time a couple exchanges some kind of intimacy, the bond between them grows deeper and more satisfying so that the satisfaction of two becoming one displaces the satisfaction of being autonomous. And just as the oyster makes the pearl ever-more lustrous by adding coat after coat of shell-forming fluid, a couple can produce a relationship of priceless quality simply by reaching out to each other day in and day out through words, glances, and caresses.

Sadly, young love does not often see examples today of that kind of love. Little wonder at their youthful skepticism of Graham's claim that a couple married for over a half a century can actually experience romance that is real, that competes with what they knew when they were young. We cannot know whether such skepticism was at play when an interviewer asked the Grahams' daughter Ruth if her mom, bedridden with degenerative osteoarthritis, and her dad, infirm with Parkinson's, were still madly in love.[16] Or perhaps the interviewer expressed the wistful hope of a postmodern mind. If so, the Graham daughter nourished that hope when she replied, "Very much so. Very much so...They look at each other with such love and tenderness. It's very sweet. And he says that this is the best time of their lives."

New love compared to old love is somewhat akin to the comparison of new silver with old silver. Certainly the former possesses a dazzling brilliance. But the latter's tarnish defines the elegance and artistry of its design. The marks of old silver's age speak to the history of its service, its significance, and its value. Old silver embodies a rich storehouse of memories, which gives it a luster that an immature piece of new silver, for all its inherent value and shiny surface, has not yet attained.

Keeping Love and Romance in the Marriage Relationship

The rarity of couples celebrating double-digit anniversaries seems to indicate that as a culture, we seem to have forgotten the simple truth that life "don't come easy."[17] Certainly, strong marriages, full of love and romance, require a lot of work; marriage is definitely an area where things "don't come easy." Perhaps, people give up too soon because they have absorbed the attitude that civilization is more advanced when things are faster, better, cheaper, and human life easier and more effortless. From Easy Bake Ovens to Easy Chairs, America is a culture striving for Easy Street.

And what is wrong with that? What exactly are we missing in today's quest to avoid difficulty?

The multimillion spectators and viewers of Olympic-level athletic events indicate that Americans still do appreciate achievements that "don't come easy." No pain, no gain—it is easy to see in athletics; year after year of grinding practice and mind-numbing drills, all coming together for one do-or-die competition. Still, while millions of us tune in for the spectacle and pomp of the Olympic Games or World Series and vicariously share the thrill of seeing the Stars and Stripes rising above other contenders for the laurels, we mere mortals are not very likely to have that singular moment of triumph and glory.

So what do the rest of us gain from pain—especially when it comes to working at establishing and building a happy, successful marriage?

Artists will tell you that perspective is everything. Photographers wait hours for just the right lighting, or they take hundreds of pictures to get just the right expression on a model's face. They also carry several lenses in order to have just the right one for the current circumstances when taking a special photograph. It does not take much to distort the view and ruin the effect that the artist or photographer wants to capture. There are many warped perspectives on love, romance, and marriage. An Egyptian writer and educator, Sayyid Outb, who is credited with laying the groundwork for the radical Islamic movement, spent time in the United States in 1949 and wrote what he saw as proof of animalistic American sexuality. He described ordinary American scenes with sex-drenched imagery and overheated language.[18] No wonder he thought all women should be hidden in shapeless black robes and their faces covered. Some feminists, on the other hand, denounce marriage as "legalized rape," and pseudopsychologists compare marriage to slavery and declare that marriage is bad for women's mental health and self-esteem.

How interesting that these "experts" deny the significance of romance and marriage in a woman's life yet accept tawdry encounters. Several years ago, Lisa Robertson, a Qantas flight attendant[19] described her tryst in a cramped airplane lavatory with a famous movie star, Ralph Fiennes, as "making love."

In the sexual arena, the number of ways for referring to sexual behavior are too numerous to catalog. Some are too crude to bring up in polite company while others are vague and lyrically poetic. Often a term that is wonderfully appropriate when applied to one situation is stripped of its true meaning when applied inappropriately. Exhibit A would be the frequent false usage of the expression "make love." I cannot think of a more egregious example of this than the flight attendant admitting that she and the academy-award nominated actor, a man she had never met before, engaged in sexual intercourse in the first-class toilet at 35,000 feet. She is quoted as saying, "It's true. We did make love on the plane that night. At first I denied it because I was so desperate to keep my job..."

The true character of their brief, pathetic affair was further clarified in her account when she described her subsequent stay overnight in his hotel room as ending at 7 a.m. the next morning with him saying, "I'm going to have to kick you out now." And then, she quotes him as saying in a sincere, gentle voice (being the consummate actor that he is), "I really like you."

Is this what passes for romance with postmodern women? For "making love"?

Such delusion may comfort the flight attendant but that does not make it true. It may be as she claims, that "we were both fantastically attracted to each other." But mere physical attraction does not warrant her conclusion that "I am sure he cared about me." Whoa. Cared about her? Lusted for her is more like it.

In the end, when he refused to cooperate in fabricating a story that might have helped her keep her job, she said, "I am upset by his betrayal."

Words like naked, vulnerable, exposed, intimate, personal, private, personhood, and human dignity are all terms we understand and might find useful in teaching a child about sexual behavior, even if it would be hard for us to give the child clear, explicit definitions of some of them. With several of them, we would likely resort to giving a definition by pointing to an example, such as when we point to the sky on a clear day and say to a child, "The sky is blue." It is hard to imagine, however, anyone using the encounter between the actor and flight attendant at 35,000 feet as a good example of "making love."

Using euphemisms (substituting a mild, indirect, or vague term for one considered harsh, blunt, or offensive) to describe sexual intercourse is not new. The ancient Scriptures frequently use the verb "to know" in lieu of something more explicit to recount the occurrence of sexual relations. But this euphemism, though somewhat vague, is nevertheless laden with meaning. It points to the fact that sexual intercourse is a means to an extremely intimate private knowledge of our personhood. In intercourse, the raw unadorned animalistic side of our humanity is exposed whether little or all clothing is removed. Logically, we know that the sexual part of our nature is universal; but each individual's personhood is unique and, at some level, intensely private. Hence, we find that being revealed to another individual through intimate sexual contact is one of life's moments of greatest vulnerability. We could not feel more exposed if we stood before an audience of thousands naked, having forgotten to don our costume and not knowing our lines.

That is why dating, courtship, and romance are so important as a prelude to marriage and equally important in keeping the marriage alive and vital. "Knowing" encompasses more than just physical lovemaking; it involves a commitment to the whole person and an understanding of that person's needs—including the need for love and romance.

When the cloak of our rationality is pushed aside and our intellect no longer provides a covering, it is then most important that both partners be clothed in love and the confident certainty of a permanent commitment to each other—in a word, married. Then the couple can progress to a state of being totally liberated from their inhibitions and the innate fear we all have of being exposed—to wit, of being known. What would under other circumstances be rape (a despicable violation of personhood) is now a physical expression of the union of two hearts in tender devotion and passionate desire.

This union is the only experience that genuinely warrants the term "making love." Anything short of this, no matter how it is spoken of, is a counterfeit, a fake experience of intimacy.

Notes

1. Janice Shaw Crouse, "It don't Come Easy," *Concerned Women for America*, August 25, 2004, http://cathoicexchange.com/2004/09/08/82158/ (accessed October 5, 2011).

2. Dr. Neil Clark Warren, "The Cohabitation Epidemic," *Focus on the Family*, June/July 2003, 10–11, http://www.josh.org/site/c.ddKDIMNtEqG/b.4186681/apps/s/content.asp?ct=5426739 (accessed October 5, 2011).

3. Barbara Dafoe Whitehead and David Popenoe, "The Marrying Kind: Which Men Marry and Why," In *The State of Our Unions: The Social Health of Marriage in America, 2004* (Rutgers University: The National Marriage Project, 2004), http://marriage.rutgers.edu/Publications/SOOU/TEXTSOOU2004.htm#Marriage (accessed February 17, 2009).

4. Janice Shaw Crouse, *Gaining Ground: A Profile of American Women in the 20th Century* (Washington, DC: The Beverly LaHaye Institute, 2000): 37–42.

5. Vera B. Tejada and Paul D. Sutton, "Births, Marriages, Divorces, and Deaths: Provisional Data for 2007," *National Vital Statistics Reports* 56, no. 21 (July 14, 2008): 1, Table A; and earlier reports, http://www.cdc.gov/nchs/data/nvsr/nvsr56/nvsr56_21.htm#TA (accessed February 16, 2009).

6. Lyrics from a song made popular by both Frank Sinatra and Dinah Shore, "Love and Marriage," has been recorded by numerous artists, http://www.lyricsg.com/101613/lyrics/franksinatra/loveandmarriage.html (accessed October 5, 2011).

7. Ibid.

8. Carol Platt Liebau, *Prude: How the Sex-Obsessed Culture Damages Girls* (New York: Center Street Hachette Book Group USA, 2007), 119.

9. D. C. Gentile, *Teen-Oriented Radio and CD Sexual Content Analysis* (Minneapolis, MN: National Institute on Media and the Family, 1999) as cited in Liebau, *Prude* 121.

10. "Hot 100," Billboard's Week of August 21, 2010, *Billboard.com*, http://www.billboard.com/charts/hot-100#/charts/hot-100 (accessed August 13, 2010).

11. Alexander Grant and others, "Eminem: Love the Way You Lie Lyrics. Featuring Rihanna," *Metrolyrics*, http://www.metrolyrics.com/love-the-way-you-lie-lyrics-eminem.html#ixzz0wVTTTsGw (accessed October 5, 2011).

12. Larry King, "Interview with Billy Graham," *Larry King Live*, CNN Transcripts, June 16, 2005, http://transcripts.cnn.com/TRANSCRIPTS/0506/16/lkl.01.html (accessed July 10, 2010).

13. Jon Meacham, "Pilgrim's Progress," *Newsweek*, August 14, 2006, http://www.newsweek.com/2006/08/13/pilgrim-s-progress.html (accessed October 5, 2011).

14. From William Shakespeare's *A Midsummer Night's Dream*, Act 1, scene 1, line 134. The line was spoken by Lysander in the play that was written about 1595. http://www.enotes.com/shakespeare-quotes/course-true-love-never-did-run-smooth (accessed October 5, 2011).

15. From William Shakespeare's *A Midsummer Night's Dream*, Act III, scene 2, line 115. The line was spoken by the character Puck. The play was written about 1595. http://www.bartleby.com/70/1832.html (accessed October 5, 2011).

16. CNN PRESENTS, "Encore Presentation: Billy Graham, America's Pastor," *Larry King Live*, CNN Transcripts, September 10, 2006, http://transcripts.cnn.com/TRANSCRIPTS/0609/10/cp.01.html (accessed July 10, 2010).

17. Ringo Starr and George Harrison, "It don't Come Easy," *Apple Records*, April 1971. This song reached number four in both the U.S. and U.K. singles charts. It was Starr's first solo single in the U.K., but his second in the United States following the breakup of the Beatles. Information about this song can be found at *Wikipedia*, "It don't Come Easy," page last modified April 10, 2011, http://en.wikipedia.org/wiki/It_Don%27t_Come_Easy (accessed April 14, 2011).

18. Robert Siegel, "Sayyid Qutb's America: Al Qaeda Inspiration Denounced U.S. Greed, Sexuality," *National Public Radio*, May 6, 2003, http://www.npr.org/templates/story/story.php?storyId=1253796 (accessed October 5, 2011).

19. Janice Shaw Crouse, "Plane Talk about Making Love," *Townhall*, February 21, 2007, http://townhall.com/columnists/JaniceShawCrouse/2007/02/21/plane_talk_about_making_love (accessed October 5, 2011).

3

Bring Back Dating

I must go down to the seas again, to the lonely sea and the sky,
And all I ask is a tall ship and a star to steer her by...
I must go down to the seas again, for the call of the running tide
Is a wild call and a clear call that may not be denied...
    —"Sea-Fever" by John Masefield (English writer, 1878–1967)

The irrepressible God-given urge of man and woman to find a connection with each other is like the wild call to the seamen of the running tide—it is an urgent, clear call that few can or would want to deny. As the sailor needs a fixed north star by which to navigate, just so young people, today as always, need "true" truths to successfully negotiate dating relationships in today's world brim with challenges—some that can be seen as clearly as the winds and waves; some that are hidden threats as menacing as undertows, rip tides, reefs, and sand bars—not always obvious to the untrained eye but capable of inflicting great harm all the same.

Since the sexual revolution of the 1960s, subsequent postmodern generations—three or more television generations followed by two Internet generations—have decreed that the old constellations that guided in the past have no relevance. Among the spiritually minded, there once were issues of morality (the virtue of chastity, now supposedly "out-of-date," required sexual intercourse to be reserved for marriage) that guided couples' behavior. The cultural guidelines for the secular-minded, though not bound by religious teaching, still demanded that couples behave so as "not to embarrass" the family. A girl who "slept around" or even was known to have had sex with a boyfriend or fiancé was considered "loose" or "promiscuous," and a boy who "got a girl pregnant" was "blamed." Today, however, very little is cause to blush; in today's "anything goes" culture, few behaviors, no matter how crude and vulgar, embarrass or are forbidden. And what of the church? Much of it, certainly the mainline denominations, with the Catholics and evangelicals not far behind, have largely abandoned their role in keeping the moral constellations burnished. Few pastors speak out about sexual promiscuity or cohabitation, and many churches have largely capitulated to the pagan secular culture.

In TV shows such as *90210*, everyone sleeping around was portrayed as normal. Similarly in *Friends,* and particularly so in the case of Jennifer Anniston's character "Rachel," an obsession with finding "the one" led her to sleep around, desperately searching for "the one." *Sex and the City* carried these ideas further and had an enormous effect, shaping young people's perceptions of how they should behave. The media's portrayal of casual sex as fun and glamorous, rather than promiscuous, risky, and slutty, led to new attitudes and values that displaced traditional ones.

With the old moral principles that had guided dating and sexual behavior lampooned and discredited by Hollywood and television on the entertainment front, and with feminism adding an intellectual façade of sorts to supposed "free love" (more about this later), new voices—some religious and some secular—began to be raised to fill this void.

In 1997, Joshua Harris, a popular speaker on high school and college campuses, wrote a book called *I Kissed Dating Goodbye.*[1] The book struck a chord; it sold far more than a million copies, was the number one paperback nonfiction book for all of 1998 and number two for all of 1999. Today, Harris claims that he was more interested in deepening his spiritual life than in spawning a no-dating fad. Whatever his intent in writing the book and in speaking on the subject across the United States, the idea of "kissing dating goodbye" had great appeal among many religious youths, particularly since they were facing mounting pressure from the secular culture to treat their virginity as though it were a plague that needed eradication. One young woman said to me, "You need to understand. The question in my high school is not whether you're going to kiss a guy on a first date, but whether you are going to sleep with him." So, no date, no hassle about sex.

While Harris is certainly not solely to blame for the nondating trend among religiously oriented young people, his book helped to spark widespread disenchantment with traditional dating by articulating a rationale for not doing so. I suppose one could be forgiven to think that such a serious decision as marriage could be decided through such a random process as dating. On one college campus, guys started wearing T-shirts trumpeting their disdain for dating, which read: "We don't date chicks!"

The "no-dating" climate has not, however, silenced the "wild clear call" of John Mansfield's lines heading this chapter. Dating just morphed into the avalanche of guys and girls texting each other non-stop day and night. One teenager lamented a slow day when he received only seventy-five texts between the time after school and bedtime.

Instead of formal dates where a guy asks a girl out, picks her up at her home or residence and is responsible for an evening of entertainment and her safe return, young people are more likely to participate in "group dates" where everyone is on their own—or not date at all. Worse, large segments of today's college population are more likely to "hookup" than to date.

Obviously, there is nothing wrong and much that is right with group activities for teens and young adults. During the 1970s and 1980s, numerous research studies pointed out the importance of friendship networks in helping members of both sexes find their future mates.[2] Psychologists note that considerable courage and self-confidence are required to initiate a conversation with a total stranger, whereas even shy or anxious personalities can relate relatively easily with someone with whom the person has mutual friends.[3] But there is a huge difference between the skills required for group interaction and those required for one-on-one interpersonal communication. There is definitely a place for group activities where young people can enjoy being with members of the opposite sex in casual and comfortable interaction, but intentional casual dating is also very helpful in the maturation process.

> *Watching your daughter being collected by her date feels like handing over a million-dollar Stradivarius to a gorilla.*
> —Jim Bishop (American Writer, 1907–1987)

The Purpose of Dating

There are definitely generational differences in perceptions about dating as well as differing customs in various communities, high schools, and colleges. I will be very clear. In my opinion, dating can have numerous benefits: developing self-confidence and social skills for young people, helping young people discern who they are in relation to the opposite sex, helping young people hone in on those characteristics that they want in a husband or wife, teaching young people good judgment in terms of assessing character and integrity, and helping young people develop the "antenna" that they need in order to recognize when others are not who they present themselves to be.

For the purposes of preparation for marriage, dating should be guided by the following considerations. During high school and college, dating should be viewed as an opportunity to schedule time with a person of the opposite sex in order to get to know him or her. The dates should be times of fun, fellowship, and good times—opportunities to discover the infinite variety in personalities and to learn about yourself and others. One of the important lessons that students learn is that different people bring out different aspects of our personalities; in many respects, we are different people when we are around different types of persons.

Such dating should not be burdened with pressure and an overlay of seriousness. Though certainly the ultimate purpose of dating is to find a mate, treating dating too seriously at the outset smacks of desperation, and it is inhibiting and counterproductive to the maturation process. High school and college students should realize that dating a person does not necessarily lead to marriage; dating is for fun and friendship—understanding, of course, that neither of these is possible if each is not treated with the courtesy, kindness, and respect that adds to the self-esteem of each of them. Along the way, most young people will generally fall in love with someone special, yet another "incidental" benefit of the dating "game."

Even though the goal is to have fun and enjoy getting to know the other person, each individual needs to have specific boundaries that reflect his or her own values and plans for the future. Those boundaries need to be clear and clearly communicated through both words and actions. This is the point at which much of today's "dating" fails and becomes risky or destructive behavior. To avoid getting involved in risky behaviors, young people should not spend time with persons who will not respect their boundaries or attend parties where their values are disrespected or flaunted. Young people need to realize that casual sex is heavy baggage to bring into a marriage, and they should avoid being in isolated places or at parties where they might face compromising situations. Since drinking often precedes sexual intimacy on campus—when inhibitions are freed and students behave in ways they regret later—students should avoid parties where alcohol and subsequent sex are likely. More than one in ten high-school girls will have been physically forced to have sexual intercourse in or out of school by the time they graduate and, usually, alcohol is involved. Nearly 20 percent of young women in college will be victims of attempted or actual sexual assault; again, alcohol is typically involved.

Wise young people will use imagination and creativity in dating—planning trips to museums or galleries, trying bowling or miniature golfing, visiting amusement parks, playing tennis, or going biking. They will engage in activities where conversation is possible rather than activities, like going to a movie, where it is possible to be together for a couple of hours without really interacting with each other.

Developing Social Skills through Dating and Vice Versa

I do not view dating as a frivolous activity. In a safe, social situation with someone who can be trusted to respect your values, dating can be preparation for life over and beyond the dating scene. The skills required to keep the interest of a girl or guy at a party require the same traits and skills that are necessary for getting along with others in a working situation or other social situations. It is about carrying on a conversation with someone that you do not know very well and presenting yourself as an interesting, well-informed person. Those skills that help a person get along with people in general are the same ones that enable a girl or guy to be a good date. Generally, the skills that make a person a "good date" as a teen or twenty-something are the same ones that, later on, make the person a reliable and competent "team player" at work.

Dating can be an excellent way to develop social skills. Likewise, dating skills are developed during all social interactions; in that way, the two skills—dating and social interaction—are linked. I am convinced that appropriate dating in high school and college prepares young people for successful relationships in adult life. Many a promising adult relationship is short-circuited because one or the other of the participants lacks the social skills necessary for successful interaction. In the same way, many a career path is derailed because the employee lacks the social skills for the next level of career advancement.

Marriage counselors tell us that marriages often flounder because of a basic lack of communication skills—the husband or wife is unable to talk with his or her spouse about essential matters in their marriage or is unable to express his or her emotions well enough to forge the intimate "connection" that makes for close marital bonds. Hundreds of books are written on communication breakdowns in marriage because one or the other of the marriage partners lacks the necessary skills to form a solid relationship. According to the American Counseling Association, the most common thread throughout all broken marriages is breakdown in communication. How much better it is when couples enter marriage with the skills they need to appropriately and accurately communicate with each other and carry on conversations with friends and co-workers.

Thus, I argue that dating matters to marriage, just as it matters in life. Here are just a few of the skills that can be developed in the social situations that constitute a typical traditional date:Learning to carry on interesting conversation in a variety of circumstances.

- Learning to get along with different types of personalities and people of different backgrounds.
- Learning and practicing the social protocols (including manners) required of polite society.
- Learning to recognize and adopt appropriate words and behaviors for different circumstances and situations.
- Developing the skills necessary for making and keeping friends.
- Developing poise and self-confidence through interacting successfully with a variety of people in a variety of situations.
- Learning the appropriate dress and acquiring the conversational polish required to be an appealing companion.

Social skills, as well as dating skills, are learned slowly and through practice; that is why dating can be helpful beginning in high school. The consequences of awkwardness at that time in life are much less significant than later in college or as young adults. The basic rule is simple: to get better at a specific skill—like thinking of things to say in social conversations—means to observe others who are skillful and to find situations where you can practice until you become as comfortable with it and as proficient at it as are your role models. These efforts will, inevitably, make a person more adept at all human relationships, including marriage.

Dating under Attack; Free Love Launched

This type of dating, however, has been under attack since the early 1960s when Helen Gurley Brown wrote *Sex and the Single Girl*,[4] advising girls that sex was the best way to have fun, be in control of their lives, and step onto the fast track of career success. Dating, declared Gurley Brown, was passé; smart, savvy women used men to get ahead and manipulated them for their own purposes. Marriage was a trap to be avoided.

Helen Gurley Brown made a career out of getting what she wanted out of relationships.[5] Everything that Brown has written in her extraordinarily prolific career—as a celebrity author, glamorous New

York socialite, and editor at *Cosmopolitan* for three decades—has advanced the idea that women have to look out for themselves, "play" by their own rules, and work the system for their advantage in order to get ahead.

In her signature style—breezy, irreverent, playful, sexy, humorous, and confessional—Brown sold several generations of women on the idea that promiscuity is sophisticated and that smart women use sex to move up in the world. After living the sexually liberated life until age thirty-seven, Helen decided she was ready for marriage. I cynically note that, obviously, with every passing year, her opportunities for using sex to get ahead were narrowing. She also realized, perhaps unconsciously—but given her philosophy and pragmatic approach to life and career, it was probably a conscious decision—that she could not make the jump from phenomenally successful executive secretary to member of the upper-crust professional class without marrying someone who bridged that chasm for her. Wealthy film studio executive, David Brown, was the perfect candidate; she "fell in love with his credentials." While she knew that he did not love her, that David respected her financial and career accomplishments was enough. She set out on a "lengthy and frustrating" crusade to become his wife. Not surprisingly, from her point of view, "men who help women with their careers are sexier than men with flat stomachs, large biceps, and other remarkable assets."

In 1964, a reporter asked Brown if she had changed her mind and decided that "a woman's priority in life should be to please the man in her life." Helen responded that "pleasing your man" is merely being "self-serving" because pleasing a man enables you to get the man and have a happier time and a better marriage. "Man pleasing has to do with keeping your relationship desirable and happy," she answered in the interview, "It also has to do with getting a man to commit to you if he hasn't yet done so."

How ironic that the queen of sexual liberation ends up in a marriage and focused on securing her husband's commitment to fidelity. It is doubly ironic that a woman who built a career on warning other women to avoid needing a man ends up realizing that happiness depends on getting a certain man to marry her and then making that husband happy. To further compound the irony, Brown, who wrote extensively about the importance of a woman controlling her own destiny, recognizes her dependence upon her husband for her professional success, just as he comes to realize his dependence upon her for his personal well-being.

So the woman who turned dating on its ear in favor of sex games ends up living a life that repudiates the lifestyle that she advocated for everyone else. We have no way of looking inside Gurley Brown's relationship with her husband, but it is hard to imagine David Brown writing to Helen with "all the tenderness of [his] heart" like John Adams wrote to Abigail, calling her his "best, dearest, worthiest, wisest friend in this world."

The "New" Dating Game

The crude and promiscuous nature of the "new dating game" is vividly laid out in Charlotte Allen's article in the *Weekly Standard*[6]. Allen writes, "Louts who might as well be clad in bearskins and wielding spears trample over every nicety developed over millennia to mark out a ritual of courtship as a prelude to sex: Not just marriage (that went years ago with the sexual revolution and the mass-marketing of the birth-control pill) or formal dating (the hookup culture finished that)—but amorous preliminaries and other civilities once regarded as elementary, at least among the college-educated classes."[7] Allen blames demographics, contraception, and divorce, but she also blames "the feminist-driven academic and journalistic culture celebrating that yesterday's 'loose' women are today's 'liberated' women, able to proudly 'explore their sexuality' without 'getting punished for their lust,' as the feminist writer Naomi Wolf put it..."[8]

Allen cites numerous cultural influences that contribute to the hookup culture. But, she adds, "If it all sounds cheesy, tedious, manipulative, obvious, condescending to women, maybe kind of gay, it's because it is. But here's the rub: *This stuff works.*" Why? Allen declares, "Women crave dominant men. And it seems that when men are forbidden to dominate in a socially beneficial way—as husbands and fathers, for example—women will seek out assertive, self-confident men whose displays of power aren't so socially beneficial...many women satisfy their yearning for dominance by throwing themselves at bad boys or even worse." The net result: "[W]e have met the Stone Age, and it is us."[9]

As Allen explained:

> The whole point of the sexual and feminist revolutions was to obliterate the sexual double standard that supposedly stood in the way of ultimate female freedom. The twin revolutions obliterated much more, but the double standard has reemerged in a harsher, crueler form: wreaking havoc on beta men and on beta women, too, who,

as the declining marriage rate indicates, have trouble finding and securing long-term mates in a supply-saturated short-term sexual marketplace. Gorgeous alpha women fare fine—for a few years until the younger competition comes of age. But no woman, alpha or beta, seems able to escape the atavistic preference of men both alpha and beta for ladylike and virginal wives (the Darwinist explanation is that those traits are predictors of marital fidelity, assuring men that the offspring that their spouses bear are theirs, too). And every aspect of New Paleolithic mating culture discourages the sexual restraint once imposed on both sexes that constituted a firm foundation for both family life and civilization.[10]

Why the Hookup Culture that Replaced Dating Is a Hideously Bad Idea

Today in the hookup culture that Allen describes so well, anyone who advocates abstinence before marriage is considered a prude with outdated, archaic ideas who is advocating something that is both impossible and unrealistic. Nothing generates more vicious "hate mail" and personal attacks than when I write articles about the benefits of abstinence before marriage—approving of the new trends toward abstinence that have led to reductions in teen sexual activity, teen births, and teen abortions. Expressing these views has brought howls of protest and filled my e-mail box to overflowing with verbal abuse from readers who hold the notion that uninhibited, promiscuous sexual activity is the key to the good life. They are happy to let me know, sometimes in the rudest possible terms, that I am unrealistic, prudish, and sexually repressed.

One correspondent was incensed when I reported a study from the *American Journal of Preventive Medicine* that linked teen sex with depression.[11] This person volunteered that he/she had been intent on getting rid of his/her virginity at the first opportunity. I wanted to ask, "How is that going for you?" because magazines periodically run supposedly funny features recounting how various people "lost their virginity." Inevitably, such features make for sad reading; the writers recount embarrassment, frustration, awkwardness, and disgust for themselves and their partner. Before listing ways that college students lose their virginity (most during drunken or drug-induced stupors), one blog put it this way: "You always remember where you were when you lost your virginity, and most of the time, you wish you could forget it."

What causes people to get so defensive and angry over the issue of people's ability to control their sexual impulse—that it is, indeed, beneficial to learn self-control in the area of sexual behavior? Self-control is not "in," and the sexual revolution, according to a variety of informed observers, "seems complete: Young women now engage in premarital sex at almost the same rate as young men."[12] Two researchers at San Diego State University report a stronger correlation between attitudes and behavior about premarital sex among young women than among young men, indicating that "culture has a larger effect on women's sexuality."[13] They also report a significant change of attitude toward premarital sex from 1940 to 2000: "Both young men and women became more sexually active over time, as measured by age at first intercourse (decreasing from 19 to 15 years among young women) and percentage sexually active (increasing from 13 percent to 47 percent among young women). Attitudes toward premarital intercourse became more lenient, with approval increasing from 12 percent to 73 percent among young women and from 40 percent to 79 percent among young men."[14] [Though there are signs that abstinence until marriage may be making a comeback, as the latest trends indicate some decline in sexual activity, teen births, and teen abortions.]

Romance Is Thrown Aside

In his informative and provocative article in *The Chronicle of Higher Education*, Steven E. Rhoads, a professor of politics at the University of Virginia who specializes in the issues of gender, culture, and public policy, declared, "[R]omance has no place in the mating culture in college today, where the 'hookup'—a commitment-free sexual encounter with a stranger or acquaintance—reigns."[15] He believes, based on twelve years of teaching a course on sex differences to college juniors and seniors, that women typically are not happy with hookups. "Time and again, women see their girlfriends' posthookup traumas, even if they themselves manage to avoid such outcomes," he wrote. "If the men call again, it's often just for another hookup. But as soon as the women push for a real relationship, the men break it off." Women, he observed, "don't want sex for long without an emotional connection, a sense of caring, if not real commitment, from their partners. As one student wrote in a paper for my class, 'We are told not to be sexual prudes, but to enjoy casual sex, we have to be emotional prudes.'"

Further, Rhoads reported, "My female students tell me that the emotional pain caused by casual sex goes largely unreported by women, because they are often ashamed that they care about men who treat them like strangers the next morning. They don't want the men involved or the rest of the campus to know about their tears." After all, "[f]eelings don't change with the times in quite the same way that behaviors and attitudes do...and will not disappear anytime soon."

Bonding Is Short-Circuited

These days, nothing causes some people's ire to rise more than to suggest that sex is not "free" and should not be taken "casually." Yet, the science is clear: casual sex short-circuits the bonding process. Years ago, several rock groups, including the "Searchers," sang about "Love Potion Number Nine,"[16] which would keep a guy from being a "flop with the chicks." What those rock stars did not know—but, we now know—is that there really is a love potion—a miracle, God-designed chemical that is induced when a couple shares touch, closeness, and/or intimacy. Called "oxytocin," the neuropeptide isolated by neuroscientists and dubbed the "cuddle hormone," has crucial influence on a couple's bonding.[17]

Researchers know that oxytocin is produced naturally in the brain—in the hypothalamus—and that it is released when a couple becomes physically intimate, most especially during sexual orgasm, producing strong bonding in both men and women. For women, it increases trust and immediately produces feelings of attachment, just as dozens of prefeminist Hollywood movies dramatized. What researchers have discovered, however, is something a movie could not show. Amazingly, oxytocin also increases a man's sperm count, facilitates sperm transport, and strengthens male ejaculation. In short, it causes greater male potency.

The researchers' experiments have shown that this natural chemical dramatically affects many species and that blocking the hormone can short-circuit a mother's maternal nurturing instincts and cause her to reject her offspring. On the positive side, oxytocin is also released in the mother when an infant nurses, and it stimulates contractions during the birth process—it is used in the delivery room to trigger labor. Its long-run contribution to the infant's well-being, though, is that oxytocin (and the closely related male hormone vasopressin) is a key ingredient in the process of pair bonding—creating a family that can become a safe, nurturing environment for the child. When a couple cuddles, the chemical is released and the woman, especially, becomes attached to the man. A couple's repeated intimate encounters strengthen their bonding.

We are used to musicians singing and poets waxing eloquent stanzas about love, but it is quite a jolt to have scientific researchers bluntly call love a "chemical addiction" between a man and a woman. In fact, they claim that the brains of people who say that they are deeply in love use the same neural mechanisms that are activated during the process of addiction. The affected brain areas are relatively small, but have powerful influence on deep emotional responses—one's "gut" feelings. A Rutgers University study indicates that the feelings of romantic love are among the strongest drives on earth—even more powerful than hunger.[18] Other researchers indicate that oxytocin has other long-range implications—that individuals develop a "template" for a partner based on their previous pair-bonding.

Interestingly, there is a prairie vole (a small burrowing rodent less than two inches long) that is one of the few animal species (only 3 percent) that forms monogamous relationships.[19] These voles have an intense, extended mating ritual and then mate for life. Another type of vole, the montane vole, has vastly different behavior—monogamy plays no role in its reproductive activities, even though, genetically, the two vole species are 99 percent alike. Scientists say that the montane vole brain lacks a receptor for oxytocin and vasopressin. If the oxytocin receptor—called OTR in research lingo—is missing, mating does not produce bonding. The monogamous relationships that are part of God's plan for us as humans are not an accidental feature, but purposive, a matter of intentional design. And like the prairie vole as opposed to the montane vole, He put all of the elements into our nature to accommodate that purpose and propel us in that direction.

A study from the University of California, San Francisco (UCSF),[20] found that the production of oxytocin varied among women according to the level of distress and anxiety or the degree of security in their relationships. The women who had fewer negative emotional relationships in their lifetimes experienced greater oxytocin production. Likewise, they were better able to set appropriate boundaries for their subsequent relationships. Numerous studies indicate that stress and fright inhibit oxytocin release. In other words, if relationships are not grounded in the kind of explicit commitment evidenced by loving, trustworthy, considerate, selfless behavior, the amount of oxytocin produced by intimacy decreases, and it becomes increasingly difficult for bonding to take place. On the other hand, the researchers at UCSF said bluntly, "[A] close, regular relationship may influence the responsiveness of the hormone."[21]

Why did we need scientists to reintroduce us to these basics? Generations have known about these responses from Biblical precepts and, intuitively, from experience—even if they did not know the exact chemical mechanism. Why did mothers ever stop teaching the common sense lessons of love? How did we come to reject all that Scripture and experience traditionally taught and to depend upon so-called experts—"professionals" who have taught us so many false notions in the last fifty years—to tell us how to ruin our lives?

The truth is simple. To love deeply and with greater enthusiasm, we must be highly discriminating about our relationships with the opposite sex. Oxytocin is instrumental in regulating the sex drive in both males and females; it creates a natural feedback loop so that the more sex a couple has, the more they want. Sex with the right person (read husband/wife) produces a psychochemical cocktail that can yield absolute, unconditional, and uninhibited love for each other—orgasm causes levels of oxytocin to increase three to five times above normal.

The warning is equally simple—to casually "hookup" is to risk short-circuiting future relationships. The chemical reaction that takes place during orgasm prepares the body and heart for a relationship. When the relationship does not develop, the person's bonding ability and ability to trust is undermined. Further, the stress of uncommitted mating produces the same effect. In short, promiscuity can weaken the long-range bonding potential of sex. The bottom line is this: Sex has consequences. The cocktail of chemicals that is unleashed when a couple touches is powerful and has long-lasting, as well as wide-ranging, effects on that specific relationship as well as all subsequent ones.

In short, the oxytocin effect can also lose its potency to draw the couple together if the couple has sex repeatedly without a corresponding emotional intimacy. In such a case, the emotions will "freeze" and refuse to bond. In his seminal writing on bonding, Dr. Donald Joy[22] reports that a study of 100,000 women indicated that "early sexual experience" was linked to low self-esteem, unhappiness in sexual intimacy, and dissatisfaction in eventual marriages. Dr. Joy stated unequivocally, "Humans are uniquely hungry for establishing significant relationships."

There Are Physical Risks and Relationship Consequences

So much for the myth, "Sex is no big deal!" It always has been "a big deal" and always will be. Even if contraception and the prevention of disease transmission were 100 percent effective—which they most certainly are not, the psychological impact of meaningless, casual sexual intimacy, particularly upon young females, can never be eliminated. No amount of argument to the contrary will change that basic biological reality.

Oddly enough, the promotion of sexual promiscuity gets coupled with messages about empowering women. Some feminists argue that women "have a right" to be sexually promiscuous "just like men," and some even claim that being a "slut" is positive proof of women's power. In April 2011, over two thousand people participated in what was called Slut Walk Toronto to emphasize a woman's "right" to dress provocatively.[23] However, the evidence shows that so-called sexual freedom has hidden costs; along with a loss of "power," women have paid other hefty prices. Women still bear the responsibilities and consequences of casual sex, with the difference between now and fifty to one hundred years ago being that men are not pressured to marry their "baby mamas." Too often, the woman is left with only regrettable "choices." Too many choose abortion, many living with guilt and regret, while others choose single motherhood with its substantial risk factors for children and unrelenting stresses on the mother; too few choose adoption.

Casual sex is a great recipe for getting sexually transmitted diseases. [See Chapter 5] Though modern medicine has made these somewhat less disastrous, a high percentage are incurable and highly contagious; they can leave women with a lifelong disease, many of which can make them sterile. Sadly, STDs are rampant among young adults and increasingly so among teens. So, while many celebrity feminists and the entertainment industry promote recreational sex as empowering for women, nothing could be further from the truth.

Having sex without entering a publicly committed relationship—marriage—puts a couple's relationship at risk and brings considerable emotional baggage into that relationship as well as any future relationships. In addition, trust is jeopardized; if the individual was unwilling and/or unable to maintain self-control prior to marriage, why would a marriage partner believe that spouse would be able to resist temptation after marriage. In his 1987 surprising bestseller, *Super-Marital Sex: Loving for Life*, Paul Pearsall described the ideal lead-up to an ideal marriage, based on ten years of careful records from the thousands of couples that he counseled: "Slow development of the original sexual bond, with an absolute boundary by which no penetration occurred before marriage." Further, he asserted, "Premarital sex is counterproductive of a good martial relationship."[24]

The fact is that despite the wholesale repudiation of traditional Judeo-Christian moral values relating to sex and marriage by a large majority of the elites—as well as many of the general public, the reality is that chastity is a virtue and that virginity is one of the most priceless gifts a couple can give to each other in consummation of their nuptial vows.

The idea that valuing virginity equates to being sexually repressed is, of course, patent nonsense. One might as well try to make the argument that back in the 1970s and 1980s, being a nonsmoker or a teetotaler was tantamount to being antisocial.

Logically, the benefits of going into marriage unencumbered by the emotional scars and the health consequences that often go with sexual experimentation and promiscuity have not changed. But we know—and have known since the days of the Greek philosopher Aristotle—that persons are persuaded not just by logic (*logos*) but by emotions as well (*pathos*). Moreover, the strongest arguments come from persons with credibility and charisma (*ethos*), who combine the force of logical arguments with emotional appeals.

Those who defend traditional morality today, however, are at a distinct disadvantage in terms of persuading teens who evaluate arguments within the context of today's popular culture and not from the *logical*, factual content of the argument. For teens willing to consider the evidence carefully and clearly, it is blindingly obvious that casual sexual experimentation (often fueled by drinking and drugs) is a terribly inferior proposition compared to the joys of experiencing sexual intimacy as the seal of a marriage commitment to the love of one's life. However, this requires long-term thinking. It requires valuing an experience that you can only dimly imagine. For both of these, strong parental guidance and support are crucial assets.

The persuasiveness of logic by itself is often insufficient in the face of the *emotional* counterforces with which young people have to deal. On the one hand, there is the strong temptation of the excitement associated with sexual exploration, and, on the other, there is the fear of group ridicule for sexual abstinence.

It would be difficult enough if it were only peer group pressures driving teens in the wrong direction. However, far too many of today's sexual revolution veterans of the 1960s, now aging Baby Boomers, have spent a long time telling themselves and any audience that will listen that their momentary sexual thrills were worth the bad stuff they have lived with ever since, namely the "complications" in their relationships with their spouses and children. The emotional wreckage littering the landscape for the last thirty to forty years is like the elephant in the corner that everyone pretends not to see. Yet it does not take a psychologist to recognize that avoidance is ineffective in dealing with the relationship messes and destroyed dreams. The trends indicate that many teenagers are now seeing that "elephant" and thus are valuing virginity.

In an earlier era, one counterbalance to the forces pushing for sexual experimentation by teens and young adults was the moral authority of traditional Judeo-Christian teaching regarding the sanctity of sexual activity and the imperative for limiting sexual intercourse to the marriage bed. Sadly, rather than facing the ridicule from those among the educated elites, many religious leaders have abandoned the teachings regarding moral purity before marriage and fidelity within marriage.

We must do a better job of instilling in young people a healthy fear of violating our human dignity, which we diminish by ignoring the full realities involved in sexual intimacy, by truncating the multidimensional nature of sex, by robbing it of its significance, and by reducing it to merely a means of momentary physical pleasure rather than reserving intercourse to be the means of bonding a husband and wife into one flesh—making them both rapturous and whole—and providing a love-bathed secure setting should the miracle of new life bless their union.

When we accept that our human dignity is God-given, we have the *logically persuasive reason* to follow moral law as the surest—and the only—safe path to love and happiness. We also have the *emotionally persuasive reason* to be afraid of acting in violation of the boundaries laid down by the Creator of the Universe; in His universe we see the laws of cause and effect at work everywhere. Ignorance of, or indifference to, these boundaries brings consequences as surely, if not as swiftly, as jumping out the window of a fifty-story building brings destruction. Moral laws are built into our humanity, and they order the world we live in. Best of all, we are made in His image, and when His law is instilled within us, we have the guidance to love and to forgive, which sustains love over the long haul.

There is a quiet revolution happening on the nation's school and college campuses. There is good news from the Centers for Disease Control and Prevention (CDC) that today's trends indicate more sexual abstinence by teens and college students, as well as a decrease in teen pregnancy (a trend that began in the 1990s as the abstinence movement took shape). Among fifteen- to twenty-four-year-olds, just under 30 percent report no sexual contact ever. The current percentages (29 percent for females and 27 percent for males) are a significant increase of abstinent young people from 2002, when the percentage was 22 percent. Other recent trends indicate less sexual activity, fewer teen pregnancies and births, and lower abortion rates.

Two Notre Dame professors, Mark Regnerus and Jeremy Uecker, note that as sex has increasingly been separated from marriage, 70 percent of contemporary young adults regret their first sexual encounter. Regnerus and Uecker document some of the realities that are prompting today's young people to be abstinent.[25] The move back to abstinence is good news indeed and certainly substantiates our claims that providing better information leads to better decision-making by adolescents and young adults. All these new, more positive trends mean a brighter future for the nation's young people.

I need to add, in passing, that there remains a dark and growing cloud on our future: the rising proportion of unwed births (41 percent in 2009) for women continues to be problematic. And it is not, as it used to be in the 1960s and 1970s, primarily a problem of raging teen hormones. In 1973, the teen population contributed 53 percent of all unwed births. However, in 2009, it had declined to only 21 percent. It is now the twenty-something women who are driving the share of out-of-wedlock births higher and higher. Among today's young women, "baby bumps" are not just culturally acceptable; they are glamorized in the media, which has filtered down to the high-school level and spread throughout American culture.

Among teens, however, there are encouraging signs of a new respect for abstinence and traditional dating, instead of recreational sex and "hookups." The CDC reports that teenage birth rates have significantly declined. The statistics from 2009, the most recent year for data collection, show that teenage birth rates "were at the lowest levels ever reported in the United States, declining a significant 37 percent over the last two decades."

According to the CDC report, birth rates for teens aged fifteen to seventeen dropped in thirty-one states during a two-year period, 2007–2009, and rates for older teenagers aged eighteen to nineteen also declined a significant amount in forty-five states during this same time period.

55

This seventy-year low in teen birth rates raises questions about the reason for such a significant decline—especially after years of increased birth rates and popular TV shows such as "16 and Pregnant" being the standard for modern adolescent culture.

With an increasingly sexualized culture, fewer and later marriages, and reports about rampant promiscuity, questions about what might be leading to this decrease in teen birth rates are very legitimate.

Answers include speculation about the influence of abortion, the economic recession, and better use of contraceptives.

The Decline in Teen Births Is Clearly Not Due to Increased Abortions

Actually, the abortion rate in the United States is also at record lows—the lowest in more than thirty years. Just over one in five pregnancies ends in abortion (down from one in four in 2000). The actual number of abortions has been on a steady decline, having reached their peak in 1990. In another important indicator of shifting attitudes about abortion, the number of abortion providers has also dropped to under 2,000 (a decrease of more than 2 percent).

The Decline Is Not Due to the Recession

Some suggest that the recession has increased awareness of how much it costs to sustain a family, making teens think twice about their choices. Research released earlier in the spring by the Pew Research Center found that states hit hardest by the recession experienced the biggest drops in births. Obviously, hard economic times can have a potential impact, but it would be a stretch to think that teens immersed in a culture of instant gratification and "just do it" messages are good candidates—especially when sexually stirred—for making decisions based on their understanding of the economy. Sexual activity is typically motivated by emotions and not restrained by fiscal concerns. This leads to a huge decrease in second and third births by teen mothers.

Economics may indeed have had an effect, but not in the way that the above statement suggests. The downward trend in teen births has persisted through three recessions and two economic expansions during the last two decades. One notable instance where economics was a factor resulted from changes in welfare policy. Beginning in the early 1990s, states began requiring teen mothers receiving assistance to stay in school and live with a parent or other approved adult, thus ending a teenager's ability to set up and maintain their own residence at government expense. Also, under welfare reform, a teen having an additional child did not automatically receive an increase in income.

The Decline Is Not Due to Better Teen Contraception

Increased use of contraception has also been cited as playing a role in the decrease of teen pregnancies; however, significant numbers of sexually active teens do not use contraception. The increase in implantable contraception has been accompanied by a decrease in use of the pill. The CDC reported that 46 percent of teens have had sexual intercourse, but 14 percent of girls and 10 percent of boys say that they do not use any type of birth control.

Abstinence and Better Knowledge About the Consequences of Too-Early Sexual Activity Is a More Likely Reason for the Decline in Teen Pregnancy

"Sex-education" proponents and those who benefit financially from teen sexual activity would like to cite reasons other than abstinence for the decline in teen pregnancies; they downplay the influence of more widespread support for the benefits of abstinence and getting the abstinence message spread to young people. The data, however, is most consistent with the conclusion that the abstinence message is making inroads and influencing today's youth. Our teens are more aware of the variety and prevalence of sexually transmitted diseases, the harms of promiscuity, and the disruption that an unplanned pregnancy brings to a teen's life—in spite of Planned Parenthood and MTV's attempts to normalize the consequences and profit from increased teen sexual activity. They are also, thanks to abstinence education, more self-confident and see more possibilities for their future as they learn the benefits of saying "no" to too-early sexual activity.

Teens living with the consequences of their over-sexualized environment are confronting the not-so-glamorous truths about the "hookup" culture. College counselors report that they are seeing a dramatic increase in sex-related problems on campuses. An article in *Professional Psychology* reveals over three-quarters of clinic directors (77.1 percent) noted increases in "severe psychological problems." Over the past decade, counselors report that depression cases *doubled*, suicidal students *tripled*, and sexual assault cases *quadrupled*.

Sexually transmitted diseases are rampant in a culture where it is not uncommon for students to have sex with several partners; researchers refer to it as "concurrency." About one in four women and about one in five men have HPV. Other STDs, like Herpes, Gonorrhea, and Chlamydia, are also common among students—an estimated two-thirds of STDs occur among those under age twenty-five. The prevailing message about abortion is that it is a "choice," but far too many of today's college women have seen a friend be abandoned by a guy or coerced to have an abortion when he finds out she is pregnant.

Conclusion

Wonderful books about today's dating culture are available and are having an impact on college students and young careerists.Wendy Shalit's book, *The Good Girl Revolution: Young Rebels with Self-Esteem and High Standards*, and her original book on modesty, *A Return to Modesty: Discovering the Lost Virtue*, are having profound influence.

Miriam Grossman's *Unprotected* lays out the consequences of promiscuity.

Carol Platt Liebau's book, *Prude: How the Sex-Obsessed Culture Damages Girls*, reveals the "minefields" that today's students have to navigate in their sexually "ramped up" world.

Julie Klausner warns smart women not to be reckless with their hearts or bodies in *I Don't Care about Your Band*.

Joe McIlhaney Jr. and Freda McKissic Bush have written a book of scientific data on casual sex, *New Science on How Casual Sex is Affecting our Children*.

Laura Sessions Stepp, author of *Unhooked: How Young Women Pursue Sex, Delay Love and Lose at Both*, describes the shift of "power" away from women in the hookup culture and noted that many young women cannot handle the physical and emotional battering that they suffer in the new hookup landscape.

Meg Meeker's *Your Kids at Risk: How Teen Sex Threatens Our Sons and Daughters* is also a no-holds-barred treatise about consequences.

In her book, *Hooking Up: Sex, Dating, and Relationships on Campus*, Kathleen Bogle writes about how co-eds long for a return to traditional dating. All these books, and numerous others, are being read by today's generation of students, and they are having a positive impact on student behavior.

In addition, there are some very savvy outreach programs gaining popularity on college campuses that promote a more healthy approach to dating and building relationships between the two sexes. Foremost among them is the Love and Fidelity Network, which currently has chapters on about two dozen high-profile campuses, including Princeton, Harvard, and Notre Dame. This very popular program, with distinguished Princeton professor Robert George in leadership, provides well-attended forums and discussion groups promoting abstinence, sexual integrity, and marriage. The Ruth Institute, headed by Dr. Jennifer Roback Morse, provides speakers for campus events and quality research on the benefits of marriage.

We are also seeing some intriguing pop cultural changes afoot with pop stars sending countercultural messages. Lady Gaga created a media frenzy in 2010 when she told the press that she was going celibate and suggested that others do the same. Former American Idol winner Kelly Clarkson released a song, "I Don't Hook Up," where she declared that she did not hook up and she did not "come cheap." On Facebook, there is a girls' group called "Bring Dating Back" for girls who want guys to take them out on a real date rather than head straight for a bed.

But arguably, the most influential cultural statement lately among the youngest teens was a few subtle lines in a #1 hit song, "Fifteen." Taylor Swift, one of the most popular of today's country music stars, sang poignantly about "realizing bigger dreams" than the high-school boyfriend, and about crying with Abigail "who gave everything" to a boy who "changed his mind." She said in a recent interview, "I wouldn't be a party girl even if I wasn't doing this [songwriter and performer]; that's just not the way I live my life."

At last, our young people are beginning to hear the truth from some pop stars, and they are getting solid information about sex, including the quality abstinence programs that have been given wider distribution over the past decade. Today's youth are hearing from multiple sources about the benefits of self-respect, self-restraint, and learning to say "no." Perhaps a trend is underway after all; we can only hope and continue to challenge the nation's young people to live up to their highest potential.

To my delight, many in today's generation long for the "good ole days" of dating. Both *Glamour* and *Salon* have written about the desire to "bring back dating."

Salon recounts a mother/daughter conversation, where the daughter says to the mother, "I envy you. You lived in an era when dating really existed." The mother declares that it was not all that great: "Things were much more defined in those days. Boys asked girls out. Girls played hard to get. A good girl never phoned a boy. You know the story."

The daughter laments, "People don't date anymore. They go out once, they go out twice, and then they're a couple. This getting to know lots of people, try on new experiences—it just doesn't exist anymore."[26]

Glamour magazine listed fifteen "vintage dating terms" that needed to make a comeback.[27] Number one on the list was "woo, court" because "they imply effort on the man's part." The same reason was given for "When can I see you?" and "Can I call you?" The phrase, "Little Black Book," also made the list because it required the guy to know the girl's name, not just write a description and phone number. Girls also wanted a return of romantic-sounding terms like "beau, paramour, suitor, and lover." The unifying theme of the "bring back dating" movement seems to be a desire to have more intentionality on the part of the guys and more romance in male/female relationships.

It is too soon, of course, to be certain of whether the Internet generation, seeing the wreckage of the last fifty years, will gain understanding and rediscover the wisdom of the old constellations, those tried and proven moral principles that once guided young people to navigate the turbulent waters of dating and courtship. There are hopeful signs.

Notes

1.   Joshua Harris, *I Kissed Dating Goodbye* (Sisters, OR: Multnomah Books, 1997).
2.   Brian G. Gilmartin, *Shyness & Love: Causes, Consequences, and Treatment* (Lanham, MD: University Press of America, 1987), 227–28.
3.   Ibid., 227.
4.   Helen Gurley Brown, *Sex and the Single Girl*, 1st ed. (New York: Giant Cardinal, 1963).
5.   This section on Helen Gurley Brown was published in the journal, *The Family in America*. Janice Shaw Crouse, "The Marriage Tango," *The Family in America* 23, no. 3 (Fall 2009): http://www.familyinamerica.org/index.php?rid=17&cat_id=4 (accessed October 5, 2011).
6.   Charlotte Allen, "The New Dating Game: Back to the New Paleolithic Age," *Weekly Standard* 15, no. 21 (February 15, 2010): http://www.weeklystandard.com/print/articles/new-dating-game (accessed October 5, 2011).
7.   Ibid.
8.   Naomi Wolf wrote *Promiscuities* as an attempt to remove the stigma from being a "Slut"—she capitalized the new label to give it dignity and to "remove the puritanical social norms."
9.   Allen, "New Dating Game."
10.   Ibid.
11.   Janice Shaw Crouse, "Teen Sex Leads to Depression and Drug Use," *Townhall*, January 30, 2007, http://townhall.com/columnists/JaniceShawCrouse/2007/01/30/teen_sex_leads_to_depression_and_drug_use/ (accessed October 5, 2011).

12. Steven E. Rhoads and others, "The Emotional Costs of Hooking Up," *Chronicle of Higher Education*, June 20, 2010, http://chronicle.com/article/The-Emotional-Costs-of-Hooking/65960/?key=QWkgLgJoZXVINnFieyJEfSVQO3N5KUsqbnwTY3caZlBV (accessed October 5, 2011).

13. Brooke E. Wells and Jean M. Twenge, "Changes in Young People's Sexual Behavior and Attitudes, 1943-1999: A Cross-Temporal Meta-Analysis," *Review of General Psychology* 9, no 3 (September 2005): 249–61.

14. Ibid.

15. Rhoads et al., "Emotional Costs."

16. Information about the song and a history of artists performing the hit can be found at *Wikipedia*, "Love Potion No. 9 (song)," http://en.wikipedia.org/wiki/Love_Potion_No._9_%28song%29 (accessed October 5, 2011).

17. University of California, San Francisco, "Hormone Involved in Reproduction may have Role in the Maintenance of Relationships," *ScienceDaily*, July 15, 1999, http://www.sciencedaily.com/releases/1999/07/990715062344.htm (accessed August 18, 2010).

18. Helen Fisher, *Why We Love: The Nature and Chemistry of Romance* (New York: Henry Holt, 2004): 182.

19. Christopher Mims, "Addicted to Love," *ZooGoer* 33, no. 3 (2004), http://nationalzoo.si.edu/Publications/ZooGoer/2004/3/monogamy.cfm (accessed October 6, 2011).

20. University of California, San Francisco, "Hormone Involved in Reproduction."

21. Ibid.

22. Donald M. Joy, *Bonding: Relationship in the Image of God*, 2nd ed. (Nappanee, IN: Evangel Publishing House, 1999), 86.

23. Tooble Team, "Slut Power," *Tooble* (blog), April 6, 2011, http://tooble.tv/2011/04/slut-power/ (accessed October 5, 2011).

24. Paul Pearsall, *Super-Marital Sex: Loving for Life*, Book Club ed. (New York: Doubleday, September 16, 1987), 75.

25. Mark Regnerus and Jeremy Uecker, *Premarital Sex in America: How Young Americans Meet, Mate, and Think about Marrying* (New York: Oxford University Press, 2011), 22.

26. Courtney Weaver, "Prevent Wandering Eyes: Bring Back Dating!" *Salon*, September 24, 1997, http://www.salon.com/books/feature/1997/09/24/unzipped (accessed October 5, 2011).

27. "Fifteen Dating Terms We Want to Bring Back," *Glamour*, December 30, 2010, http://www.glamour.com/sex-love-life/blogs/smitten/2010/12/15-dating-terms-we-want-to-bri.html (accessed October 5, 2011).

Part II

Marriage: Safe Haven for Sexuality

4

Centrality of Sex

There is no greater nor keener pleasure than that of bodily love and none which is more irrational.

—Plato, The Republic III.403

According to the popular television personality and psychologist, Dr. Phil, who wades through the intimate details of his guests'—as well as his professional clients'—lives, there is an epidemic of "sexless marriages" these days. His observations coincide with articles in popular magazines like *Time* and *Newsweek* and in more upscale journals like *The Atlantic, Salon, Psychology Today*, and *First Things*. In the midst of a sex-saturated culture, overflowing with dramatic, intimate, and explicit images of the female anatomy, a new phenomenon has developed—men losing interest in sex.[1] Even the prolific political columnist, Mark Steyn, has weighed in, asking, "Do you notice anything shriveling?"[2] In his essay, he reports that the lack of sexual enthusiasm has even extended to the Netherlands, a place renowned for sexual permissiveness. Now, according to a survey in the ANP news agency, "the Dutch now derive more pleasure from going to the bathroom than from sex." So much for "free" love. Has sex become a casualty of the sexual revolution?

Clearly, something is weird when everybody is talking about it, but fewer and fewer are doing it. Could it be that sex has become just another item to periodically check off the "to do" lists of too-busy couples? Popular icon, Oprah Winfrey, also highlighted what she called a "growing cultural phenomenon: the sexless marriage."[3] In spite of the vaunted privacy surrounding the bedrooms in American homes, the General Social Survey[4]—which tracks the social behaviors of Americans—has kept track of bedroom behavior of couples since 1972. They report "wide variations" in the importance and frequency of sex between married men and women. The average is 58 times a year (a little more than once a week), but couples under age 30 average 111 times a year.[5] Still, about 14–16 percent of married men and women "have not had sex with their spouse in the last six months to one year."[6] *Newsweek* quotes psychologists who "estimate that 15 to 20 percent of couples have sex no more than 10 times a year, which is how the experts define sexless marriage."[7] The author of *The Sex-Starved Marriage*, Michele Weiner Davis,[8] asserts that the number of sexless marriages is "a grossly underreported statistic." *Newsweek*, who did not limit its research to the experts, agrees: "Judging from the conversation of the young moms at the next table at Starbucks, it sounds like we're in the midst of a long dry spell."[9]

One commentator noted that "sex is used to sell everything from toothpaste to transmissions," yet a large percentage of married couples have limited or no sexual contact. Lest someone use these comments to support sex outside of marriage, the figures in those relationships are even less frequent. Married people have 6.9 more sexual encounters per year than those who are "sexually active" but not married.[10] According to the University of Chicago's National Opinion Research Center, sexual activity, depending on the age of the couple, ranges from 25 to 300 percent greater for married couples versus unmarried ones.[11] Younger married couples (aged 18–29) have sexual relations an average of nearly 112 times per year (slightly more than twice a week), but couples over 70 years of age have sex only 16 times a year on average.[12]

While couples typically have numerous reasons for ceasing sexual relations—childbirth, an affair, establishing a career, midlife crisis, low sex drive, guilt, body insecurities, belief that sex is "dirty" or that sex is for procreation only[13]—there is general agreement that couples are happier if they enjoy regular sex. Even though there is no universally recommended or ideal level of sexual activity, "happy couples have more sex, and the more sex a couple has, the happier they report being."[14] Michele Weiner Davis underscores the importance sex plays in a healthy relationship: "When it's good, it offers couples opportunities to give and receive physical pleasure, to connect emotionally and spiritually. It builds closeness, intimacy and a sense of partnership. It defines their relationship as different from all others. In short, sex is a powerful tie that binds." The reverse is also true. She writes, "People in sexless marriages report that they are more likely to have considered divorce, and that they are less happy in their marriages."[15]

At a more grassroots level, every time I write a column about marriage, I hear from readers who lament their sexless marriages.[16]

The comments are all from men, and they tell of years—sometimes decades—of living together without love, affection, or sexual intimacy. The writers describe an arid life of "going separate ways" and "living separate lives." Often a man will speak admiringly of his wife as the mother of their children and a fine person, but sadly relate that there is no longer any personal interaction between them as a couple. These are the ones who have not bothered to divorce, yet they lead lives of quiet, grinding frustration, if not desperation, hostility, anger, and depression. Such responses have come so often that I have taken note and related them to the social science research that reveals even younger couples are increasingly under so much stress that a noticeable number of them are "too tired" for marital intimacy.

Some experts explain that too-stressed couples are so tired that, if given a choice, they would choose eight hours of sleep over sex.[17] Therapists have coined two new syndromes to describe the modern phenomenon of couples too tired and/or too stressed to have sex: the "DINS" (Double Income, No Sex) syndrome and the "TTFS" (Too Tired For Sex) syndrome. There are some very practical explanations for the DINS or TTFS syndromes. According to Dr. Pepper Schwartz, a sociology professor at the University of Washington and author of numerous relationship books, ongoing stress causes high levels of cortisol, commonly known as the "stress hormone." Cortisol "interferes with erotic feelings" and "lowers libido."[18] Other therapists point out that chronic stress "pushes down levels of testosterone, which govern libido, energy and sense of well-being."[19]

We have all seen it happen; a young couple steps onto the fast track and the treadmill of life begins to take its toll. An overly stressful lifestyle becomes habitual, with an inevitably corrosive effect upon health and relationships. Natural exuberance gets ground down, laughter seldom breaks through the grim determination and drive, and the little touches of endearment ebb away.

Are these the inevitable, natural effects of building careers or businesses? Of having children? Of simply getting older? Of two people with different temperaments, expectations, and tastes, trying to navigate their disagreements? Yes, yes, yes, and yes—if a couple does not pay attention to the actions that are needed to counter the negative side effects, these factors can generate. The once vibrant joy of life, fueled by sexual passion that a couple shared, need not be blasted to pieces by some dramatic, explosive turn of events like the celebrity blowups reported daily in the tabloids. More often than not, their tender feelings for each other are destroyed much more subtly—almost imperceptibly, eroded away day by day in tiny grains until a chasm is opened up between them; call it marriage's second law of entropy.

In a happy marriage, where the couple is giving attention to the proper maintenance of their relationship, the physical intimacies they share and the time they spend together strengthen the bond between them, and their love for each other is both rejuvenated and deepened. But this takes effort, a conscious commitment of both time and energy.

Nearly all couples experience times of stress, whether caused by external circumstances or their own mistakes, when closeness and intimacy get neglected. Given the vicissitudes of life, this is pretty much to be expected; it could hardly be otherwise. But problems nearly always arise if the couple fails to draw back when the stress lessens to make refurbishing their relationship a priority.

Too often, couples fail to realize that intimacy lubricates the gears of their life and relationship. Problems that once would have been sloughed off as insignificant—not worth interfering with the pleasure they find in each other—get taken more seriously, and conflicts multiply and grow. Clearly this gradual escalation of conflict and/or indifference to each other is not what God had in mind, or He would never have used marriage as an example of the kind of relationship that He wanted to share with us.

In other words, though lovemaking may seem like a luxury good that can be deferred without consequences, nothing could be further from the truth. Couples err when they allow the temporary absence of intimacy—during the stressful times that are sure to come—to become the norm of their lives. Those couples that become preoccupied with those things that are considered "necessary" find their existence increasingly dull and their relationship increasingly strained. Ironically, the things that seem so "necessary" in the present moment often turn out to be of little consequence in the long run.

Marital intimacy would not be so intensely pleasurable if God had merely meant it to be an optional ingredient in our marriage relationships. The bait of sexual attraction is there to lure us to court each other to the point of being intimate on a routine basis and, thus, keep our marriages vibrant and alive—certainly an enterprise that is not a waste of time and energy. Continually reviving our love through courtship and intimacy in our physical lives produces a model for what our spiritual relationship with God should be.

Even the marriage professionals tell us that "intimacy is often the glue that holds a couple together over time."[20] Two Wharton economists analyzed what they called "declining female happiness,"[21] using thirty-five years of data collected by the National Bureau of Economic Research. Their startling finding: none of the recent societal trends benefiting women has increased their happiness. In fact, the opposite has happened. Throughout the industrialized world, women's happiness has declined in absolute terms and in comparison to men's happiness.

In her October 2009 *First Things* article, "What Does Woman Want? The War Between the Sexless,"[22] Mary Eberstadt gives her explanation for so much unhappiness troubling today's driven women. Perhaps some of the modern misery of which so many women today authentically speak is springing not from a sexual desert but from a sexual flood—a torrent of poisonous imagery, beginning even in childhood, that has engulfed women and men, only to beach them eventually somewhere alone and apart, far from the reach of one another.

At least that way of looking at the puzzle might explain part of the paradox of female promiscuity and unhappiness. Between bad ideas of gender neutrality and even worse ideas about the innocence of pornography, we reach the world where men act like stereotypical women and retreat from a real marriage into a fantasy life via pornography. Conversely, women act like stereotypical men, taking the lead in leaving their marriages and firing angry charges on the way, largely due to frustration and withheld sex. Yet, the last three decades illustrate that as individuals increasingly focus on their own happiness, they are unwilling to put forth the hard work to make the dream a reality. Or, there are so many demands on their time and energy that couples can no longer bestir themselves to meet someone else's needs. One Manhattan therapist described today's women as "exhausted and resentful."

Sandra Tsing Loh's article in *The Atlantic*, "Let's call the whole thing off,"[23] details all the things that are on her "staggering mother's to-do list" and concludes, "I cannot take on yet another arduous home and self-improvement project, that of rekindling our romance." Most everyone, however, has a hectic schedule in today's fast-paced world; so one can only wonder if the crux of her misery lies in her unfunny punchline: "and, then, in the bedroom, to be ignored—it's a bum deal."

What Loh and others do not mention is that often pornography is the cause of the emotional distance between couples and men's inability to feel desire for their wives or to perform in the bedroom. At a press conference at the National Press Club, scholars from Princeton's Witherspoon Institute sounded an alarm, telling the nation that pornography is more prevalent and more harmful than most people realize. Their findings contradict the current attitude that pornography is harmless entertainment. They also exposed the fact that pornography has moved out of the sleazy dives into our homes through twenty-four-hours-a-day, easy Internet access. Actually, the data show that porn has taken over much of the nation's entertainment; it is addictive, it is pervasive, and it is harmful.[24]

- Americans rent 800 million pornographic videos every year—that is one in five of all video rentals.
- One in four women worry that their partner's pornography habit is "out of control."
- More than two-thirds (66 percent) of men ages eighteen to thirty-four years visit one or more of the 40,000-plus pornography websites *every month*.
- The pornography industry produces 11,000 new porn movies annually—far more than Hollywood's annual output of 400 mainstream movies.

These movies are more than the "skin flicks" of old; they are far more violent with hard-core degradation and sexual exploitation. There is a total absence of sexual and/or emotional attachment; instead, there is a sad and often horrific objectification of girls and women. Gail Dines,[25] author of *Pornland: How Porn has Hijacked our Sexuality*, says that today's pornography is nothing like the early editions of *Playboy*—titillating nudes and pin-ups in provocative poses. Instead, it is increasingly violent, degrading, and dehumanizing.[26]

Mary Ann Layden, psychologist and scholar at the University of Pennsylvania, described a client who she said is typical of the hundreds of porn addicts that she counsels: "He had a beautiful and eager wife waiting in bed for him; but instead of a 'real' sex partner, he preferred to go online." Dr. Layden cited studies indicating that men who consume porn typically find real women less attractive and often become impotent or less satisfied with their partners than those who avoid pornography. She said that the more porn a man watches, the less satisfied he is in the bedroom.

Pamela Paul, author of *Pornified: How Pornography is Damaging our Lives, Our Relationships and Our Families*, explained the effect on men who consume pornography: "Pornography touches all aspects of their existence. Their work days become interrupted, their hobbies were tossed aside, and their family lives were disrupted. Some men even lost their jobs, their wives, and their children." Dr. Layden added, "The marriage relationship is traumatically damaged and decreased in terms of the emotional intimacy, which is actually the cornerstone of the marriage." In the preface to her book, Miss Paul comments that the use of sexually explicit language and crudity—especially as it relates to terms referring to girls and women—illustrates the ways that pornography has changed our culture. Pornography is "contaminating all our relationships between men and women," said Dr. Layden.

William Struthers, a neuroscientist, psychology professor at Wheaton College, and author of *Wired for Intimacy: How Pornography Hijacks the Male Brain*, has researched how pornography alters the anatomy and physiology of the brain. He says that pornography results in an "anatomical rewiring of the brain," suggesting that "Internet porn is the crack cocaine of sexual addiction." A simple explanation is that the brain becomes neurochemically dependent or addicted—that is, it will crave activities (such as looking at pornography) that elevate those neurochemicals to produce the surge of feelings and sensations that result.

It is a well-established fact that the brain is the most important sex organ in the human body. In recent years, there has been significant research and debate about the origins of physical response during sexual activity—with general agreement that what happens physically depends on what is going on in the brain. Researchers tell us that there are more than 8,000 nerve endings in the clitoris[27]—and a huge number in other areas of the female sexual organs—that send messages about sexual stimulation to the brain.

> In the late 1990s and the mid-2000s, a team of scientists at the University of Groningen in the Netherlands conducted several studies of both men and women to determine brain activity during sexual stimulation. The team used PET scans to illustrate the different areas of the brain that would light up and shut off during sexual activity.... [T]hey discovered that there aren't many differences between men's and women's brains when it comes to sex.[28]

The major differences, however, between men's and women's brains regarding sex is that the area of a woman's brain that deals with fear and anxiety shuts down when she is enjoying sex. I believe that this

71

is important evidence that marriage matters: "Women have more of a need to feel safe and relaxed in order to enjoy sex."[29] Casual, recreational sex does not work very well for women because the area of their brains controlling fear and anxiety does not shut down.[30] The bottom line: Researchers using PET scans have found that the brain only "lights up" during comfortable, safe, enjoyable sexual activity; the scans show the truth—they do not light up—when a woman is faking an orgasm.[31] Further, the production of dopamine, vasopressin, and oxytocin is inhibited in the brain by the emotions of fear and anxiety, thus reducing the pleasure and the desire to repeat the action, as well as preventing trust and bonding with the partner.[32]

Weiner Davis explains that couples who want to keep the passion in their relationship have to use the mind to make that happen. "Desire is really a decision. You have to decide to make it priority to have a vibrant, exciting, emotionally satisfying sexual relationship. You have to continually discover and rediscover new ways to keep your sexual energy alive." She makes a number of suggestions to help couples keep their sexual energy high—from buying silky lingerie to changing their approach to sex. Many couples, she notes, "just wait for the mood to strike" when, instead, they need to make time for sex. Some counselors refuse to work with couples who are not willing to make intimacy in their relationship a priority. Denise A. Donnelly, associate professor of sociology at Georgia State University, is a researcher focusing on sexless marriages. She reports, "Once a marriage has been sexless for a long time, it's very hard" to rekindle the fire of sexual passion. Typically, she says, such couples have "established a pattern of non-communication."[33] Jan Sinatra, a psychotherapist and coauthor of *Heart Sense for Women*, says that communication "is the barometer of the relationship."[34] While lack of communication can indicate a problem, the solution is not simple and the situations "are just so complicated."[35]

Not all researchers agree. In fact, Charles and Elizabeth Schmitz, bestselling and multiple-award-winning authors, wrote in *Psychology Today*, "...[O]n a scale of 1-10 with 10 high, the average rank [of sex] was only 6! This finding has held true over the nearly 27 years of our research." The Schmitzes report that of the "seven pervasive characteristics present in all successful marriages," sex is "not one of them," but "only part of one of the seven characteristics of a successful marriage."[36]

But numerous psychologists disagree with Charles and Elizabeth Schmitz. They say that intimacy is one of the most important parts of a marital relationship. Psychologist Kevin Leman says, "A good sex life colors a marriage from top to bottom and is the most powerful marital glue a couple can have."[37] According to Leman, if sex is not an integral part of your life as a married couple, "the chances of you staying married, quite frankly, are not real high."[38] He notes that a sexually fulfilled man will "normally be a better father and a better employee" and a sexually fulfilled woman will have "less stress and more joy in her life."

There are certain behaviors that are guaranteed to produce "marital mayhem." Dr. Dave Currie identifies four such principles that will "mess up" any good marriage.[39] Not surprisingly, the first is to be selfish—to think first and foremost about your own personal happiness; to look out for number one! That attitude ignores the needs and desires of the other spouse. Second is to justify unfaithfulness—with unfaithfulness rightly understood broadly. As Currie put it, "Unfaithfulness...doesn't start at the bedroom door, but in the windows of your mind. A look here, some lust there, maybe throw in a bit of pornography and a dose of flirtation with others, and you're well on the way before you even leave your spouse."[40] Since rough times are guaranteed, expecting marriage to be easy can cause a couple to be blindsided by life's difficulties and destroy the relationship. When a couple prepares for the storms of life, the ordeal can become the "glue that binds them together" rather than the "wedge that drives them apart."[41] The fourth thing is to depend on quick fixes. Marriages buckle under the strain of problems that are ignored. Like a flame, "deny it oxygen, and it goes out." Think of "time and effort as the oxygen" in the marital relationship.[42]

Yet, over and over again, couples put everything ahead of their relationship: career, children, hobbies, even television. The wrong priorities will keep a potentially good relationship from flaming into "torrid."

"Torrid" is the word the nearly sixty-year-old congressman used to describe his extended adulterous relationship with a married staffer that destroyed his political career. He is possibly the last politician in this town that most observers—especially those of us who knew him and respected him—would have expected to have an affair.

When he and the woman met, he said, they spontaneously felt a "spark." As they worked closely together, the spark ignited a flame of passion that eventually engulfed them. The congressman added, as a matter of context, that his vulnerability stemmed, in part, from the loneliness of his bachelor existence in the nation's capital with his family back home. He paints a Spinozan picture of a spark landing in dry tender (i.e., a lonely man) with their close proximity fanning the blaze into a hot, torrid affair. While he felt terrible guilt over the affair, he both blamed himself and the circumstance, as well as the chemistry between them, for overwhelming his scruples.

In the end, he stood alone with his shame before the media, the public, and his family—dismayed and disgraced, with his life and hers in shambles.

His confession, resignation, and quick departure from Congress and the Capitol at least spared us some of the embarrassing spectacle we have endured from so many politicians who struggled to hang on to office even after their "indiscretions" became public. Typically, our sensibilities have been assaulted by the pathetic, demeaning ploy of the tanned, botoxed, cheating husband dragging his wounded wife in front of the cameras in a cynical effort to gain sympathy and salvage the situation. With this congressman's solo *mea culpa*, his sordid story faded quickly from the news and was replaced by the next scandal *du jour* coming out of Washington.

Nonetheless, his story keeps bubbling up in my thoughts. When my husband and I first came to Washington twenty years ago, the then-senatorial aide spent two hours explaining the "ropes" of Washington politics to two new friends from his home state. He was unforgettable—so very intense about his conservative values, so sincere and open about his religious faith, and so very knowledgeable about issues and "the way things work" inside the beltway.

I have wondered why he felt it necessary to make bad matters worse by calling their relationship "torrid." From his tone, he was not castigating himself for immature impetuosity and bad judgment; nor did his remarks smack of locker room braggadocio. Rather, he seemed to be trying to convey the impact of being overcome, undone, and overwhelmed by a wondrously powerful and intoxicating physical and emotional attraction. He seemed to be saying that he did not know that he was capable of those types of feelings. He seemed unaware that he subconsciously wanted to experience "torrid," and, thus, was blindsided and then tripped up. If he had realized the potential, might he possibly have had his defenses up and avoided succumbing to temptation?

I am puzzled by why I cringe at this part of his confession. In part, it is because his characterization of their relationship as "torrid" seems to violate the little dignity he had left, to expose what should have remained private in a pointless attempt to convey the strength of the temptation he faced. I also wonder if, with the cynicism and negative characterization of love's short shelf life that abound in the culture, perhaps I have unknowingly absorbed cultural myths. Have I, despite experience that should teach me better, subconsciously let the conventional notion rub off on me that "torrid" is for newlyweds, not paunchy, graying, past-middle-age types who have long ago grown past such nonsense?

Do I see "torrid" as evidence of immaturity? Is it?

Today, we think of passion as being mostly related to young romance. An older view, however, is that passion is an emotional response arising from our "lower nature." The former view is clearly shallow and incomplete; this nontheologian wonders if the latter view is not a vestigial remnant of the Gnostic heresy. The plain fact is that the Old Testament Scriptures picture the Creator as a being who feels strong emotions such as anger and jealousy (unbelievers, of course, sneer at this as thinking anthropomorphically). And in the New Testament, it is stated explicitly that the Heavenly Father loved His creatures so passionately that He gave His beloved Son to redeem them (John 3:16) at the cost of the Son's suffering and tragic death by crucifixion. Couple these elements with the Scripture's teaching that God created us in His own image, and it becomes difficult to see how our need to love passionately is anything less than a fundamental aspect of our divinely ordained humanity.

So, who needs "torrid"?

As long as "torrid" is viewed as, at best, unseemly and immature, couples who are middle-aged and older—experiencing the frenetic pace and relentless demands of modern life, coupled with a growing awareness of the inevitable diminution of physical and emotional resources—may feel indifferent to a gradual loss of intimacy and the affection it nourishes, viewing it as a normal, natural progression in life. There is an old humorous but fallacious jibe that says, "Cooking lasts; kissing don't." Adopting this mistaken view means millions of couples drift apart, and, thus, deprive themselves of the intimacy that I am convinced God intended to contribute to maintaining the fidelity of the marriage bond.

I believe it is fair to ask, "Is it honest to conceal this element of our humanity?" (Let us be clear as to what my point is. Although I genuinely enjoy seeing young couples flirting, I have little patience for undignified public displays of affection and absolutely none for aging Romeos sporting younger trophy wives.) From the multitude of public figures (and others) whose careers have been destroyed by affairs, is it healthy to pretend that a desire for a torrid love life is not part of who we are? I can only wonder if the devout congressman's lack of understanding of this part of his nature is not what blindsided him and caused him to fall prey to temptation?

Look at it this way: it is plainly evident that the conjugal union from which new life comes was designed by the Creator to produce one of life's most intense pleasures, thereby ensuring that we would want to marry and have children. In a parallel fashion (in order to fulfill Christ's explicit teaching that God intended the marriage covenant to be a life-long proposition), passionate marital love contributes to the accomplishment of an enduring bond and is, thus, an integral part of the Creator's plan to make life-long fidelity not merely feasible, but immensely gratifying. Hence, as I see it, the capacity for "torrid" is not to be disparaged, nor, as bitter experience devastatingly shows, is it safe to ignore our need for it.

Frankly, life-long marriage without "torrid" is not an appealing picture. Despite the claims of the cynics, life-long marriage with "torrid" is possible, even if only a minority is willing to make the investment to enable it to flourish. What experience shows for certain is that a marriage not nurtured and refreshed by intimacy will not prove the secure haven God intended it to be.

Obviously, there is nothing new about selfishness, betrayal, or mistreatment—such behaviors have been staples from both men *and* women. Just as there is a multitude of unhealthy ways to eat (I know from personal experience), there are also countless ways to mess up a marriage. But that does not make either poor nutrition or dysfunctional relationships normative. Why should we teach young women that all men are not to be trusted, to expect that sooner or later divorce will follow the wedding?

Mature voices have always warned that marriages will inevitably go through rough patches. My marriage has needed healing on more than one occasion, as has that of most couples since the Garden of Eden. But that does not validate the cynics' claim that bitter irreconcilable relationships inevitably result in all marriages. Clearly, the *need* for redemption is universal—but so is the *possibility*.

Sex, properly understood, can play a very significant role in that needed redemption. Nothing exceeds the potential of loving marital relations in this regard. (That by itself, even without its potential for procreation, would be enough to put an end to the pernicious lie that sex is no big deal.) Counselors make much of the human need for hugs. We all need, as researcher Eric Berne put it, "strokes"—both physical and emotional. He argued graphically that "without stroking, our spinal cord will shrivel up." Berne's analysis of research on foundlings showed that, with infants, touch can mean literally the difference between life and death. Certainly, either emotional or physical distance can destroy marriage.

The emotions involved in sexual intercourse are so powerful that they defy our ability to fully analyze or explain them. "Making love" is *magical*. What so many young people do not reckon with is that the intense physical feelings produced by sex are matched "ounce-for-ounce" by the emotions stirred. The power of the emotions unleashed by sex is such that the experience of "making love" remains something of a *mystery* to those who try to grasp it rationally. The poets tell us that it can even be a *mystical* experience. Little wonder then that sexual intercourse is considered the consummation of the marriage relationship. Little wonder then that sex should be reserved for the marriage relationship.

A number of years ago, our neighbor's sixteen-year-old daughter made the common assumption that her boyfriend was serious about her and that the relationship was destined for marriage. She certainly was serious about him and thought that she loved him. When she got pregnant and quickly discovered he was not going to marry her, she lamented, "I just wanted him to love me."

We listened in dismay to the raw pain as she repeated the phrase again and again, like a mantra. Adding insult to injury, the boy's mother—not wanting her teenage son (and the family) to be saddled with the responsibilities of a wife and child—caustically suggested (in the pre-DNA era) that the child might not even be her son's.

Not a single element of this sad, tawdry story surprises any adult over thirty. It is an old and totally predictable tale. Today, it bears repeating, though, because heartbroken responses like our young neighbor's appear to surprise folks when the same thing happens in current circumstances, despite all the sex-ed in school and despite all the supposed sexual equality and freedom.

Today's teens talk breezily and brazenly about sexual matters. They claim that "sex is no big deal." They have their own vocabulary to describe the cavalier intimacy. "Hooking up," "scoring"—there seem to be plenty of convenient euphemisms for sexual experimentation.

The latest lingo is a re-run: "fooling around." It all sounds casual enough—blasé enough. But, somebody needs to ask, "Who is fooling whom?" Where have all the adults gone? Where are the grown-ups who know from experience that sex *is* a big deal, that sexual intimacy is about mating and bonding, that sex, pregnancy, and birth are the absolute *biggest* deals in life—that sex is (or can be and should be) a magical, mysterious, and mystical experience.

Where are the realists who will admit that, for all our culture's "mainstreaming of gender equality," outside of marriage, women are *still* left rocking the baby and paying the rent—on their own. This heartbreak and difficulty are compounded by the fact that literally millions of girls and women are left with physical, emotional, and psychological damage from sexually transmitted diseases or the aftermath of abortion. It is not surprising that an immature, inexperienced teenage girl might be misled into thinking that sexual experimentation, "fooling around," is relatively harmless. The attention it brings from the boys can be intoxicating—at first. In addition, the inherent excitement of first infatuation is super-charged by sexual intimacy. It is not surprising that many young men, breathing the air of an MTV-permeated culture, believe that they can and must establish their manhood with sexual initiation. But where are the parents? Where is the father? Where is the mother? Sadly, too many are not around, are otherwise engaged or are themselves products of a culture forged in the experimentation of the 1960s Woodstock Generation.

Raised in an era awash in feminist efforts to promote the androgyny myth, many parents, as well as young people, have bought into the ideology of male and female sexual equality. Others have bought into the credo that enshrines the negative consequences of sexual experimentation as an inescapable rite of passage. Still, others flounder in guilt and confusion, unable to sort through what to say to their children; too many end up saying nothing. Many want their children to *do as they say*—what they know to be right—even if it is *not what they did.* Often, these parents know the price they paid and they do not want to think about it, much less talk with their children about it. Ironically, these same adults feel no discomfort in giving young people very direct messages about other issues: what to eat, not to smoke, and how to vote. We even have public service announcements encouraging families to have an evening meal together. But we flinch before the prospect of teaching them about sexuality within a moral context.

Perhaps the social sciences have outpaced our moral understanding and convictions. We may not have learned anything from the pain and heartbreak brought on by sexual promiscuity, but, as a society, surely we should learn from the vast amount of data amassed from the last fifty to sixty years of cultural change. We know now that living together or having sex together does not usually end in marriage. During the 1970s, about 60 percent of cohabiting couples married each other within three years, but this proportion has since declined to less than 40 percent. Numerous studies of college students have found that women typically expect that "living together will lead to marriage." Men, on the other hand, typically cohabit because it is...ah, "convenient." Right! Sex without commitment conflicts with our human nature; it is likely to have negative consequences such as uncertainty and insecurity. Live-in sexual arrangements carry with them innate instability (as noted above) and lack community acceptance and support.

For years, those with a special agenda have tried to say that sexual relationships are symmetrical: that males and females are equal in their emotional or physical responses. Yet both common sense and research tell a completely different story. There is a fundamental *asymmetry*, both physiologically and emotionally, that makes the female far more vulnerable in sexual relations than the male. Marriage balances out the female's disadvantage by involving family and community. Families in enlightened societies said, historically, to unattached males: "You must agree to be faithful, to fulfill the obligations of fatherhood and make those commitments publicly before you have sex with our daughters." The marriage contract, then, was a public statement that protected not just women and children, but the community as well.

Let me offer a simple, effective lesson in how parents can talk with their children about sex. It might even be helpful for adults who need to understand that the foundation on which great sex is built consists of values, relationships, and emotions, not just mechanics and circumstances.

Here is a "sex pyramid"[43] similar to the familiar "food pyramid," which gives a hierarchy of balanced nutrition. The "sex pyramid" provides a "roadmap" for parents to talk about the hierarchy of elements in sexuality. Instead of "THE TALK," which is sometimes stilted to the parent and irrelevant for the child, parents should find and manufacture opportunities to talk about the elements of the pyramid as observed in everyday situations.

The Sex Pyramid

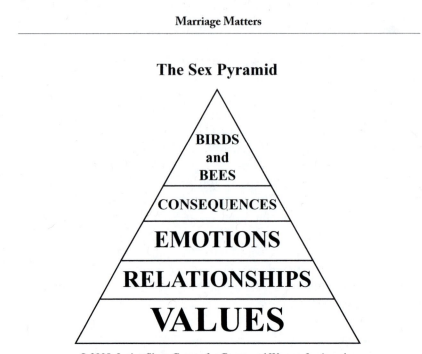

© 2005, Janice Shaw Crouse for Concerned Women for America

Such conversations can begin in early childhood and continue through older adolescence. For instance, when viewing a movie where a couple goes to bed right after being introduced, comment in an age-appropriate manner about how they could not possibly be ready to trust each other and build a relationship. Comment about the woman's foolishness in thinking the guy is serious about her, how the guy is taking advantage of the woman, and the consequences of such inappropriate sexual activity. You can contrast that behavior with the positive consequences of a sexual relationship within a loving marriage between a man and a woman committed for a lifetime. Each of the pyramid's elements can be covered in a casual, conversational manner that communicates the family's values, how sex impacts relationships and emotions, and the circumstances that produce positive or negative consequences.

Let us consider each of the five elements:

- **The foundation is "Values."** Parents must communicate their values clearly, unequivocally, often, and effectively. They should be confident in the knowledge that Biblical values do not go "out of style" or become outdated. All truth is God's truth and, regardless of cultural trends, Biblical values remain true and reliable compasses to guide believers through all the situations of life. Judeo-Christian values of respect, dignity, and honor are universal values that need to be applied specifically to sexual behavior so that our boys learn to respect and honor girls, and girls learn dignity and self-respect so that they can effectively say "no."

- **The second step is "Relationships."** Parents must communicate the importance of establishing a relationship of trust and respect before intimacy develops. Parents need to communicate basic principles about character development, honor, and individual responsibility. Young people need to know that they are not victims of their hormones and that they need to develop discernment in assessing a potential mate's worthiness and ability to behave honorably and respectfully.

- **The third step is "Emotions."** Young people are seldom aware of just how extensive is the emotional aspect of relationships—especially when sex is part of the mix. Parents can help their children develop emotional control and teach them to analyze their feelings. Parents need to focus on helping their children to separate their emotions from their judgments and to be careful in getting emotionally involved before laying a foundation of trust and respect. Our children need to learn not to commit beyond the level of trust. They need to trust, but to also use discernment.

- **The fourth step is "Consequences."** It is vitally important that parents cover both positive and negative consequences. Young people today rarely understand the prevalence of sexually transmitted diseases and even those who are aware of them think that they will not get one. In a similar manner, most young people think that they are "mature" and they believe that their relationships will "last forever." Likewise, today's generation has not heard much about the "sacred covenant" of marriage and the importance of abstinence until marriage and fidelity afterward. Parental expectations play an extremely important role in a child's behavior, and parents need to realize how much impact they have on their children's attitudes toward sex and marriage. When fair and loving parents hold high standards, generally, the children will live up to them. There are no guarantees, of course, but parents never err in expecting the best behavior from their children.

- **At the top of the sex pyramid is the mechanics of the sexual act— the "birds and bees" aspect.** This actually should receive the least attention because it is the easiest part of sexual interaction to explain and understand, though, ironically, comprehensive sex education tends to focus on the biology of sexuality rather than the foundation on which sex is built. Ideally, though in our sex-saturated culture it gets harder and harder, each couple needs to "discover" sex on their own. Wise parents will focus on the foundational aspects of the sex pyramid throughout their kids' childhood and, at the appropriate time, give accurate and complete biological information. During the dating years, parents should be available for counsel, as requested.

It is past time that responsible adults in our culture—parents, teachers, community and religious teachers, leaders and pastors—prepare young people to make wise and informed decisions by telling them the full and moral truth. These adults need to plainly say, "The best choice for you is to remain abstinent until marriage and to be faithful within marriage." Those choices lead to the greatest wellbeing in life—as well as the greatest sexual happiness. The "Sex Pyramid" provides a framework to help parents and other influential adults communicate these messages effectively to the young people in their care.

Sex is the ultimate intimacy, and it can be the ultimate baring of the soul. It is a vital part of bonding two hearts together. When you add that sex is the means to participate in the creation of life, it is of monumental significance.

These are not novel ideas, not new truths. They have been with us for millennium upon millennium. Sex was never meant to be just an itch to be scratched, a way to enjoy some pleasant sensations—like eating a Thanksgiving dinner or a hot fudge sundae. So how could we have ever bought the insidious lie that sexual intercourse can be indulged in casually with just anyone?

A good man or a good woman is hard to find. And our culture's epidemic of promiscuous sex is not going to make it any easier. The more someone plays the "relax-it's-just-sex" game, the less capable he or she becomes of finding a good husband or wife with whom to share the deep emotional intimacy that is an essential ingredient of the sexual experience. Without that intimacy, bonding is incomplete, and when a rough patch comes along, the relationship will not be worth the self-sacrifice needed to set it right, to grow and mature through apology and forgiveness. It will—in this day and age—simply be "not worth the hassle."

Caitlin Flanagan, in her 2003 article "The Wifely Duty,"[44] declared, "Marriage used to provide access to sex. Now it provides access to celibacy."

> To many contemporary women, however, the notion that sex might have any function other than personal fulfillment (and the occasional bit of carefully scheduled baby making) is a violation of the very tenets of the sexual revolution that so deeply shaped their attitudes on such matters. Under these conditions, pity the poor married man hoping to get a bit of comfort from the wife at day's end. He must somehow seduce a woman who is economically independent of him, bone tired, philosophically disinclined to have sex unless she

is jolly well in the mood, numbingly familiar with his every sexual maneuver, and still doing a slow burn over his failure to wipe down the countertops and fold the dish towel after cooking the kids' dinner. He can hardly be blamed for opting instead to check his e-mail, catch a few minutes of SportsCenter, and call it a night.

Flanagan proposed a simple solution to "restoring the joy and happiness to your marriage":

> [It] is not complicated; it requires putting the children to bed at a decent hour and adopting a good attitude. The rare and enviable woman is not the one liberated enough to tell hurtful secrets about her marriage to her girlfriends or the reading public. Nor is she the one capable of attracting the sexual attentions of a variety of worthy suitors. The rare woman—the good wife, and the happy one—is the woman who maintains her husband's sexual interest and who returns it in full measure.

In the long, dry spells of responsibility and drudgery that establishing careers and raising children entails, marital sex offers brief but vital reprieves from the daily grind. It is impossible to rationally explain exactly how physical intimacy's fresh assurances that we are not alone in carrying heavy responsibilities can have such a miraculous, rejuvenating effect. It is simply one of love's beautiful mysteries. Nothing can quite compare with knowing that the love of our youth is still there—despite all the wear and tear, the give and take. Such compromise and forgiveness of hurts are needed to restore joy, rekindle enthusiasm and renew the promise to stay side-by-side over the long haul—forever needing and being needed—as the two become one flesh.

There will come a time in every marriage—after the thrill of fiery passion has been dulled by difficulties and stress—when the only thing to do is put one foot in front of the other or find satisfaction in caring more for someone else's fulfillment than your own.

I know there are sometimes real reasons for ending a marriage—abuse and infidelity, for sure. But many of the justifications do not cut it: "We weren't getting along"; "We're not in love any more"; "I've got to find out who I really am"; or, "People aren't meant to live together for so many years."

I have been married to the love of my youth for a very long time. I have experienced the highest highs and some pretty miserable lows. What I have learned is that some of the conflicts of marriage are not really about the immediate event that causes the flare-up of feelings.

Looking back on some of the low places in our marriage, neither my husband nor I can remember what started the conflict. What we do remember was that the low times came during prolonged stress—dark days when money was tight, pressures and demands on time and energy unrelenting, or our hopes and ambitions had crashed and burned. Times when it seemed as though all we had dreamed of had been smashed by circumstances beyond our control. There were times when the whole idea of a fresh start or positive outcome seemed utterly impossible.

No, we did not immediately join hands, draw close to each other, and bravely face our fate. Those times were bleak, and we were knee-deep in despair. Sometimes we hurled angry, hateful, hurtful words at each other. Other times, we were distant but maintained a detached civility to each other so as not to embarrass ourselves in front of the kids, family, and friends. Basically, we plodded on—"till-death-do-us-part," our only option—even though yammering thoughts warned, "This is the way it is going to be the rest of your life."

Of course, that was not true. The stresses of winter do eventually give way to spring. And with proper pruning and tender loving care, a plant that looks dead can bloom again. We were passionately in love when we married, and with the pruning of forgiveness, love blossomed again, passionate as ever; actually, even more so.

It is strange to look back at those dark times and try to figure them out. Part of it was our own fault. We put a lot of stress on ourselves through our own ambitions, tendency to take on too much, and our pig-headed determination to see our expectations realized. But part of it was circumstances—investments that went belly up, jobs that were lost, the illnesses and deaths of loved ones. Put simply, there were lessons about life that we had to learn—accepting and valuing each other for who and what each of us was, not what we, through the rose-colored glasses of early romance, imagined that the other was going to be; being willing to apologize and ask for forgiveness, whether it was our turn or not; getting up and dusting ourselves off when fortune did not smile or failure knocked us smack on our backsides, and, by God's grace, embarking on the painful business of starting all over from scratch when all around us there were others whose lives seemed so much less troubled or when life seemed unfair.

Running a marathon has some lessons for marriage. No matter how easy things are in the beginning, there are going to be difficult periods. But when those times come, if you keep going through the pain, you and those who love and depend on you will drink deeply from the cup of satisfaction that only those who cross the finish line can know. After all, if a life-long marriage were an impossibility, would God, through the prophets, have used the institution of marriage—which He designed—as a metaphor for the relationship He desires to have with His people?

Notes

1.   Janice Shaw Crouse, "Being Sexually Deprived in a Sex-Saturated Culture," *Concerned Women for America*, September 15, 2009, http://www.cwfa. org/articledisplay.asp?id=17719&department=BLI&categoryid=dotcom mentary (accessed September 29, 2011).

2.   Mark Steyn, "Do You Notice Anything Shriveling?" *Macleans.ca*, August 27, 2009, http://www2.macleans.ca/2009/08/27/do-you-notice-anything-shrivelling/ (accessed September 29, 2011).

3.   Connie Matthiessen, "The Sex-Starved Marriage: When Couples Stop Coupling," *CDPHP My Online Wellness Webpage*, last updated February 20, 2009, http://drugtools.caremark.com/topic/sexstarve (accessed October 1, 2011).

4.   The General Social Survey (GSS) conducts basic scientific research on the structure and development of American society with a data-collection program designed to both monitor social change within the United States and to compare the United States to other nations. http://www.norc.uchicago.edu/GSS+Website/ (accessed September 29, 2011).

5.   Tara Parker-Pope, "When Sex Leaves the Marriage," *New York Times Well Blog*, June 3, 2009, http://well.blogs.nytimes.com/2009/06/03/when-sex-leaves-the-marriage/ (accessed September 29, 2011).

6.   Denise Donnelly and others, "Involuntary Celibacy: A Life Course Analysis – Statistical Data Included," *Journal of Sex Research* (May 2001): http://findarticles.com/p/articles/mi_m2372/is_2_38/ai_79439406/ (accessed September 29, 2011).

7.   Kathleen Deveny, "We're not in the Mood," *The Daily Beast*, June 29, 2003, http://www.thedailybeast.com/newsweek/2003/06/29/we-re-not-in-the-mood.print.html (accessed September 29, 2011).

8.   Michele Weiner Davis, *The Sex-Starved Marriage* (New York: Simon and Schuster, 2003), 146.

9.   Deveny, "We're not in the Mood."

10.   Ibid.

11.   DiscoveryHealth.com writers, "Marriage and Sex," *HowStuffWorks.com*, April 28, 2005, http://healthguide.howstuffworks.com/marriage-and-sex-dictionary.html (accessed March 2011).

12.   Ibid.

13.   Parker-Pope, "When Sex Leaves the Marriage."

14.   Ibid.

15.   Ibid.

16.   Janice Shaw Crouse, "Stress and Martial Happiness," *Concerned Women for America*, January 4, 2010, http://www.cwfa.org/printerfriendly.asp?id=18

222&department=bli&categoryid=dotcommentary (accessed September 29, 2011).

17. Kristen Russell Dobson, "Too Tired for Sex?" *ParentMap.com*, July 9, 2010, http://www.parentmap.com/sex-romance/publications/parentmap/too-tired-for-sex (accessed September 29, 2011).

18. Dr. Pepper Schwartz, as quoted in Dobson, "Too Tired for Sex?"

19. Dr. Diana Wiley, "Seduction Tips for Men," *AskApril.com*, http://www.askapril.com/print.php?type=1&id=62 (accessed September 29, 2011).

20. Deveny, "We're not in the Mood."

21. Betsey Stevenson and Justin Wolfers, "The Paradox of Declining Female Happiness," *American Economic Journal: Economic Policy* 1, no. 2 (August 2009): 190–225.

22. Mary Eberstadt, "What does Woman Want? The War between the Sexless," *First Things*, October 2009, http://www.firstthings.com/article/2009/10/what-does-woman-want (accessed September 29, 2011).

23. Sandra Tsing Loh, "Let's Call the Whole Thing Off," *The Atlantic*, July/August 2009, http://www.theatlantic.com/magazine/archive/2009/07/let-8217-s-call-the-whole-thing-off/7488/ (accessed September 29, 2011).

24. Janice Shaw Crouse, "Pornography is Addictive, Pervasive and Harmful," *Townhall*, January 4, 2010, http://townhall.com/columnists/JaniceShaw-Crouse/2010/04/01/pornography_is_addictive,_pervasive_and_harmful/ (accessed September 29, 2011).

25. Gail Dines' Presentation to the Feminist Anti-pornography Conference: Pornography and Pop Culture—Rethinking Theory, Reframing Activism, "Pornography and Pop Culture: Putting the Text in Context," March, 24, 2007, video clip, http://video.google.com/videoplay?docid=50031551140 18800220# (accessed September 29, 2011).

26. Julie Bindel, "The Truth about the Porn Industry," *Guardian*, July 2, 2010, http://www.guardian.co.uk/lifeandstyle/2010/jul/02/gail-dines-pornography/print (accessed September 29, 2011).

27. Shanna Freeman, "What Happens in the Brain during an Orgasm?" *How-StuffWorks.com*, October 7, 2008, http://health.howstuffworks.com/sexual-health/sexuality/brain-during-orgasm.htm (accessed March 2011).

28. Ibid.

29. Ibid.

30. Ibid.

31. Ibid.

32. Ibid.

33. Ibid.

34. DiscoveryHealth.com, "Marriage and Sex."

35. Parker-Pope, "When Sex Leaves the Marriage."

36. Charles D. Schmitz and Elizabeth A. Schmitz, "How Important is Sex in a Successful Marriage?" *Psychology Today Blog*, December 25, 2009, http://www.psychologytoday.com/blog/building-great-marriages/200912/how-important-is-sex-in-successful-marriage (accessed September 29, 2011).

37. Interviewer Dick Staub, "The Dick Staub Interview: Kevin Leman Talks about Sex, Baby," *Christianity Today*, August 1, 2003 (web-only), http://www.christianitytoday.com/ct/2003/augustweb-only/22.0.html (accessed September 29, 2011).

38. Ibid.
39. Dave Currie, "Marital Mayhem: 4 Principles Guaranteed to Mess up Any Good Relationship," *PowertoChange.com*, http://powertochange.com/sex-love/mayhem/ (accessed January 2011).
40. Ibid.
41. Ibid.
42. Ibid.
43. Janice Shaw Crouse, "How to Talk to Your Child about Sex: The Sex Pyramid," *Concerned Women for America*, March 16, 2005, http://www.cdrcp.com/pdf/How%20to%20Talk%20to%20Your%20Child%20About%20Sex%20-%20The%20Sex%20Pyramid.pdf (accessed October 3, 2011).
44. Caitlin Flanagan, "The Wifely Duty," *The Atlantic*, January/February 2003, http://www.theatlantic.com/past/docs/issues/2003/01/flanagan.htm (accessed September 29, 2011).

5

Why Casual Sex Causes Harm

A good man is hard to find,
You always get the other kind.
Just when you think he is your pal,
You look for him and find him fooling 'round some other gal.
Then you rave, you even crave, to see him laying in his grave.
—Eddie Green (1918)

Ever since *Time* grabbed the spotlight with in their 1966 cover story blaring the question, "Is God Dead?"[1] their competitor *Newsweek* has been trying to get the upper hand in the popular media public relations stakes. In 2010, *Newsweek* turned attention away from questions about God and speculation about their own impending demise to report on the "death" of marriage. Two reporters, Jessica Bennett and Jesse Ellison, wrote the cover story, "The Case Against Marriage,"[2] where they claimed that, while marriage once "made sense," it is "no longer necessary." As Dr. Al Mohler pointed out, this is the "most direct journalistic attack on marriage in our time"[3] and, likely, represents increased frontal attacks from the mainstream media.

Conventional wisdom says that if you tell a lie often enough, people will begin to believe it. Certainly, that has happened in the case of arguments promoting "free love" and denigrating marriage. After forty years of increasingly more prevalent and pervasive casual sex, experts claim that more than 60 percent of couples who get married today have lived together prior to their marriage ceremony. Further, casual sex—it could more accurately be called "promiscuous sex"—is common on many college campuses and even among certain segments of high-school populations.

Sophistication today is achieved through sexual cynicism. Compare attitudes toward casual sex with attitudes toward smoking and drinking. In today's era, smoking and drinking to excess are considered déclassé and have been replaced by health club memberships and mineral water.

In the 1920s era of the Flapper,[4] both smoking and hard drinking were considered sophisticated. It was chic to smoke and both the elegant movie stars and urbane socialites dangled their cigarettes and drank their cocktails with élan. Remember the three-martini lunch? It took fifty years for data to finally get through to the elites that drinking during working hours is counterproductive; that smoking is bad for health; that alcoholic beverages are dangerous for the fetus of a pregnant woman; and that to drink and drive is dangerous, stupid, and unforgivably irresponsible.

On sexual realities, however, the truth still has not broken through—though elsewhere in this book, I discuss seeing glimmers of hope in the more conservative attitudes of many of today's young people. The radical feminist rhetoric of the past forty years is not quite as in vogue as it used to be, but its ethic of sexual experimentation is widespread and firmly rooted in the popular culture—not surprising really, since the media has saturated our culture with the feminist myth of sexual freedom, and the public schools, along with Planned Parenthood and the Sexuality Information and Education Council of the United States (SIECUS), have implicitly condoned, if not actually promoted, sexual permissiveness via so-called "comprehensive" sex education which sells the idea that causal, recreational sex is acceptable for singles as long as the persons involved are "responsible" and use a condom.

According to a *People*/NBC poll,[5] only 67 percent of young teens having sex say that they use a condom every time even though roughly 20 percent claim to be sexually active (depending on the poll). In fact, the *People* article begins with the story of a fourteen-year-old who has had two "pregnancy scares"—the first because "the condom broke" and the second because of a "heat-of-the-moment" encounter. The current lingo is "friends with benefits," where the "guys get the pleasure" without commitment and the girls "are willing to give them that."[6]

What the girls (and guys) do not realize is that they are getting more than they bargained for. Dr. Meg Meeker, a pediatrician in Traverse City, Michigan, and author of *Epidemic: How Teen Sex is Killing Our Kids*, said that when "almost half of all girls are likely to become infected with an STD *during their very first sexual experience* [emphasis hers], we have a serious problem on our hands."[7] In her frequent public speeches, Dr. Meeker warns doctors that they have to update their assumptions these days: "When a preteen or teen comes in with a sore throat, you can't just think mono and strep. With the dramatic increase in oral sex, you have to also think herpes and gonorrhea."

Early sexual activity means more sexual partners; if a girl begins sexual activity in her early teens, she is, on average, likely to have more than a dozen partners over her lifetime, and the "turnover" rate of partners is more than four times as high as among those who begin sexual activity in their early twenties. Such girls are also more than twice as likely to become infected with sexually transmitted diseases (STDs). And, about 40 percent of teens who are sexually active eventually become pregnant out-of-wedlock.[8]

Less well known are the psychological and emotional problems associated with early sexual activity. Only one-third of girls who had early sexual activity describe themselves as "happy" as compared with over half of those who waited. Sexually active teens are more likely to be depressed; more than a quarter of the girls report depression, and boys are twice as likely to be depressed as those who are abstinent. Sexually active teens are more likely to attempt suicide; girls are three times more likely, and boys are eight times more likely. The bottom line is that more than two-thirds of teens who are sexually active admit that they wish they could go back to sexual innocence again and desperately wish they had waited.[9]

But casual sex is not just a teen thing. Nor are the disastrous results limited to teen sex.

On a recent plane trip, I watched a real-life *Sex and the City*[10] vignette unfold in front of me. While I was waiting in a gate area of a Florida airport, a very confident, well-dressed and handsome forty-something "Mr. Big"[11] entered and sat near me. His expensive country-club clothing and self-assurance set him apart from the other travelers—many of them waiting in jeans and t-shirts. Shortly, he was joined by a lovely, equally elegant woman around his age.

She was not a jaded sophisticate; nor was she an angry, hard woman. Instead, her demeanor was diffident and uncertain. I watched as he looked everywhere but at her; aloof and detached, he never even glanced in her direction. She, on the other hand, would glance at him and then look away. She would lean toward him and make a hesitant, brief comment with a slight, tentative smile. He would nod, but never did he even turn in her direction or make eye contact.

Intrigued by the difference in their self-confidence and the lack of "connection" between them, I noticed that neither was wearing a wedding ring. They were obviously returning from a vacation together.

Equally apparent was the fact that the man held all the cards in their relationship.

Watching their *pas de deux*, it all seemed so dismally predictable to anyone with an ounce of real-world experience, not indoctrinated by the faux cheer (and easy resolution during sweeps time) of a *Friends*[12] storyline. She appeared insecure and uncertain about her role in the life of a man she loved. Was she worried about their future as a couple after their tryst at the beach? He appeared to be giving her ample reason for concern.

She had traveled a boulevard of sexual freedom to a relationship cul-de-sac where there was emotionally neither an easy way out nor a way to turn back the clock. Their future as a couple was now totally dependent upon his whims. She may have been yearning for permanence and a future together, but to all appearances, she would have to settle for merely that vacation in Florida. Such are the paltry rewards of sexual freedom.

The adherence to this hollow pseudosophisticated sexual-liberation credo is particularly evident at conferences and on college campuses. At times, the hostility toward traditional views of family and motherhood is palpable; more often, it is merely a below-the-surface attitude that today's women do not particularly need men or that "piece of paper" that constitutes, for them, marriage, nor do they want to step off the fast-track of career success in order to accommodate the needs of a husband and children. The men, likewise, are not eager to take on the responsibilities of a wife and family—one that might be snatched from them through a no-fault (but not no-liability) divorce—when they have plenty of opportunities for sex without the encumbering commitment that goes with marriage.

Sadly, the data tell us that contemporary cultural trends are not any more female-friendly than they have been for millennia. Sexual competition is still a young woman's playing field. But apparently, many of today's young women, fooling around with a no-commitments "Mr. Big," are not aware that they should be competing to find "Mr. Right" before their fertility runs out. Most of them do not realize that, after college, their marital options greatly shrink at the same time that their window of opportunity for children is closing.

Because of profound misrepresentations, many women focus exclusively on career in their twenties and, thus, pass their window of opportunity for finding a husband and having children. After age thirty, a woman's chances of conceiving drop by 75 percent; if she gets pregnant, her chance of miscarriage triples, the rate of stillbirth doubles, and the risk of genetic abnormality is six times greater. Sadly, the waiting rooms of infertility centers are crowded with professional women who bought into the myth that they should focus on career first and wait to have a husband and children later—if and when it fits into their plans.

Young women need to hear the whole truth: by giving career priority over marriage and family in their twenties and thirties, they strengthen the likelihood that career is all that they will have left in their forties. And, contrary to the message from *Newsweek* and other sources about marriage being passé, the vast majority of young people (92 percent) think marriage would make them happy and want to be married some day; most also want to have kids.[13]

A new generation needs to get the news before they end up like the lovely woman in Florida, impeccably dressed, undeniably free, and achingly lonely. I saw the pair again at baggage claim when we arrived at our destination. Apparently, she had finally succeeded in securing his attention. He reached over and fondled her intimately, indiscreetly, and possessively. I could not see her facial expression, but her body stiffened, and she leaned away from the inappropriateness of his public groping.

It is not news to anybody these days—not if they watch any television or glance at the covers of the magazines lining the checkout counters in the grocery stores—that we live in a sex-saturated society where supposedly the majority of young people are "doing it," more often than not without "benefit of marriage." The "Playboy philosophy"[14] is trumpeted by a myriad of media voices that glamorize casual sex while most of the shrinking mainline churches present pitifully watered-down messages about morality that confuse rather than clarify. Academic institutions, particularly the women's studies programs, promote the idea that marriage is at most an option for the distant future, and women are advised that the present is the time to "just do it!" The secular mantra, heard from middle school onward, is that sex will make you popular and happy; it is great recreation that is free and fun. For coeds and adult women, the message is blunt: women "must have sex to have a man."[15]

There is a mountain of media out there promoting a phony philosophy about the joys of casual, risky sexual experimentation; one need look no further than the junk advice featured in magazines like *Cosmopolitan* to see just how pernicious it is. According to one analysis, "Cosmo" is primarily about advertisements (59 percent ads, 23 percent ad-related, and 18 percent nonad-related, which included seven hard stories and twenty-four soft ones). Research indicates that the magazine objectifies women through the articles, advertisements, and illustrations. It sends distinct messages that women are sexual objects without individuality, personality, or intelligence—a woman's worth is nothing more than looking and acting sexy.[16] Even the "Dear Abby" column in many daily newspapers spreads the expectation of sexual activity even for the youngest of our teens.[17]

The assault on women—that, ironically, in light of feminist dogma, has convinced them that their only worth is being a sex object—will not be neutralized until a brigade of those who know better find their voices to convince today's *Sex and the City* generation of young women that only discipline and restraint will open the gateway to achieving their dreams and ambitions. Our culture must change to cultivate the attitude among women that says, "I won't mess up my tomorrows by fooling around today."

In part, such a cultural change can only come through straight talk about casual sex. Such conversations are long overdue. Every young person needs to know the following truths:

Truth #1: Casual Sex Impairs the Ability to Establish a Lasting Emotional Bond

When natural human emotional responses are repeatedly denied, those emotions are hardened, and the capacity to bond is weakened. Dr. Donald Joy published groundbreaking research in the early 1980s and has updated it periodically in the intervening years.[18] He chronicles the ways that intimacy produces oxytocin and, thus, bonding. His research indicates that human beings respond to sexual intercourse by affection and bonding, and they are driven to make that connection permanent and exclusive.

Dr. Joy reported on the work of a researcher at a hospital clinic in Detroit who worked with 1,000 couples for 10 years studying their marital problems and recording their sexual histories. He concluded that sexual intercourse is constructive only within marriage. His evidence is overwhelming that one or the other of the partners in casual sex (usually the girl or woman) experiences immediate emotional pain even in the absence of acknowledged injury. The experience of casual sexual intimacy produces memories that can contaminate future relationships and create lingering problems later on, when the person eventually marries. When the married couples in his research had problems, he said, "The pain in the marriages was rooted in their promiscuity."[19]

As early as the fourth century BC, the Greek philosopher Plato argued that love creates bonds and that those bonds strengthen society. In 1809, Johann Wolfgang von Goethe wrote about marriage as unifying human beings in passionate relationships similar to the unifying aspects of some chemical reactions. Later, scientific studies identified a natural brain chemical produced by affection and touching—oxytocin. Also called the "cuddle chemical," oxytocin is known as the "attachment hormone that produces bonding and trust."[20]

A campus psychiatrist at a major American university has written a book attempting to answer questions about the consequences of casual sex. The book is *Unprotected: A Campus Psychiatrist Reveals How Political Correctness in Her Profession Endangers Every Student.* *Unprotected*, written anonymously, was later revealed to be Dr. Miriam Grossman from the student health services of the University of California, Los Angeles.[21] Dr. Grossman says that the "hookup" culture has become the norm on the nation's campuses. "Depending on the study, 40-80 percent of students 'hook-up,' and by graduation, the average number of these nearly anonymous encounters is ten. Yet we wonder why so many young people suffer from depression, anxiety, eating disorders, and self-abuse." She adds, "A young woman is not warned that she is hard-wired to attach through sexual behavior, and that no condom will protect her from the heartache and confusion that may result.... This is information every incoming freshman must know; it will optimize her chances of staying emotionally and physically healthy as she navigates her way through the anything-goes campus environment."[22]

In fact, consequences are never mentioned except in the context of smoking, diet, exercise, or sleep. Certainly, as mentioned earlier, no one mentions the "fascinating research on the biochemistry of bonding," which reveals that casual sex is hazardous to a woman's mental health.

When I was an academic dean, I found that there was often (though not always) a relationship problem—usually a broken romance—behind a sudden drop in a student's grades. Dr. Grossman describes story after story of students who came in with academic and psychological problems that, she discovered with a little probing, turned out to coincide with sexual intimacy that produced one-sided attachment.

She quotes a neuropsychologist (I have mentioned this elsewhere, but it is so important for young women to know that it bears repeating) who described the effect of oxytocin: "You first meet him and he is passable. The second time you go out with him, he's OK. The third time you go out with him, you have sex. And from that point on you can't imagine what life would be like without him."[23]

Ironically, and in contrast to prevailing attitudes, men need love just as much as women. The conventional wisdom is that women need relationships, while men just want sex. Researchers say that young men and women just express their distress at a breakup differently. Women are more likely to feel depressed after a breakup, while men are more likely to have substance-abuse problems. Researchers say that women may shed more tears over a busted romantic relationship, but men suffer the greater emotional toll. In a study of more than 1,000 men and women, ages eighteen to twenty-three,[24] researchers found that unhappy romances cause men more emotional grief, including threatening their identity and feelings of self-worth. The study's author, Robin Simon of Wake Forest University, wrote, "The advantages of partner support and disadvantages of partner strain are more closely associated with men's than women's mental health."[25]

The life of actor Heath Ledger illustrates the male side of heartbreak.[26] Reports about Heath's tragic death include remarks by friends concerning his reaction to the recent breakup of his relationship (accounts differ on whether or not they were married) with Michelle Williams, the mother of their two-year-old daughter, Matilda. One source said, "Heath was shattered by his split from Michelle. He became a recluse. He barely slept; he was dealing with terrible mood swings." Friends say that he became an introvert, "hardly venturing out anymore," "barely slept," and was obviously "headed in a downward spiral." One analyst said that "a picture is fast emerging" from friends' discussions: "he's been battling some pretty serious demons," "he lost his grip on life"—both personally and professionally, and he has behaved increasingly in an "unhinged" way. One of his friends saw him at a party after the estrangement from Michelle and said, "It was obvious something awful had happened to him." The host of a recent party said that he arrived at the event "looking like a homeless" vagrant.

No one can know what was really going on in Heath's life, and his tragic, untimely death was likely due to an accidental overdose of sleeping pills. He is known to have had pneumonia and to have been treated for substance-abuse problems, including heroin addiction. All of those physical and emotional factors, including a reliance on sleeping pills, would make an accidental overdose plausible. He told friends that he was sleeping only two or three hours a night. He admitted that the psychological demands of his new role as the Joker in the Batman film, *The Dark Knight*, were exhausting. He said that he could not get his mind to turn off the intensity of his role as a "murderous psychopath." A critic praising his role in *Brokeback Mountain* commented that he got into the character so deeply that it was hard to imagine how he would be able to get back out. Heath, however, claimed that after a scene was filmed, "I just walk out the door, and I'm back into my regular life." Critics have compared the "intense, brooding actor" to a young Marlon Brando and James Dean. He seemed headed for stardom.

But, in a culture where recreational sex is fast becoming the norm for young adults, tragic deaths like Heath's (even when the cause is murky) should be a wake-up call. The narrative young people hear and see depicted in the entertainment media is that casual sex has no great significance beyond being a brief episode of pleasure, a purely temporary event of no lasting importance. Heath's depression following the breakup of his relationship with Michelle Williams is just one example of the fact that not even sexy hunks are exempt from broken hearts. Heath and Michelle fell in love at first sight on the set of the movie, *Brokeback Mountain*. A reporter who covered Heath extensively said that he stood in "awe of [Heath's] devotion and attention to [Michelle]." Everyone agrees that Heath was devoted to his "two girls," but that their later arguments over his drug use were "quite nasty."

Another wake-up call from the values of our throw-away culture is Heath's statement that he felt like he had lived out of a suitcase ever since his parents divorced when he was ten years old. In spite of children's supposed resilience, divorce leaves predictable negative outcomes, and father-absence leaves a vacuum that is virtually impossible to fill. Heath talked openly about his difficulty in dealing with his parents' divorce; he felt close to both of his parents and, like so many children run over by divorce, he blamed himself. He said that getting into acting helped him deal with his dark emotions after his parents' divorce.

None of these things alone, of course, led to Heath's death, but combined, they were obviously a factor in his deep depression and his life spiraling out of control. We do a disservice to young people when we promote the myth that sex is meaningless and shrug off the impact of divorce on children.

The bottom line is that sex *does* have consequences. The cocktail of chemicals that is unleashed when a couple touches is powerful and has long-lasting, as well as wide-ranging, effects on that specific relationship as well as all subsequent ones.

Truth #2: Casual Sex Leaves Young People Alone and Lonely

It is impossible to ignore or dictate to nature. Young people need to choose carefully. Even without the risk of STDs and/or pregnancy, sex can never be free of consequences. The choice to engage in sexual intimacy *always* has consequences. We cannot expect young people to choose wisely when adults—whose thinking is sometimes clouded by their rationalization of their own hurtful and toxic sexual experimentation—are irresponsible by not providing the best possible information to encourage self-discipline and self-control, which are the surest keys to young peoples' long-term well-being.

Dr. Meg Meeker writes, "Teenage sexual activity routinely leads to emotional turmoil and psychological distress…[Sexual permissiveness leads] to empty relationships, to feelings of self-contempt and worthlessness. All, of course, precursors to depression."[27] Sexually active teens are more likely than their abstinent counterparts to attempt suicide (girls 15 percent to 5 percent and boys 6 percent to 1 percent).[28] But the most telling fact is that the majority of teenagers, 72 percent of the girls and 55 percent of the boys, acknowledge regret over early sexual activity and wish that they had waited longer to have sex.[29] So much for today's cultural mantra that "sex is no big deal!"

Dr. Miriam Grossman's first book—the bestselling *Unprotected*—explains what happened to produce such dramatic changes on campuses. She reveals that "radical politics" has replaced "common sense" in the campus health and counseling centers to the detriment of students' well-being. In short, Dr. Grossman declared that her profession was "hijacked" and that college students are the "casualties" of the "radical activism" of health professionals on college campuses.[30]

The nation's seventeen million college and university students are being denied truth while their risky behavior is condoned by the prevalent social agenda on campus. Dispassionate objectivity and compassionate concern for an individual's health and well-being have been replaced by social activism. Now, the "polarization" of "opposite" sexes and a "binary gender system" must be replaced by androgyny and "alternative sexualities."[31] Nobody dares mention that promiscuous intimate behavior produces emotionally destructive consequences.

Ideology takes precedence over equipping students with the knowledge they need to cope with the inherent vulnerabilities and pitfalls of male–female interaction.

Ironically, Dr. Grossman, who laments political correctness, often uses the term, "sexually transmitted infections" (the politically correct designation for STDs because "infections" seem less serious than "diseases") instead of "sexually transmitted diseases." Today, on and off campus, STDs are considered no big deal. Yet, human papillomavirus (HPV)—a major cause of cervical cancer—is so common and so contagious that some doctors recommend that women "assume" that a partner has the infection. She also reveals that chlamydia is far more serious than generally perceived and that the college years are a good time to address the ramifications effectively; instead, the dangers of chlamydia are ignored or profoundly sugarcoated. As a result, untold numbers of women discover too late for intervention that they have become infertile from an undiagnosed STD.[32]

The idea of consistent condom use among college students is a joke—one study revealed that less than half of college students used a condom during their last vaginal intercourse. Discussions about HIV/AIDS are even more off-limits. While definitive information is available about the specific *behavioral* risk factors that cause HIV/AIDS, two myths continue to be disseminated—anybody can get it and AIDS does not discriminate. In contrast, Dr. Grossman lays out the specific, undeniable facts: HIV is spread primarily (and almost entirely) by three means: (1) anal sex, (2) shared needles, or (3) a partner who is involved in those things.[33]

Dr. Grossman reveals, too, that God is not welcomed in college health clinics. In fact, psychologists are almost five times more likely to be agnostic or atheist than the general public. Almost 90 percent of Americans believe in God. Among students, over three-quarters say they pray, and an equal number say that they are "searching for meaning and purpose in life." In fact, "cultural competency" (respecting the values of inclusion, respect and equality, especially in regard to gender, race, sexual orientation, disability, and other identities) is replacing religion, even though evidence overwhelmingly reveals that religion protects against drug and alcohol use, early sexual activity, and suicide.[34]

While the public generally sees abortion as a "woman's issue," Dr. Grossman cites a *Los Angeles Times* survey indicating that postabortion men experience more regret and guilt than postabortion women do.[35]

As Dr. Grossman and Dr. Meeker note so effectively, today's teens and young adults are amazingly misinformed and unprotected. Casual sex has consequences, and the steady flow of students crowding campus health centers is a clear indication that somebody needs to be telling them the truth about these consequences.

Truth #3: The "Sexual Revolution" Has Unleashed an Epidemic of Sexually Transmitted Diseases (STDs) and a Flood of Nonmarital Childbearing

In their March 2011 report, the Centers for Disease Control and Prevention (CDC) published the latest National Health Statistics Reports (NHSR). The report estimates that about "19 million new cases of STIs [sexually transmitted infections] occur each year," and "about half of those occur among those who are 15-24 years of age." The "direct medical cost" of these diseases to the fifteen- to twenty-four-year-olds alone was estimated at $6.5 billion in the year 2000. The racial disparities are significant—black teens have the highest rates of Chlamydia and gonorrhea, with black females ages twenty to twenty-four not far behind as next highest.[36]

Concerned Women for America released a major study on STDs in July 2011 that indicates forty-nine types of STDs; some curable, others not.[37] Fully 20 percent of all AIDS cases are among college-aged young people. Having three or more sexual partners in a lifetime increases a woman's odds of cervical cancer by fifteen times.

The shocking facts about the extent of STDs among young people are documented by the Centers for Disease Control. At the same time, they are hidden by the glossy advertisements in the media that downplay STDs, making them appear to be an insignificant health threat and suggesting that all are easily cured or controlled (as anyone who has seen the TV ads for herpes medications "knows"). Sadly, most of the young people with STDs will be dealing with the symptoms and consequences for the rest of their lives. In the United States, new cases of STDs are triple what they were just six years ago. Many of the STDs are incurable and others have persistent, significant symptoms requiring bothersome, expensive, and lifelong treatment.

The NHSR report[39] is troubling in that it purports to be "relevant to demographic and public health concerns, including fertility and sexually transmitted diseases among teenagers and adults" and focuses on those who are fifteen to forty-four years of age. Nearly 14,000 respondents entered their answers into a computer without an interviewer. The report found "twice as many women having same-sex contact in their lifetimes compared with men (12 percent of women and 5.2 percent of men)." NHSR also found less than 10 percent of teenagers aged fifteen to nineteen have had oral sex with an opposite sex partner, but not vaginal intercourse (7 percent of females and 9 percent of males).

I noted that statisticians have adopted the use of STIs instead of STDs (sexually transmitted infections rather than sexually transmitted diseases). Representatives of Planned Parenthood and SEICUS told me, when I asked at a meeting about the difference between the two terms, that "infections" carry less stigma than "diseases," because "anybody can get an infection, but a disease is more serious and carries a connotation of blame."

While the focus of the NHSR report ostensibly is on STIs, there are ten graphs of same-sex attraction, sexual identity, sexual behavior, and sexual activity. All this attention produced evidence, not surprisingly, that 86 percent of HIV cases are acquired through sexual behavior (others acquire HIV through transmission from an infected spouse or partner, or from a pregnant mother to her baby) and that the cost of the 50,000 new cases of HIV each year is approximately $20,000 per person. Amazingly, the study noted that, in addition to terms such as "heterosexual" and "homosexual," they used the terms, "straight," "gay," and "lesbian" so that respondents could easily "recognize" the meaning. Is this really necessary?

Among women who had fifteen or more sexual partners, black women topped the list at 11.3 percent, with whites at 8.9 percent, and Hispanics far behind at 4.4 percent. Among men having more than fifteen sexual partners, black men topped the list at 30 percent, whites at 21 percent, and Hispanics were a close third at 19 percent. Women reported more same-sex sexual activity over their lifetimes than men (12 percent of women and 5.2 percent of men).

Further, in contrast to the overwhelming impression conveyed by popular culture, contraception is not a reliable means of preventing pregnancy among those who engage in recreational sex. In 2000, approximately 822,000 pregnancies occurred among fifteen- to nineteen-year-olds. And what are the results? Seven out of ten adolescent mothers drop out of high school.[40] The National Center for Health Statistics analyzed data from the 2002 National Survey of Family Growth and found two startling facts. Among young women who used contraception at first intercourse, the probability of giving birth at each age is, surprisingly, only half that of those who did not use contraception. Further, the probability of a sexually active female giving birth approximately doubles between eighteen and twenty years of age, whether or not the young woman uses contraception at first intercourse.[41]

What the data are telling us is that out of every twenty-four girls in sex-education classes where they are handing out condoms, the odds are that about four of the sexually active ones can forget about going to college—even if all of them told the guys they must wear those condoms they got in sex-education class. When a girl just says "no" to five to ten minutes of awkward fumbling around in the back seat of some guy's car, what is it going to cost her? Maybe five to ten minutes of popularity with a guy who probably will not be around to help pick up the pieces of her future.

As promiscuous sex has become "normalized"—thanks, in part, to Hollywood's incessant push to expand the borders of the sexual revolution—the percentage of children born outside of marriage from 1970 to 2009 mushroomed. In the United States, the percentage rose from 11 percent to more than 40 percent.[42] In the United Kingdom, the percentage climbed from 8 percent to 46 percent.[43] The rates for France and Sweden rose to 54 percent,[44] and Germany's rate increased to more than four times its 1970 level.[45]

The big question is: Why have our values changed? Why are young people falling for these contemporary trends? Once again, the answer is that the popular culture inundates them with myths and literally pushes them to "find themselves" through risky, promiscuous sexual experimentation. Young people are fed lies and are encouraged in their rebellion against moral boundaries by the aging veterans of the sexual revolution. Several years ago, Anna Quindlen, a Pulitzer Prize-winning author and *New York Times* columnist, told one group of graduates at their college graduating ceremonies, "Begin with that most terrifying of all things, a clean slate. Then look, every day, at the choices you are making, and when you ask yourself why you are making them, find this answer: For me! For me!"

It is sad to think about how encouragement of "me-centered-ness" and the need for a little attention—and maybe even a little affection—prompt a lot of girls to say "okay" and then have to contend with the very real possibility of ending up pregnant or infected with an STD, even when the guy wears a condom. To my mind, clearly facing the hard realities of sex makes the choice about sexual activity very simple and very uncomplicated. Just saying "no" is a pretty good idea, after all.

Truth #4: Casual Sex Is Dangerous in the Age of HIV/AIDS, but It Is a Myth that "Everybody Is Vulnerable to Getting it"

The politically correct mantra about HIV/AIDS is that "anybody can get it." This half-truth is as bizarre as pointing to the tragic death of professional naturalist Steve Irwin, best known as "The Crocodile Hunter," and saying, "Anyone can die from the barb of a stingray." There is an obvious missing piece in both instances. You are not going to die from a stingray's barb *unless* you dive in waters that are home to stingrays. Likewise, unless you (1) have intimate sexual contact with someone who is infected with the HIV/AIDS virus, (2) share contaminated needles to do drugs, or (3) are a healthcare worker who comes in direct contact with the body fluids of an infected person (or as in the heartrending case of Kimberly Bergalis, who contracted AIDS from her infected dentist), you will not—I repeat, you will NOT—contract HIV/AIDS.

Another phony slogan foisted upon the public is that women are the "new face of HIV/AIDS." These myths are among the pernicious efforts to disperse the stigma associated with a disease that is almost exclusively a homosexual male and drug addict epidemic. Insidious myths like these leave today's young people misinformed, misled, and, thus, unprotected.

In Unprotected, Dr. Grossman reveals that basic medical knowledge about the transmission of the HIV/AIDS virus is kept from students. In spite of the fact that we are now well past the quarter century mark in the AIDS epidemic, and in spite of the fact that 1 in every 500 college students may be HIV-positive, basic HIV/AIDS information is not known by the general public; our students, in particular—the very ones most in need of truth to reinforce self-discipline, are not fully informed about the facts.

We treat HIV/AIDS differently from any other public health threat. While doctors are required by law to report nearly fifty communicable diseases (including tuberculosis, measles, syphilis, and meningitis), and people with those communicable diseases are ordered by law to get treatment or go to jail, U.S. laws prohibit disclosure of anyone's HIV status. Even the HIV tests use a code name to avoid identifying any infected persons. Thus, the only way anyone knows that a person has the virus is if that information is voluntarily given.

Yet, the CDC reports that in the United States, there are 40,000 new HIV cases per year and about 900,000 people living with the disease, with nearly 250,000 of those people unaware that they are infected. In response, the CDC recommends that the public be nonjudgmental and that they identify racism, discrimination, stigma, and homophobia as reasons for the spread of the epidemic! As Dr. Grossman points out, instead of the public health programs that successfully controlled cholera, polio, and syphilis, we fight the AIDS epidemic, a disease that has already claimed half a million victims in the United States, with programs about cultural sensitivity. Such is the power of homosexual activists who waged a "privacy" campaign and, as noted by Dr. Grossman, won special status for HIV/AIDS among infectious diseases through voluntary and anonymous testing and no requirement for partner notification.

As a result of the shortsightedness of homosexual activists' campaign, people who are at risk for the disease are blasé about their behavior and their disease status. At the same time, politically correct slogans like "anyone can get it" and "women are the new face of HIV/AIDS" blatantly misstate the nature of the risk faced by the general public.

While signs everywhere warn that "anybody can get it," those who are highly vulnerable to HIV/AIDS remain the same as nearly thirty years ago. HIV is still (and has been since the outset) primarily concentrated in the same high-risk groups—men having sex with men, and intravenous drug users. Some studies are now claiming that heterosexual victims constitute up to 30 percent of the total number of cases. Look closely, though, and the definitions in those studies have changed. The fine print reveals that the heterosexual category *includes* persons who have had sex with bisexual men and drug users. The most common route of sexual transmission of HIV remains anal intercourse. Yet billboards proclaim, "HIV is here to stay and anybody can get it!" Just as 80 percent of lung cancers are related to tobacco use, the vast majority of HIV/AIDS victims are homosexual men or drug addicts. It is their *behavior*—anal intercourse and sharing needles—that puts them at risk. To be blunt, the rectal lining, unlike the vaginal lining, is a relatively porous barrier that is only one cell thick (the lower intestine is designed to absorb fluids—that is the very essence of its function); thus, it is quite easy for the HIV virus to transit through the intestinal wall into the blood stream and target cells. Some experts estimate that it only takes about ten minutes for the virus to break through the barriers to infect the victim.

To be blunt again, in regard to women's vulnerability to HIV, the virus can burrow through natural barriers, enter the bloodstream, gain access to deeper tissues, and reproduce much more easily in the rectum than in the vagina. Thus, women are better protected against the virus. Dirty needles bypass the skin barrier of addicts; likewise, a nursing infant of an infected mother is directly vulnerable to the virus. The healthy vagina, however, has a strong lining that is infection-resistant, and under normal circumstances, its tremendous elastic-ity minimizes the risk of tears and abrasions so that the HIV virus, barring a weakening of the system, has great difficulty breaching its natural barriers. Thus, according to Dr. Grossman, some researchers contend that vaginal transmission is very rare. This view is supported by the fact that studies of prostituted women reveal that AIDS is found overwhelmingly only among those who are also intravenous drug abusers.

In spite of the availability of this information in the medical lit-erature, the politically correct messages still mislead the American public. Billboards still brazenly declare that "anybody can get it" and "women are the new face of HIV/AIDS." It is time that we told it like it is: HIV/AIDS is spread primarily by anal sex, sharing needles, or hav-ing a sexual partner who does those things. Health care professionals aside, if you do not dive into the waters of promiscuous sex and drug use, you will not have to fear the deadly barb of AIDS.

Truth #5: On Another Front, Replacing Marriage with Casual Sex is Especially Harmful to a Young Adult's Long-term Well-being

A young person's choices about sex reveal his or her attitudes about others. Sexual intercourse can be an intense and pleasurable experience, but it is more—much more. Sexual intimacy triggers the strongest and deepest, most exhilarating passions in life. Its purpose is to bond a man and a woman into "one flesh" in the deepest intimacy that human beings can share. Further, sex is designed to both create life and build a strong relationship to protect and provide for that life. Little wonder that the Creator fashioned the means of creating life in such a way that it is one of the most awesome forces in our lives and then linked it to marriage so as to signify to us, "Priceless. Handle with great care."

Although young people know the mechanics of sex, they know little to nothing about the magic, the mystery, or the meaning of a man "knowing" a woman, to use the Biblical term that implies so much.

How can we ever manage to teach our children what is real and true when so many corrupt fallacies about sex reverberate throughout our culture? Sex is no big deal? Tell that to anyone whose marriage was destroyed by infidelity or to someone whose heart has been broken when he or she felt sexually manipulated or his or her body was "used" by sexual exploitation wrapped up as "free sex." Amazingly, Google reveals dozens of heart-wrenching popular songs about "broken hearts," attesting to the pain and anger associated with faithless lovers.

I ran into this just the other day at the hair salon. Women around me talked about how terrible men are; what jerks they always turn out to be. Perhaps sensing that I was not joining in the conversation, one of them put a question directly to me: "A woman would have to be crazy to trust a man, wouldn't she?" On the spot, I replied, "Well, not all men are terrible or untrustworthy." Stony silence greeted my remark; it was like I had betrayed the Sisterhood. It was like I was delusional or in denial, though one woman seemed embarrassed to have exposed her private pain in such a public way.

Obviously, there is nothing new about selfishness, betrayal, exploitation, manipulation, or mistreatment—such behaviors have been staples from both men *and* women. How sad, though, to teach young women to be cynical; that all men are not to be trusted, that sex is demeaning or humiliating, or to expect that relationships will not last and that divorce inevitably follows the wedding?

Mature voices have always warned that marriages will inevitably go through rough patches, but that does not make the cynics' claim true: that all marriages inevitably end up as bitter, irreconcilable relationships. Sex, properly understood, can play a very significant role in the needed redemption when relationships sour. Nothing exceeds the potential of loving marital relations in this regard. (That by itself, even without its potential for procreation, would be enough to put an end to the pernicious lie that sex is no big deal.)

We have already mentioned the frequent Scriptural use of the verb "to know" in lieu of more explicit terms to recount the occurrence of sexual relations. But this euphemism, though somewhat vague, is, nevertheless, laden with meaning. It points to the fact that sexual intercourse is a means to an extremely intimate, private knowledge of our personhood. In intercourse, the raw unadorned animalistic side of our humanity is exposed whether little or all clothing is removed. Logically, we know that the sexual part of our nature is universal; but each individual's personhood is unique and, at some level, intensely private. Hence, we find that being revealed to another individual through intimate sexual contact is one of life's moments of greatest vulnerability. We could not feel more exposed if we stood before an audience of thousands naked, having forgotten to don our costume and not knowing our lines.

When the cloak of our rationality is pushed aside and our intellect no longer provides a covering, it is then most important that both partners be clothed in love and the certainty of a permanent commitment to each other—in a word, married. Then the couple can progress to a state of being totally liberated from their inhibitions and the innate fear we all have of being exposed—to wit, of being known. What would under other circumstances be rape (a despicable violation of personhood) is now a physical expression of the union of two hearts in tender devotion and passionate desire. This union is the only experience that genuinely warrants the term "making love." Anything short of this, no matter how it is spoken of, is a counterfeit, a fake experience of intimacy. Yet, the term, "making love," is part of our common lingo, and even when the encounter is meaningless, one or the other of the participants can feel betrayed afterward, when the meaninglessness is exposed.

Ultimately, however, casual sex—sex without commitment—is a betrayal. It is a short slide from the *sunum bonum* of this age, self-actualization, to the crass position of "you gotta do your own thing." The problem is that "doing your own thing" ends up affecting many others besides you. Even if it were not immoral behavior—an old-fashioned concept these days—casual sex, by its very nature, is an exercise in foolishness. For the woman, there are the risks to health and personal safety of sex with a man not emotionally equipped to make the commitments required of a husband and father. Even if he has good looks and charm, a "nice" guy does not take advantage of the "something-for-nothing" deal that uncommitted sex entails. A young woman's heart is a delicate, priceless treasure, and any male who is a real man—someone worthy to be the father of her children—does not take something of such value unless he is willing to give some-thing of equal worth in exchange, namely the lifetime commitment of marriage.

I like the challenge of "doing our own thing"—four-wheeling treacherous passes in the Rocky Mountains, for instance. But I am compelled to accept another, more important, challenge—combating the dangerous trends of today when young people "doing their own thing" end up broken and deserted at the bottom of the treacherous passage from youth to maturity.

My husband and I had done our thing—going over Engineer Pass and Cinnamon Pass, barely passable four-wheel drive trails across the Rockies between Lake City and Silverton, Colorado.[46] You know the type; you have seen them in those television commercials designed to convince you that their truck is tough enough to go anywhere a goat can go. Not only were the vistas beyond description, but we were fortunate enough, indeed, to come across a herd of wild mountain goats—the first we had ever seen in any of our trips to the Rocky Mountain outback. Then there was Ophir Pass between Silverton and Telluride. Although it is rated as only moderately difficult, the half-mile-long stretch is a narrow shelf cut into an enormous talus slope. My husband was smart enough not to point out, far below, the hulk of a broken, deserted vehicle that had not made it across.

Our reward was breakfast at the locally renowned Butterhorn Bakery and Café in Frisco, Colorado. The Butterhorn Café is one of those places of Western ambiance located in a rustic, picture-perfect old mining town—the kind that dots the Colorado mountains.

What I remember most, however, was not the delicious breakfast, but the brief conversation we had with our waitress.

We had assumed the waitress was a coed, soon heading back to college; she shocked us by saying that she was twenty-eight. Then, she cheerfully volunteered that she had recently moved to Frisco with her boyfriend with whom she has been living for ten years. They decided, she said, to trade the beach scene in South Carolina for snowboarding in the Rockies.

It is funny how activists have made privacy such a sacred right, yet people still want to connect by revealing themselves to others.

Our waitress had no idea how much her statement revealed to her customers—two people whose professions are to analyze the nation's social trends. While the young woman eagerly looks forward to the pleasure of snowboarding this winter, frankly, we know that the odds are she probably cannot count on a future with that boyfriend. While she is, undoubtedly, emotionally bonded to him, she does not have a commitment from him. After giving up ten years of her youth, she is unlikely to receive anything but heartbreak in return. Such relationships typically end with the girl being the loser. If and when they get married, it will be the boyfriend who makes the decision, not the girl and not them together. She probably does not know that a marriage after living together is more likely to end in divorce than if they had not lived together beforehand (this is not a fact that gets emphasized in most family life lectures in high school and college). When he decides to "get serious," it will probably be with a fresher, younger girl.

And, her biological clock is ticking; in fact, it is winding down fast. She probably does not realize how fast it is going, but, at some point, she will want a family and children. For many young women in her situation, that realization comes too late. Will her snowboarder boyfriend recognize how significant and full of meaning the life of husband and father is? Will he be willing to give up the life of freedom for one of commitment and responsibility? If she gets pregnant and has the baby, she has no assurance that her boyfriend will stick around and help her change diapers. Many abortions are prompted because the woman has a choice. The boyfriend says, "It's your choice—the baby or me!" And, for sure, a baby is an expensive proposition and would certainly hamper their snowboarding.

My heart ached that morning as I left the Butterhorn Café thinking about our waitress and the millions of other young women like her who are headed down a dead-end road. Theirs is a blighted future. They are forfeiting the priceless joys of marriage to the love of their lives. For the woman, there are the risks to health and personal safety of living with a man not emotionally equipped to make the commitments required of a husband and father.

None of us lives life without a few bumps along the way, but a life full of positive and happy times that become cherished memories is possible only in the secure bonds of a firm "till death do us part" commitment—marriage. As I think about all of the young women who have thrown away their virtue—another old-fashioned idea—I am deeply troubled. Sadly, there are far too many young people with broken hearts and incurable diseases because adults have been unwilling to state categorically that sex is meant exclusively for marriage. The era of "free love" has left a terrible legacy; it is apparent that "free love" has an extraordinarily high price tag.

Notes

1. Numerous publications—from *The Economist* to *Time* magazine—have asked the question, "Is God Dead?" *Newsweek* has led the charge in recent years with cover stories in 2005 ("God is Dead, Lennon Lives") and in 2009 ("End of Christian America").

2. Jessica Bennett and Jesse Ellison, "I don't: The Case against Marriage," *The Daily Beast*, June 11, 2010, http://www.thedailybeast.com/newsweek/2010/06/11/i-don-t.html (accessed September 29, 2011).

3.   Albert Mohler, "The Case against Marriage Courtesy of Newsweek," *AlbertMohler.com*, June 25, 2010, http://www.albertmohler.com/2010/06/25/the-case-against-marriage-courtesy-of-newsweek/ (accessed September 29, 2011).

4.   For a discussion of Flappers, see "20th Century History," *About.Com*, http://history1900s.about.com/od/1920s/a/flappers.htm (accessed September 29, 2011).

5.   "*PEOPLE* and NBC Release Poll on Teen Sex," *People* Magazine and *NBC Television Network*, January 19, 2005, http://www.people.com/people/article/0,,1017005,00.html (accessed September 29, 2011).

6.   Ibid.

7.   Dr. Meg Meeker, *Epidemic: How Teen Sex is Killing Our Kids* (Washington, DC: Regnery Publishing, 2002), 12.

8.   "People and NBC poll on Teen Sex."

9.   Ibid.

10.   For information, see the *Wikipedia* entry for "Sex and the City," http://en.wikipedia.org/wiki/Sex_and_the_City (accessed September 29, 2011).

11.   The nickname of the man who is the "love interest" for the lead character in "Sex and the City," http://en.wikipedia.org/wiki/Mr._Big_%28Sex_and_the_City%29 (accessed September 29, 2011).

12.   For more information about this television situation comedy see: http://en.wikipedia.org/wiki/Friends (accessed September 29, 2011).

13.   Associated Press, "Poll: Family Ties Key to Happy Kids," *Fox News*, August 19, 2007, http://www.foxnews.com/story/0,2933,293760,00.html (accessed September 29, 2011).

14.   Michael P. Marks, "The Playboy Philosophy as Modern Political Manifesto," Politics Department, Willamette University, Paper presented at the Annual Conference of the Western Political Science Association, Vancouver, British Columbia, March 19–21, 2009, http://www.allacademic.com//meta/p_mla_apa_research_citation/3/1/7/1/2/pages317120/p317120-1.php (accessed September 29, 2011).

15.   LeToya Singleton and others, "Cosmopolitan: An Analysis of a Popular Magazine," *Cosmo 2000*, a Powerpoint Presentation, http://virtual.clemson.edu/caah/women/ws301/ppt/**cosmo**2000.ppt (accessed September 29, 2011).

16.   Ibid.

17.   Robert Knight, "Dear Abby Tells Mom to Lose Qualms about Daughter's Porn Sites: It's Only the Latest Column to Promote Sexual License, Moral Relativism," *Concerned Women for America*, Culture and Family Institute, 2002, http://www.cultureandfamily.org/articledisplay.asp?id=2772&department=CFI&categoryid=cfreport (accessed April 1, 2011).

18.   Donald Joy, *Bonding: Relationships in the Image of God* (Nappanee, IN: Evangel Publishing House, originally Word, Inc., 1985 and 1996), http://www2.talbot.edu/ce20/educators/view.cfm?n=donald_joy#bibliography (accessed September 29, 2011).

19.   Donald and Robbie Joy, *Two Become One: God's Blueprint for Couples* (Nappanee, IN: Evangel Publishing House, 2002), (formerly *Lovers: Whatever Happened to Eden?* [Dallas, TX: Word, Inc., 1987]).

20. Janice Shaw Crouse, "Love Potion Number O," *Concerned Women for America*, January 19, 2006, http://www.cwfa.org/articlearchtemp. asp?id=9936 (accessed October 4, 2011).

21. Dr. Miriam Grossman, *Unprotected: A Campus Psychiatrist Reveals How Political Correctness in Her Profession Endangers Every Student* (New York: Sentinel, a member of The Penguin Group, 2006).

22. Kathryn Jean Lopez, "The Hook-up is In," Interview with Dr. Miriam Grossman, *National Review OnLine*, December 19, 2006, http://www.nationalreview.com/articles/219516/hook/interview (accessed September 29, 2011).

23. Grossman, *Unprotected*, 7.

24. Robin Simon, "Nonmarital Romantic Relationships and Mental Health in Early Adulthood: Does the Association Differ for Women and Men?" *Journal of Health and Social Behavior* 51 (June 2010): 168–82, http://www.wfu.edu/sociology/simon/Simon%20&%20Barrett%20JHSB%202010.pdf (accessed September 29, 2011).

25. Simon, "Nonmarital Romantic Relationships."

26. Janice Shaw Crouse, "Men's Hearts can be Broken, Too," *Townhall*, January 23, 2008, http://townhall.com/columnists/JaniceShawCrouse/2008/01/23/mens_hearts_can_be_broken_too (accessed September 29, 2011).

27. As quoted in Robert Rector and others, "Sexually Active Teenagers are More Likely to be Depressed and to Attempt Suicide," *The Center for Data Analysis Report #03-04*, Heritage Foundation, June 3, 2003, http://www.heritage.org/Research/Reports/2003/06/Sexually-Active-Teenagers-Are-More-Likely-to-Be-Depressed (accessed September 29, 2011).

28. Ibid.

29. Ibid.

30. Grossman, *Unprotected*, xiv.

31. Ibid., 36–37.

32. Ibid., 107–18.

33. Ibid., 71.

34. Ibid., 37.

35. Ibid., 100.

36. Anjani Chandra and others, "Sexual Behavior, Sexual Attraction, and Sexual Identity in the United States: Data from the 2006-2008 National Survey of Family Growth," Centers for Disease Control and Prevention, *National Health Statistics Reports (NHSR)*, Number 36, March 2011, http://www.cdc.gov/nchs/data/nhsr/nhsr036.pdf (accessed September 29, 2011).

37. Brenda Zurita, "Sexually Transmitted Diseases: The Cost of Free Love," *Concerned Women for America*, July 2011, http://www.cwfa.org/images/content/CWA_STDs-The-Cost-of-Free-Love_2011.pdf (accessed October 13, 2011).

38. Janice Shaw Crouse, *Children at Risk* (New Brunswick, NJ and London: Transaction Publishers, 2010), 60.

39. Janice Shaw Crouse, "Marriage doesn't Count," *Townhall*, March 17, 2011, http://townhall.com/columnists/janiceshawcrouse/2011/03/17/marriage_doesnt_count (accessed September 29, 2011).

40. Linda Klepacki, "What Your Teens Need to Know about Sex," *Life Challenges*, Focus on the Family, 2005, http://www.focusonthefamily.com/

lifechallenges/love_and_sex/purity/what_your_teens_need_to_know_ about_sex.aspx (accessed September 29, 2011).

41.   J. C. Abma and others, *Teenagers in the United States: Sexual Activity, Contraceptive Use, and Childbearing, 2002* (Hyattsville: National Center for Health Statistics, Vital Health Statistics 23(24), 2004).

42.   Joyce A. Martin et al., "Births: Preliminary Data for 2009," *National Vital Statistics Report* 59, no. 3 (U.S. National Center for Health Statistics, December 2010): http://www.cdc.gov/nchs/data/nvsr/nvsr59/nvsr59_03.pdf (accessed September 29, 2011).

43.   "Population, Eurostat: Your Key to European Statistics," http://epp.eurostat. ec.europa.eu/portal/page/portal/population/data/main_tables (accessed September 29, 2011).

44.   Ibid.

45.   Ibid.

46.   Janice Shaw Crouse, "Doing Your Own Thing," *Concerned Women for America*, September 14, 2004, http://www.beverlylahayeinstitute.org/ articledisplay.asp?id=6403&department=BLI&categoryid=dotcommenta ry&subcategoryid=blicul (accessed March 1, 2011).

Part III

Marriage: The Impact on the Private Sector

6

Marriage Benefits for Individuals

The greatest happiness of life is the conviction that we are loved, loved for ourselves, or rather, loved in spite of ourselves.
—Victor Hugo (1802–1885)

Introduction—the Benefits of Marriage

One memorable Sunday, my husband and I took our weekend guests to services at the Washington National Cathedral,[1] where we saw a beautiful example of marriage and the benefits that marriage brings to the individuals in the relationship. Immediately in front of us was an attractive family, seemingly tourists visiting the nation's capital. After the service, when we were complimenting the parents on their well-mannered children, we learned that the family had journeyed to Washington for the burial of the wife's father in Arlington National Cemetery earlier in the week. Her father was a Vietnam veteran, and she proudly related the fact that he had won the Silver Star for valor in combat.

Many visitors, like us, view the magnificent edifice of the National Cathedral, hear the wondrous choir and organ, worship with people from around the country, and then return home with nothing more than photographs to illustrate the majesty of the cathedral and scribbled notes about the sermon they heard. But seeing the couple with their three children imprinted a lasting image on our minds and hearts. The mutual support that the man and woman gave to each other and the caring love that they showed to each of their three children was tremendously moving—especially viewed in the context of their family's grief at the loss of a father and grandfather.

I noted that although they were not in a familiar setting and had no children's books or toys to keep them occupied, the two older children's quiet and respectful behavior spoke volumes about what they had been taught; they clearly had more than a little experience with being calm and orderly during Sunday worship. Snuggled in her carrier on the seat between the mother and father, the youngest child—an infant—slept undisturbed.

Anyone not watching closely would have missed the moment when a switch in seating arrangement occurred. During an opening hymn, in a move as smooth as any quarterback's handoff to his running back, the father shifted the baby's carrier to his own seat and moved to stand by his wife. He handled the baby carrier with such strength and deftness that it was clear the role of protector was well practiced. Later on, when the infant opened its incredibly bright eyes, the father, with sure hand, nudged the pacifier back into her mouth so gently that she fell back asleep almost immediately. Her dark eyes were so beautiful; it was a bit disappointing to have only the briefest glimpse of them. But it was wonderful to think of a little one so carefully protected and obviously cherished that she was not discomforted in the least by all that was going on around her.

As the man moved alongside his wife, her hand slid up under his elbow, almost as though it had a mind of its own, to lightly and comfortably rest on his forearm. Seeing the contact, I recognized it as yet another visible expression of the emotional bond that linked them. Even after many years together, those in the grip of love have an inexplicable need to affirm over and over again—sometimes through words, but even more often through touch—"I am yours. You are mine. We are one!" Such touches are a simple expression of love, but, somehow, they always warm our hearts and comfort our spirits.

Later, as we stood and sang another hymn, the mother leaned toward the daughter, who appeared to be about six or seven years of age, and, with her finger, traced the location of the words in the hymnal to assist the daughter's fledgling efforts. When we sat back down, the father's arm came comfortably to rest lightly on the mother's back—not in showy ostentation, but in a seeming expression of the deep-seated human need to feel directly connected to those we love.

Like a screensaver on a computer etching out an image, little by little, as they worshipped, the signs were blossoming into a clear picture of the relationship shared by this couple and their children. By the time the Eucharist was celebrated near the end of the service, I was not the least surprised—and inwardly applauded—when the father demurred at the usher's assurance that the baby would be all right if she were left sleeping in her carrier on the pew while the parents took communion with the older children. Instead, with one strong hand, the dad lifted the carrier and held it by his side as the family moved forward to receive the elements. The infant was still fast asleep when they returned to their seats.

Those in such a supportive, caring relationship usually are blithely unaware of the emotional connections and the unified front they embody that are so apparent to others observing them; but social scientists are very aware of the benefits of healthy marriage and all the positive blessings that flow to a man and woman, and their children, from their marriage and family. Study after study comparing the various types of household arrangements indicates conclusively that no other family structure produces such consistently positive outcomes as the married couple—i.e., mom and dad—family. For instance, The Urban Institute, a well-respected center-left think tank in Washington, D.C., has published information comparing family structures[2]—married couple families with cohabiting partners (where only one partner was a parent of the children in the household) and cohabiting parents with single mother households. Not surprisingly, regardless of the outcome being measured, the married couple family was far superior in measurable positive outcomes to any other household arrangement. Clearly, structure matters in important ways when it comes to living arrangements. No wonder the institution of marriage is so universal and so pervasive across otherwise diverse societies throughout history. Civilized societies have always considered marriage to be a "contract of natural law"[3] and, thus, a foundation of stable societies.

Even the liberal *New York Times* recognizes the benefits of marriage. Reporter Jennifer Steinhauer wrote, "Single people may simply not know what's good for them."[4] Michael Novak—an American Catholic philosopher, journalist, novelist, diplomat, and author of more than twenty-five books on the philosophy and theology of culture—is credited with first describing the family as the "original" Department of Health and Human Services, a comparison that is very apt since social science evidence so clearly indicates the positive outcomes that flow from a strong, caring family unit. Heritage Foundation scholar Chuck Donovan said, "The fracturing of a family is not the breaking of a single link in a chain, but the opening of a hole in a protective net."[5] When a hole develops in the net, each family member suffers consequences. When the net remains strong and whole, however, all individuals benefit.

Dr. Linda Waite, a prominent researcher on marriage, author of numerous books, and professor of sociology at the University of Chicago, said, "Marriage may provide individuals with a sense of meaning in their lives and a sense of obligation to others, inhibiting risky behaviors and encouraging healthy ones."[6] An added benefit, she tells audiences when she speaks at conferences or colleges, is that "married people report having more and better sex than single people have."[7] She frequently concludes her remarks by comparing marriage to exercise. Although many will hear and not heed the facts, some people, Dr. Waite says, will take the available information showing the superiority of marriage over cohabitation and singleness and will "have a healthier and more satisfying life."[8] That information, she adds, shows that, in numerous ways, married people are better off than those who are not married.

In her testimony before the Subcommittee on Children and Families—part of the Senate Committee on Health, Education, Labor and Pensions, Barbara Dafoe Whitehead[9] (another prominent social scientist, wife, mother of three, and University of Chicago Ph.D.), summarized the research on marriage and cited the benefits for adults.

- On average, married couples are happier, healthier, wealthier, enjoy longer lives, and report greater sexual satisfaction than single, divorced, or cohabiting individuals.
- Research indicates that married people are less likely to take moral or mortal risks, and are even less inclined to risk-taking when they have children; they have better health habits and receive more regular health care. They are very unlikely to attempt or to commit suicide.
- They are also more likely to enjoy close and supportive relationships with their close relatives and to have a wider social support network. They are better equipped to cope with major life crises, such as severe illness, job loss, and the extraordinary care needs of sick children or aging parents.
- Married parents are significantly less likely to be poor—poverty rates for married couples are half those of cohabiting couple parents and one-third that of noncohabiting single parents.
- Even poor parents gain economic advantage from marriage—though it may not lift them out of poverty; it generally reduces the degree of economic hardship because the couple can pool earnings, rely on a larger network of friends, family, and community, share risks, and, thus, mitigate the disruptions of a possible job loss.

Marriage Benefits Women

The movie *Eat, Pray, Love*,[10] released in 2010 and based on a *New York Times* bestselling book by Elizabeth Gilbert,[11] is about a woman who was "sentenced to wed"[12] in order to avoid her Latin lover's immigration problems. The author's opinion is that men benefit from marriage more than women. In an interview, she told CNN, "Looking at study after study, it becomes quite chilling to see how very much more benefited men are by marriage. Married men perform in life exceptionally better than single men, they live longer, they're richer, they're happier."[13]

Women, she declared, "often find that they've gotten the short end of the stick." She explained, "Women give more, and, as a result, they give up more. I think the other problem is that women go into marriage with such high expectations, really inflated romantic ideas about what this relationship is going to be...Ten years later, women have sort of had to take a nose dive from what they thought it was going to be."[14] But is she right? Do objective research findings support her assessment?

Benefits Are Gender-Specific

Gilbert's assumptions about marriage being better for men than for women is a common myth, one that experts say stems from the negative effect of marriage on women's careers, the stress of motherhood, and misperceptions about the danger of domestic abuse.[15] According to marriage researchers David Popenoe and Barbara Dafoe Whitehead, recent studies find that "men and women benefit about equally from marriage" but in gender-specific ways.[16] The Witherspoon Institute's "Ten Principles" project noted that both husbands and wives benefit in financial, emotional, physical, and social ways, but that the benefits of marriage for wives are more sensitive to the quality of the marriage than are the benefits of marriage for the husbands.[17] Both men and women live longer, happier, healthier, and more financially secure lives when they are married. Husbands generally gain greater health benefits, while wives gain greater financial advantages.[18]

Married Women Are Safer

One of the more distressing myths about women and marriage is the oft-repeated claim about the prevalence of domestic abuse among married women. Linda Waite found that 16 percent of cohabiting women reported that arguments with their partners could turn physical, while only 8 percent of married women have had similar experiences. The surveys also showed that 20 percent of cohabiting women reported that they had secondary sex partners, while only 4 percent of married women reported they did.[19] The United States Department of Health and Human Services reported that unmarried women were three to four times more likely to be abused by their boyfriends while pregnant than married women by their husbands.[20] Similarly, the Department of Justice estimates that "women are 62 times more likely to be assaulted by live-in boyfriends than they are by husbands."[21] Linda Waite's research found that, "even after controlling for education, race, age, and gender, people who are not married but live together are three times more likely to say their arguments get physical (such as kicking, hitting, or shoving) in the past year than do married couples."[22]

Similarly, Dr. Jan Stets, of Washington State University, also found that aggressive behavior is more than twice as common among cohabiting partners as among married couples. She found that approximately 14 percent of those who live together admit to hitting, shoving, or throwing things at their partner compared to only 5 percent among married people.[23] Numerous studies from the Family Violence Research Program at the University of New Hampshire duplicate these findings that cohabiting partners are more violent than married couples.[24] The United States Justice Department Victimization Study found that 65 percent of violent crimes against women were committed by a boyfriend or ex-husband, while only 9 percent were committed by husbands.[25] Clearly, when it comes to a woman's personal safety, she is, on average, much safer married than cohabitating.

Married Mothers Are Better off Financially

Married mothers are far less likely to live in poverty than are unmarried mothers.[26] It is tragic enough that so many young women today are skeptical about marriage because of the deluge of negative messages that they receive from the media and entertainment industries. Worse, still, is the fact that many are also convinced by the pervasive attitude that all a couple needs is passionate sex, and, thus, they do not need a "piece of paper" to prove their love. Most of them have not reckoned with the fact that having a baby out of wedlock means a 50–50 chance that they will end up in poverty. Having a second child out of wedlock raises the likelihood of ending up in poverty to more than 60 percent. Unfortunately, our nation's poverty experts continue to take the easy road and address only the derivative problems associated with poverty that are politically correct to discuss (limited job opportunities for unwed mothers, racial discrimination, and the temptation to make easy money through gambling or drugs) rather than tackle the thorny, controversial issue of the decline in marriage and mounting numbers of single mothers and absent fathers. More than forty years of failed social welfare policies have amply demonstrated that when the wrong solution is applied to a bad situation, increases in funding simply magnify the problem.

Married Women Have Greater Well-Being

In terms of their personal well-being, married women suffer less from depression than those women who are not married or who cohabitate. Marriage provides "particularly high psychological benefits" and significantly lowers the risk of suicide.[27] The Witherspoon Institute explains in its Ten Principles, "It is not just marital status but the very ideal of marriage that matters. Persons who value their marriage for its own sake—who resisted cohabitation, who think that marriage is for life, and who believe that it is best for children to be reared by a father and a mother as husband and wife—are significantly more likely to experience high-quality marriages, compared to persons who are less committed to the institution of marriage."[28] The research of W. Bradford Wilcox and Steven L. Nock, sociologists at the University of Virginia, produced similar findings: "women are happier in their marriages if they are strongly committed to the institution of marriage, if they are involved with institutions that lend social support to marriage, and if they share the normative and social support of their commitment to marriage with their husbands."[29] As the scholars somewhat cynically point out, "these women may also be more inclined to view their marriage in a positive light to legitimize their investment in married life."[30]

Of course, those familiar with the doctrines of Christianity will recognize that these attitudes reflect the Christian teachings on marriage—that marriage "helps to overcome self-absorption, egoism, pursuit of one's own pleasure, and to open oneself to the other, to mutual aid and to self-giving."[31]

The old adage, "If mama ain't happy, ain't nobody happy," is reinforced in social science research. Wilcox and Nock found that women's happiness in marriage is determined by the "emotional character" of their marriages. A husband's "emotion work"—effort to express positive emotion, to be attentive to the dynamics of the marriage relationship and the needs of the wife, or to set aside time for activities focused specifically on the marriage relationship—determines a wife's perception of their "marital quality."[32]

Several of the Wilcox and Nock findings created controversy and media attention—for instance, the result that "shared church attendance is associated with higher levels of women's marital happiness."[33] So, too, the report's statement that a husband's willingness to share housework and other domestic labor contributes greatly to the degree of a wife's marital happiness. The media focused on the finding that both men and women preferred relationships that followed gender-typical practices and roles, and also on the argument—based on their findings—that the departure from a male-breadwinning/female-home-making model may account for declines in women's marital quality. Lacking the same degree of commitment as marriage, a cohabiting relationship would be less likely to provide the kind of emotional support, sharing of responsibilities, and fidelity that engenders happiness in women comparable to that found within a strong, happy marriage; nor would cohabiting relationships be more likely to follow traditional, gender-related, and faith-based practices.

Married Women Have Better Health

Being married benefits women both physically and mentally. The research showing the differences between the health of single women compared to that of married women is remarkable. Researchers give plenty of reasons for why women have outlived men over the past few centuries. Women in the United States typically have a life expectancy five to seven years longer than men.[34] The largest longevity gap is for married couples later in life: "For women, the protective benefits of marriage" mean, "Ninety percent of married women who are alive at age 45 make it to 65, vs. slightly more than 80 percent of divorced and never-married women. Mortality rates are 50 percent higher for unmarried women."[35] Statisticians who calculate mortality risks declare, "Being unmarried is one of the greatest risks that people voluntarily subject themselves to"; for instance, being married lowers your risk of dying in the hospital, builds better immune functioning, lowers the risk of a cancer patient dying (outcomes are 8–17 percent more successful for married couples[36]), etc.[37] Married women even sleep better[38] and unmarried people spend twice as much time in hospitals as do married people.

Studies mention safer childbirth as a major factor contributing to greater women's longevity, but the foremost reason for a gender gap in mortality is that men are much more likely to engage in risky, and, sometimes, violent behavior. A writer for the *Harvard Gazette* adds, "Although women can expect to live longer than men, the gap is closing. Death rates have begun to converge in the past 20 years. Some researchers attribute the convergence to women taking on the behaviors and stresses formerly considered the domain of males."[39] Those risky behaviors include delaying or avoiding marriage in favor of casual or promiscuous sex, multiple sex partners, and cohabitation. [See Chapter 5: "Why Casual Sex Causes Harm" for the risks associated with casual sex].

Married Women Have Better Sex

Although it counters popular perceptions that sex with one person will inevitably get boring and monotonous, married couples enjoy better sex than either sexually active single couples or cohabiting couples. "The most comprehensive and recent survey of sexuality"[40] indicates that married couples enjoy more sex and are better satisfied with their sex lives—both emotionally and physically—than are either sexually active single couples or cohabiting couples.[41] Popenoe and Whitehead report, "Forty-two percent of wives said that they found sex extremely emotionally and physically satisfying, compared to just 31 percent of single women who had a sex partner. And, 48 percent of husbands said sex was extremely satisfying emotionally, compared to just 37 percent of cohabiting men."[42] The researchers explained, "The higher level of commitment in marriage is probably the reason for the high level of reported sexual satisfaction; marital commitment contributes to a greater sense of trust and security, less drug and alcohol-infused sex, and more mutual communication between the couple."[43]

Researchers have found a wide array of benefits for women who are in healthy marriages. Compared to single women in sexually active relationships and women in cohabiting relationships, women in healthy marriages are[44]:

- In a more satisfying relationship
- Emotionally healthier
- Wealthier
- Less likely to be a victim of domestic violence, sexual assault, or other violent crimes
- Less likely to attempt or commit suicide
- Less likely to abuse drugs and alcohol
- Less likely to contract STDs

- Less likely to remain or end up in poverty
- More likely to have better relationships with their children
- Physically healthier

Marriage Benefits Men

One of the old sayings that has been passed to this generation from previous ones is, "If you're susceptible to vice, find a wife."[45] Certainly, there are numerous ways that men benefit from marriage—particularly, the greater likelihood that a married man will not be involved in "vices." Instead, men who get married typically rise to the occasion and become the family's provider. Or, as is often the situation today—whether or not he is the main provider—he is one of the family's two providers along with his wife. The both of them become a "wealth-creating and wealth-preserving institution." When marriage fails to perform that function—as when single-mother families predominate, the government steps in as a surrogate (but ineffective) husband. There is a direct connection between the rise in single motherhood since the 1960s—partly due to unwed childbearing and no-fault divorce—and the growth of the big-government welfare state. As one author put it rather academically, "One proximate result of [marriage] weakening has been the growth of government as substitute provider."[46]

The attacks over the past forty years against the institution of marriage and the ensuing retreat of the young from matrimony have been driven by the attitude that marriage is a bad deal for both women and men. We have already shown that, instead of being a bad deal, marriage has numerous benefits for women. The myths that persist today about marriage being a "bad deal" for men revolve around the idea that men need more freedom and variety than marriage allows, and that men are not meant to "settle down." Years of research have surprised many by showing that marriage benefits men in a wide variety of ways. What is most surprising is that, in many ways, marriage benefits men more than women. Sadly, most of the academic research has yet to filter down to the nation's marriage-age young people. But as the facts are gradually seeping into the national dialogue, there is reason to believe that they are influencing the culture.

Married Men Are Healthier and Live Longer

In spite of all the current hype about the "swinging bachelor" life, research indicates that getting married gives individuals a powerful mental health boost. When men get married, their mental health improves—consistently and substantially. Married men (and women) are less depressed, less anxious, and less psychologically distressed than single, divorced, or widowed Americans.[47] The flip side of this is that divorced men suffer substantial deterioration in mental and emotional well-being, including increases in depression and declines in reported happiness. They also report a lower sense of personal mastery, less positive relations with others, less sense of purpose in life, and lower levels of self-acceptance than married peers.[48]

Also, married men have significantly longer life expectancies than singles with similar backgrounds and characteristics. An astounding "marriage gap" exists between married and unmarried men in terms of longevity. Nine out of ten married guys who are alive at forty-eight will live to age sixty-five, compared with just six in ten comparable single guys (controlling for race, education, and income).[49] That is a whopping 250 percent higher mortality rate. A man's health while he lives those extra years is also better. Having heart disease reduces a married man's life expectancy by just under six years. In contrast, being unmarried reduces life expectancy by ten years. Even controlling for initial health status, sick married people live longer than their unmarried counterparts.[50] A UCLA study found that single people in generally excellent health were 88 percent more likely to die over the course of the eight-year study period than were married ones. Moreover, a Norwegian study found that among male cancer patients, those who were divorced or who had never married had 11 and 16 percent higher mortality rates, respectively, than married men.[51] Clearly, the message is that marriage is good for men's health and longevity.

Married Men Have More Stable Employment, Better Earnings, and Are Wealthier

It has become a truism in American culture that men cannot afford to get married; getting married costs too much and supporting a wife is too expensive. Thus, many marriage-age men consider marriage to be simply too much of a financial burden. Many couples delay marriage for financial reasons, but the reality is that the husband could be earning more money as a married man than as a single one, and, together, they could be doing much better financially. Research indicates that married people manage their money better together than either of the partners would alone. Thus, the overwhelming message from social science research data is, once again, that many of the propositions that guide people's decision-making are, in fact, myths, perpetuated because they are politically correct and, thus, incontrovertible.

Dr. Obie Clayton, a Morehouse College professor and author of *An American Dilemma Revisited: Race Relations in a Changing World*, is another scholar who claims that marriage works out better economically for men than it does for women. He cites data indicating that marriage neither increases nor decreases a woman's personal earnings—whereas, it increases earnings for men.[52] Dr. Florence B. Bonner, a professor at Howard University, adds that the benefit is for men because women take on more of the responsibilities at home. "If you document the number of things that women do within a week to help support a man's career, it is obvious that marriage benefits males in terms of career advancement," she says. "If you are working six to seven days a week, then you have almost no time to do laundry, make the trip to the cleaners or do grocery shopping. Man can step in and do that, and we treat it as if it's a wonderful example of progress, but they do not do that consistently."[53]

The sum total effect is that marriage increases a man's income as much as a college education. Economists estimate that married men make as much as 40 percent more than single guys (even controlling for education and job history).[54] A Virginia Commonwealth University study found that married men earn 22 percent more than their similarly experienced—but single—colleagues.[55] This is true also in the military; according to a 2005 study of U.S. Navy officers, "Married men receive higher performance ratings and faster promotions than bachelors."[56] Plus, the longer a man stays married, the more his "marriage premium" is worth, including the retirement assets that have accumulated. Married couples average a net worth at retirement of about $410,000, whereas never-married couples typically accumulate only $167,000 and divorced couples end up with only $154,000. This effect is seen in the short-run as well. One study reported that married couples accumulate assets twice as fast as those who remain divorced over a five-year period.[57]

In short, "marriage is a different deal than it was 40 years ago," according to Pew economist Richard Fry. He explains, "Typically, most wives did not work, so for economic well-being, marriage penalized guys with more mouths to feed but no extra income. Now most wives work. For guys, the economics of marriage have become much more beneficial."[58] In many respects, if you think that men get a bad deal out of marriage, you are very much living in the past.

Married Men Tend to Avoid Risky Behaviors

It used to bring a knowing smile to people's faces to hear, "Marriage is necessary as a civilizing force for men." Years ago, George Gilder[59] made it gospel. In his book, *Men and Marriage*,[60] Gilder argued that in their testosterone-driven youth, men are, essentially, barbarians who damage everything in their path and need to be kept under control for the good of the community. Men need women to turn them away from "dangerous, antisocial, or self-centered activities and towards the needs of a family."[61] Without it, they tend to be destructive to everything in their paths. Most men of average talents, Gilder argued, need families to support and wives to civilize them. Marriage—with its stability and responsibilities—gives men a purpose for living as well as a sense of individuality and identity.

Diane Medved, a conservative columnist, political commentator, and author of the book, *The Case Against Divorce*, tends to agree with Gilder. She writes, "The most disturbed and destructive segment of the population is single men. When they each commit to a woman and gain the responsibility of family, they move from selfish, sexual carpe-diem behemoths to dutiful, long-term-focused adults."[62] She added that colleges are moving to coed dorms, in part, "to minimize damage to their facilities." While she does not like the idea of coed dorms, Medved agrees that the idea of "less damage" makes sense. She adds, "Just as guys together can create Animal House, guys tempered by women probably won't."

Once men are married, their lives change; they are less likely to hang out with the guys, spend time at bars, abuse alcohol or drugs, or engage in illegal activities.[63] Having a wife tends to protect husbands from being involved in crimes. According to a recent U.S. Department of Justice report, male victims of violent crime are nearly four times more likely to be single than married.[64] Married men are less likely than bachelors to take their own lives, and they are less likely to have problems with alcohol abuse or illegal drugs. A national survey reported that one out of four single men, between the ages of nineteen to twenty-six, say that their drinking causes them problems at work or that it causes them to have problems with aggression; that compares to only one in seven married guys this age who say they have those problems.[65] Some of those old truisms make sense and are being documented by computer-wielding social scientists today.

Married Men Have Better Sex, Better Relationships, and Better Emotional Health

In 2006, British researchers reviewed the sexual habits of men in thirty-eight countries and found that, in every country, married men have more sex.[66] Almost a quarter of single men and 30 percent of single women report leading lives with no sex. In addition, single men are twenty times more likely than married men, and single women are ten times more likely than married women, to report not having sex even once in the past year.[67]

Married men report personal happiness that goes beyond their pocketbooks and good health; in contrast, cohabiting men do not do as well in terms of financial or health concerns, and their happiness quotient is about a quarter of that of married men. Interestingly, married men have the "highest level of subjective well-being," followed by widowers and, subsequently, by divorced and single men, who were below both the married and the widowers.[68] One of the reasons for decreased happiness for unmarried men is the decline in relationships. Divorce makes relationships difficult between parents and children, with adult children reporting difficulty in relating to both parents after a divorce, although the father's relationship suffers most. Sixty-five percent of young adults whose parents divorced had poor relationships with their fathers (compared to 29 percent from nondivorced families).[69]

The 1992 National Health and Social Life survey reports that married men having "a readily available and willing married partner" results in them "having sex twice as frequently as most of the single men surveyed, and the married men reported higher levels of satisfaction with their sex lives than either single or cohabiting men."[70] They seem to echo the feelings of the Tom Cruise character in the 1996 hit movie *Jerry Maguire,* when Jerry uttered that memorable line to Dorothy—"You complete me."[71] And, those positive benefits and the feelings that each "completes" the other are not limited to couples living in the United States; the association between marriage and happiness is "remarkably consistent across nations."[72]

The benefits for men from marriage are just as numerous—and significant—as for women. Some of the benefits are as follows:

- Longer life expectancy
- Physically healthier
- Wealthier

- Increase in the stability of employment
- Higher wages
- Emotionally healthier
- Decrease in the risk of drug and alcohol abuse
- Better relationships with their children
- More satisfying sexual relationship
- Less likely to commit violent crimes
- Less likely to contract STDs
- Less likely to attempt or commit suicide[73]

The Economic Benefits of Marriage

Several years ago, Time's cover story heralded the "closing gap" of economic benefits of marriage. The title is misleading because the article, wisely, does not attempt to deny the research that marriage conveys economic benefits; rather, it argues for public policies to further support single mothers in order to "close the [economic] gap[s]." Once again, reading more than the headlines is important because while the article points out that "married baby boomers increase their wealth an average of 16 percent a year while those who are single increase their net worth at half that rate,"[74] the cover story is essentially a crusade to erase that disparity.

Dr. Obie Clayton, aforementioned, explained in plain language the financial benefits of being married by declaring, "For married couples there is a benefit for wealth. In terms of money, a two-parent household is going to have more. If you're making $80,000 a year and you have a spouse who is making $50,000 a year, $130,000 is going to go a lot further than that 80 or that 50. What married couples are able to do is to accumulate wealth together."[75]

An additional benefit is that married people tend to be more productive; as a result, they have higher incomes and enjoy more family time than the unmarried.[76] This can be explained, in part, by the division and specialization of labor that takes place in most families—with each person assuming responsibility for certain tasks and specific aspects of necessary family functions (such as paying the bills, taking out the garbage, running the errands, preparing the meals, cleaning, etc.).

Economists refer to the economic benefit that accrues to married couples as the "marriage premium." Not only do married men earn more money and have a higher earning potential than men who are single—whether they are cohabiting, divorced or never-married. In addition, married people receive more financial support from family members than do unmarried couples. Researchers believe that this is because families consider marriage a permanent commitment, and seeing that the couple intends to "settle down" and become established members of the community, they are viewed as a worthwhile investment. Couples who are living together are not considered a permanent unit; indeed, they themselves acknowledge that the reason for not marrying is so that either one can walk away from the relationship at will.

A recent CBS television special asked the question, "Why is marriage such an economic turn-on?" The program, MoneyWatch,[77] gave three reasons based on a report from the Pew Research Center titled "Women, Men and the New Economics of Marriage"[78]:

1. Economies of Scale—Married couples share the cost of necessary expenses, such as health insurance, utility bills, mortgage payments, etc. That is especially significant today when more than two-thirds of men have working spouses and 22 percent of wives make more than their husbands.
2. Married Couples Earn More—From 1970 to 2007, median household incomes for married couples rose more than incomes for unmarried couples. The mutual support that couples give each other and their mutual stake in the relationship means they work together toward their financial goals.
3. Married Couples Invest Better—Married women invest in stocks more than unmarried women, and, as part of a couple, they "invest more, save more and are more future-oriented."

Even during the current economic downturn, married couples are discovering that their marriage is a safe haven. According to an article in *The Washington Post*, the Great Recession that began in 2007 "exposed an economic factor" (i.e., lower unemployment rates of married men and women) that had pushed ahead of more romantic reasons for marriage, such as "emotional intimacy, sexual satisfaction and individual happiness."[79] Wilcox, mentioned earlier, is director of the National Marriage Project. He notes, "The economic downturn reminds us that marriage is more than an emotional relationship. It's also an economic partnership and a social safety net."[80]

Alex Roberts, writing for the Institute for American Values, notes that marriage is especially important for poor and working-class couples, who of late have been "drifting farther and farther away from the institution of marriage."[81] He contends that marriage, while still economically *advantageous*, is not economically *necessary* now that women are so prevalent in the workforce.[82] Ironically, this social circumstance has merely changed the dynamics of marriage; it has not changed the demand for marriage. According to Roberts, women with greater economic resources are *now significantly more likely to marry*; they just marry for different reasons—for companionship, not for financial benefits.[83]

Other researchers take a different perspective and argue that the hard financial times are increasing the importance of finding a mate with money. A study at the University of Iowa found that being a "good financial prospect" is increasingly important to men looking for a mate. For men, that attribute ranked #12 on a 2008 list of desirable attributes, while for women, it ranked #10.[84] While having a fancy car and other status symbols may serve to enhance a man's marital odds, it does not work as well for a woman to have those same status symbols when seeking marriage.[85]

In their report on "Money and Marriage," the National Marriage Project and the Institute for American Values observes that the current "Great Recession" seems to be "solidifying, not eroding" the marital bond for most couples. The divorce rate is falling as couples realize that, as they make it through this rough time, they are learning to compromise and, thus, can stick it out.[86] Indeed, a Pew Research survey found that four in ten Americans report that the recession has brought their family "closer together." "In other words," according to Wilcox, "Americans are discovering the power that family ties have to carry them—financially, socially and emotionally—through tough times."[87]

Conclusion

When people debate the benefits of marriage, they typically focus their attention primarily on the benefits for children, which are enormous and essential. I discuss those benefits and the risks of single parenting in a previous book, *Children at Risk*.[88] Less attention is given to the major and significant benefits of marriage for the two individuals and for the couple together. We have briefly surveyed those benefits in this chapter. There are, of course, many positive emotional and intangible benefits of marriage to couples; for instance, couples have fewer psychological problems when married instead of cohabiting. The research cited indicates that there are also numerous tangible and/or legal benefits that accrue to married couples.

It is also noteworthy that the latest studies indicate that couples that have been unhappily married can turn things around. Those couples on the verge of divorce who resolved to stay together and work out their problems report that, after just five years, the majority are glad that they stayed together, and 70 percent even report that their marriages are better than ever, with only 12 percent reporting that they are still dissatisfied and unhappy.

Everybody talks about the 50 percent divorce rate, and many young people disparage marriage because they believe that "half of all marriages end in divorce." But it is important to note that the risk of divorce is far below 50 percent under the following conditions:

- Couples who are educated and entering their first marriage.
- Couples who are in their midtwenties or older at the marriage.
- Couples who have not lived with different partners prior to the marriage.
- Couples who are strongly religious and marry someone of the same faith.[89]

Jennifer Steinhauer, in her article about the Population Association conference (mentioned earlier), reported, "Throughout three days of paper presentations, at least half a dozen demographers who study family structure made strong arguments against cohabitation, offering research showing that those who live together before marriage have higher divorce rates, are more likely to be incompatible and sexually disloyal and are generally less happy than married couples."[90]

At the end of their paper, "A Catalog of Risks," authors Bernard Cohen and I-Sing Lee[91] make four recommendations for priorities that should be taken into account to increase life expectancy in the United States. In this day and age of political correctness, their first recommendation comes as a jaw-dropping surprise—reduce the number of unmarried adults.

Notes

1. Janice Shaw Crouse, "The Tell-Tale Touch," *Concerned Women for America*, August 29, 2007, http://www.cwfa.org/content.asp?id=13757 (accessed September 29, 2011).
2. Laura Wherry and Kenneth Finegold, "Marriage Promotion and the Living Arrangements of Black, Hispanic, and White Children," No. B-61 in Series, *New Federalism: National Survey of America's Families*, Urban Institute, September 24, 2004, http://www.urban.org/url.cfm?ID=311064 (accessed September 29, 2011).
3. Chuck Donovan, "Marriage, Parentage, and the Constitution of the Family," *WebMemo*, No. 2783, The Heritage Foundation, January 27, 2010, http://

www.heritage.org/Research/Reports/2010/01/Marriage-Parentage-and-the-Constitution-of-the-Family (accessed September 29, 2011).

4. Jennifer Steinhauer, "Studies Find Big Benefits in Marriage," *New York Times*, April 10, 1995, http://www.nytimes.com/1995/04/10/us/studies-find-big-benefits-in-marriage.html (accessed September 29, 2011).

5. Joseph Story, *Commentaries on the Conflict of Laws*, cited by Donovan, "Marriage, Parentage."

6. Linda Waite, association president, in an address before the Population Association of America, San Francisco, CA, April 8, 1995, as cited by Steinhauer, "Studies Find Big Benefits in Marriage."

7. Linda Waite, Population Association Address, quoting from the 1992 National Health and Social Life survey, cited by Steinhauer, "Studies Find Big Benefits in Marriage."

8. Linda Waite, cited in Steinhauer, "Studies Find Big Benefits in Marriage."

9. Barbara Dafoe Whitehead, Co-Director, National Marriage Project, Rutgers, The State University of New Jersey. "Testimony before the Committee on Health, Education, Labor and Pensions: Subcommittee on Children and Families," *United States Senate*, April 28, 2004, http://www.virginia.edu/marriageproject/pdfs/print_whitehead_testimonial.pdf (accessed September 29, 2011).

10. Released in 2010, "Eat, Pray, Love" stars Julia Roberts, http://www.imdb.com/title/tt0879870/ (accessed September 29, 2011).

11. Elizabeth Gilbert, *Committed: A Skeptic Makes Peace with Marriage* (New York: Viking Press, 2010), http://www.elizabethgilbert.com/committed.htm (accessed September 29, 2011).

12. A. Pawlowski, "'Eat, Pray, Love' Author Tackles Marriage," *CNN.com*, July 5, 2010, http://edition.cnn.com/2010/LIVING/01/05/elizabeth.gilbert.marriage.book/index.html (accessed September 29, 2011).

13. Ibid.

14. Ibid.

15. David Popenoe and Barbara Dafoe Whitehead, "The Top Ten Myths of Marriage," *The Ten Things to Know Series*, The National Marriage Project, Rutgers University, March 2002, http://www.virginia.edu/marriageproject/pdfs/MythsMarriage.pdf (accessed September 29, 2011).

16. Ibid.

17. Witherspoon Institute, *Marriage and the Public Good: Ten Principles* (Princeton, NJ: Witherspoon Institute, Princeton University, August 2008), 13, http://www.winst.org/family_marriage_and_democracy/WI_Marriage.pdf (accessed September 29, 2011).

18. Popenoe and Whitehead summarize the research that is reviewed in Linda J. Waite and Maggie Gallagher, *The Case for Marriage* (New York: Doubleday, 2000), Chapter 12.

19. Linda J. Waite, "The Negative Effects of Cohabitation," *The Responsive Community Quarterly* 10, no. 1 (Winter 1999/2000): http://www.gwu.edu/~ccps/rcq/rcq_negativeeffects_waite.html (accessed February 21, 2009).

20. U.S. Department of Health and Human Services, "Domestic Violence Fact Sheet," 1994.

21. United States Department of Justice, "National Domestic Violence Fact Sheet and Statistics," March 1998.

22. Maggie Gallagher, "Why Marriage is Good for You," *City Journal* (Autumn 2000): http://www.city-Journal.org/html/10_4_why_marriage_is.html (accessed September 29, 2011).

23. Jan E. Stets, "The Link between Past and Present Intimate Relationships," *Journal of Family Issues* 14, no. 2 (1993): 636–60.

24. The Crimes against Children Research Center, The University of New Hampshire, http://www.unh.edu/ccrc/ (accessed September 29, 2011).

25. Patricia Tjaden and Nancy Thoennes, "Full Report of the Prevalence, Incidence, and Consequences of Violence against Women: Findings from the National Violence against Women Survey," U.S. Department of Justice, National Institute of Justice, NCJ 183781 (November 2000): 17, http://www.ncjrs.gov/pdffiles1/nij/183781.pdf (accessed September 29, 2011).

26. Witherspoon Institute, *Marriage and the Public Good.*

27. W. Bradley Wilcox and Steven L. Nock, "What's Love Got to do with it? Equality, Equity, Commitment and Women's Marital Quality," *Social Forces* 84, no. 3 (March 2006): http://www.virginia.edu/sociology/peopleofsociology/wilcoxpapers/Wilcox%20Nock%20marriage.pdf (accessed September 29, 2011).

28. Witherspoon Institute, *Marriage and the Public Good.*

29. Wilcox and Nock, "What's Love Got to do with it?" 1324.

30. Ibid.

31. *Catechism of the Catholic Church*, Part Two: The Celebration of the Christian Mystery, Section Two: The Seven Sacraments of the Church, Chapter Three: The Sacraments at the Service of Communion, Article 7: The Sacrament of Matrimony, #1609. http://www.vatican.va/archive/ccc_css/archive/catechism/p2s2c3a7.htm#1609 (accessed September 29, 2011).

32. Wilcox and Nock, "What's Love Got to do with it?" 1322.

33. Ibid., 1339.

34. Miranda Hitti, "Why do Women Live Longer than Men? Researcher Examine Role of Risky Behavior in Life Expectancy," *WebMD Health News*, May 11, 2006, http://women.webmd.com/news/20060511/why-women-live-longer (accessed September 29, 2011).

35. Kristen Stewart, "The Health Benefits of Marriage" [Medically reviewed by Lindsey Marcellin, MD, MPH], Family Health Center, *Everyday Health*, February 11, 2010, http://www.everydayhealth.com/family-health/understanding/benefits-of-tying-the-knot.aspx (accessed September 29, 2011).

36. Ibid.

37. Gallagher, "Why Marriage is Good for You."

38. "Study: Married Women Sleep Better than Single Women," *Reuters, Fox News*, January 29, 2009, http://www.foxnews.com/story/0,2933,484908,00.html (accessed September 29, 2011).

39. William J. Cromie, "Why Women Live Longer than Men," *The Harvard University Gazette*, October 1, 1998, http://www.news.harvard.edu/gazette/1998/10.01/WhyWomenLiveLon.html (accessed September 29, 2011).

40. David Popenoe and Barbara Dafoe Whitehead, "Ten Important Research Findings on Marriage and Choosing a Marriage Partner: Helpful Facts

for Young Adults," *Information Brief: Ten Things to Know Series*, The National Marriage Project, November 2004. http://www.virginia.edu/marriageproject/pdfs/pubTenThingsYoungAdults.pdf (accessed September 29, 2011).

41. Linda J. Waite and Kara Joyner, "Emotional and Physical Satisfaction with Sex in Married, Cohabiting, and Dating Sexual Unions: Do Men and Women Differ?" in *Sex, Love, and Health in America: Private Choices and Public Policy*, ed. Edward O. Laumann and Robert T. Michael (Chicago: The University of Chicago Press, 2000), 239–69.

42. Popenoe and Whitehead, "Ten Important Research Findings."

43. Ibid.

44. W. Bradford Wilcox, *Why Marriage Matters: Twenty-Six Conclusions from the Social Science*, 2nd ed. (New York: The Center for Marriages and Families, Institute for American Values, September 2005), http://center.americanvalues.org/?p=7 (accessed September 29, 2011).

45. Anna Maltby, "The Benefits of Being Married," *Men's Health Lists, Men's Health*, 2010, http://www.menshealth.com/mhlists/benefits_of_marriage_and_commitment/index.php (accessed September 29, 2011).

46. Donovan, "Marriage, Parentage."

47. Gallagher, "Why Marriage is Good for You."

48. Ibid.

49. Ibid.

50. Bernard Cohen and I-Sing Lee, "A Catalog of Risks: An Abstract," *Health Physics* 36 (June 1979): 707–22, http://journals.lww.com/health-physics/Abstract/1979/06000/A_Catalog_of_Risks.7.aspx (accessed September 29, 2011).

51. Maltby, "Benefits of Being Married."

52. "Who Benefits More from Marriage –– Men or Women? *Jet* 99, no. 12 (March 5, 2001), http://books.google.com/books?id=K7UDAAAAMBAJ&pg=PA15&lpg=PA15&dq=benefits+from+marriage+jet+magazine&source=bl&ots=Vcu_JCl1gB&sig=gVf-mN6_LU44D02N_brH888wI60&hl=en&ei=uCZwTNP6EYW0lQe0mKWqDw&sa=X&oi=book_result&ct=result&resnum=1&ved=0CBkQ6AEwAA#v=onepage&q=benefits%20from%20marriage%20jet%20magazine&f=false (accessed September 29, 2011).

53. Ibid.

54. Wilcox, "Why Marriage Matters."

55. Maltby, "Benefits of Being Married."

56. Ibid.

57. Gallagher, "Why Marriage is Good for You."

58. Sharon Jayson, "Study: Marriage Benefits Men Economically, Too," *USA Today*, January 19, 2010, http://www.usatoday.com/life/lifestyle/2010-01-19-1Amarriage19_ST_N.htm (accessed September 29, 2011).

59. George Gilder is Senior Fellow at the Discovery Institute, a contributing editor at *Forbes* and author of more than a dozen books, http://www.leighbureau.com/speaker.asp?id=76 (accessed September 29, 2011).

60. George Gilder, *Men and Marriage* (Gretna, LA: Pelican Publishing, 1986).

61. Wilcox, "Why Marriage Matters."

62. Diane Medved, "Coed Dorms Increase Risky Behavior? Maybe," Guest blog, *Townhall.com*, November 19, 2009, http://townhall.com/blog/g/f8b633a5-2c21-4809-b0b3-a41a8d4863e4 (accessed September 29, 2011).

63. Barbara Dafoe Whitehead, *Senate Testimony*.

64. Maltby, "Benefits of Being Married."

65. Gallagher, "Why Marriage is Good for You."

66. Maltby, "Benefits of Being Married."

67. Gallagher, "Why Marriage is Good for You."

68. Ibid.

69. Wilcox, "Why Marriage Matters."

70. As described at, http://www.socio.com/aid1213.php (accessed September 29, 2011): "The 1992 National Health and Social Life Survey (NHSLS) is the most comprehensive representative survey to date of sexual behavior in the United States general population. Conducted by a research team centered at the University of Chicago, the NHSLS was designed not only to determine the prevalence of various sexual practices, but also to examine the social and psychological contexts in which those practices occur. The NHSLS data set contains information on 1,604 variables gathered from interviews with a national probability sample of 3,432 American men and women between the ages of 18 and 59. The study explores the extent to which sexual conduct and general attitudes toward sexuality are influenced by gender, age, marital status, and other demographic characteristics. Among the numerous topics covered by the NHSLS are early sexual experiences, masturbation, contraception and fertility, sexual abuse, coercion, sexual health, satisfaction, sexual dysfunction and homosexuality."

71. The Oscar-winning movie is described at: http://www.imdb.com/title/tt0116695/ (accessed September 29, 2011) and the memorable quotes from the movie can be found at: http://www.imdb.com/title/tt0116695/quotes (accessed September 29, 2011).

72. Gallagher, "Why Marriage is Good for You."

73. "Benefits of Healthy Marriages," *The Healthy Marriages Initiative*, Administration for Children and Families, The United States Department of Health and Human Services, 2005, http://www.acf.hhs.gov/healthymarriage/benefits/index.html (accessed September 29, 2011).

74. Barbara Kiviat, "The Economic Benefits of Marriage: A Closing Gap," *Time*, September 19, 2009, http://www.time.com/time/business/article/0,8599,1924327,00.html (accessed September 29, 2011).

75. "Who Benefits More from Marriage," *Jet*.

76. Linda J. Waite and Evelyn L. Lehrer, "The Benefits of Marriage and Religion in the United States: A Comparative Analysis," *Population Development Review* 29, no. 2 (June 2003): 255–76, http://onlinelibrary.wiley.com/doi/10.1111/j.1728-4457.2003.00255.x/abstract;jsessionid=F9801DE5912DFE7824562206F42BB9C8.d01t02 (accessed September 29, 2011).

77. Kate Ashford, "Does Love Make You Richer? Research Shows that Marriage can have Financial Benefits," *MoneyWatch.com*, CBS Television Network, February 12, 2010, http://www.cbsnews.com/stories/2010/02/12/business/moneywatch/main6202431.shtml (accessed September 29, 2011).

78. Richard Fry and D'Vera Cohn, "Women, Men and the New Economics of Marriage," *A Social and Demographic Trends Report*, Pew Research Center, January 19, 2010, http://pewsocialtrends.org/assets/pdf/new-economics-of-marriage.pdf (accessed September 29, 2011).

79. Michelle Singletary, "Money Matters in a Marriage," *The Washington Post*, February 14, 2010, http://www.washingtonpost.com/wp-dyn/content/article/2010/02/12/AR2010021205908_pf.html (accessed September 29, 2011).

80. As quoted in Singletary, "Money Matters."

81. Alex Roberts, "Marriage and the Great Recession," *The State of Our Unions*, Institute for American Values and the National Marriage Project, 2009, http://stateofourunions.org/2009/marriage_and_the_recession.php (accessed September 29, 2011).

82. Ibid.

83. Ibid.

84. As quoted in Ashford, "Does Love Make You Richer?"

85. Ibid.

86. W. Bradford Wilcox, "Can the Recession Save Marriage?" *The Wall Street Journal*, December 11, 2009, http://online.wsj.com/article/SB10001424052748703558004574584042851448128.html#printMode (accessed September 29, 2011).

87. Ibid.

88. Janice Shaw Crouse, *Children at Risk: The Precarious State of Children's Well-Being in America* (New Brunswick, NJ and London: Transaction Publishers, 2010), http://www.JaniceShawCrouse.com (accessed September 29, 2011).

89. Popenoe and Whitehead, "Ten Important Research Findings."

90. Steinhauer, "Studies Find Big Benefits in Marriage."

91. Cohen and Lee, "Catalog of Risks."

7

The Benefits of Marriage for Children

To be loved for what one is, is the greatest exception.
The great majority love in others only what they lend him,
their own selves, their version of him.
—Johann Wolfgang von Goethe

Prominently displayed in the lobby of the Herbert Humphrey Building, which houses the U.S. Department of Health and Human Services, is a large bronze sculpture of a woman playing with her three children, titled "Happy Mother." The subtle implication is that no father is required, that marriage is unnecessary—even undesirable. Nothing is more illustrative of the problems facing children today than the mythology about family conveyed by that sculpture. The false values embodied in it—primarily, that a woman alone with her children comprises the archetype of happy motherhood—are at the root of forty years of failure by the research communities and by the federal government to honestly report on the problems that are undermining the foundations of the American family and devastating American children's well-being.[1]

Putting the myths aside, the social science research consistently reveals that children need a married mother and father. Children need the protection and nurturing of not just any variety of two-parent family, but a married-couple family—made up of a mother and a father to—instill those qualities that will enable the child to become an ethical and productive citizen. Moreover, children need society to support, rather than thwart, the family's efforts to provide a strong moral and spiritual foundation for children's emotional and psychological development.

The majority of Americans agree that marriage is very important. In fact, while opinion leaders may not be willing to face the facts, ordinary people agree with the family researchers—nearly 70 percent of the general public believes that a child needs both a mother and a father to grow up happily.[2] More than 65 percent of adults think that single motherhood is bad for children and society.[3] Most Americans—90 percent—will marry in their lifetime.[4] Yet, while the mom-and-dad family is still the rule rather than the exception for white America (66 percent of Americans live in a married-couple household), the proportion of married Americans continues to decline and reflects changing cultural values and attitudes. The combined effect of ideology and policy changes on values and behavior is clearly visible in the sharp drop in marriage rates from seventy-eight per thousand (women age fifteen and older) in 1972 to sixty-four per thousand by 1977, just five years later.[5] Marriage rates have continued to decline—both in periods of recession and economic boom—to less than one-half the median rate during the first seventy years of the twentieth century, and, as of yet, there is no end to the decline in sight. The impact of the decline in marriage shows up clearly in the proportion of American women who are married. In 1960, 67 percent of the total number of women were married, now it is a little less than 54 percent.[6] Among black women, the percentage has dropped from 60 percent to 34 percent.[7]

The percentage of children not living with both of their own biological parents has increased from about one out of five to two out of five since 1960 (22.3 percent to 39.2 percent[8]). The number of single mothers is at record levels, with some inner city areas having 80–90 percent out-of-wedlock births. The number of cohabiting couples is ten times larger than in 1970, and about 40 percent of these are couples with children.[9]

This precipitous decline of marriage means that the nation's children are losing their safe haven as well as the effective place for character and values to be inculcated by precept and example. The absence of marriage in the child's home life means that one or both of the parents' obligation to care for the child—whether out of love or duty—has been severely impaired, if not entirely abrogated. In his book, *The Marriage Problem*, the eminent political scientist James Q. Wilson[10] questioned why marriage has universally endured. He concluded that marriage is a "reproductive alliance" that people enter into freely because, as Robert P. George said, "Experience teaches that the marriage relationship is indispensable to the rearing of the young."[11] The hope for marriage rests, in Wilson's analysis, on the fact that "human nature makes people responsive to an overriding concern—child care." Our task then is to design and maintain a culture that will "keep [a married couple] together in achieving what most want, and when they get it, cherish. Their own child."[12]

Marriage Provides Children with a Safe Haven

The logo of the Children's Defense Fund[13] is a simple line drawing of a small child alone in a boat on a wide-open sea. The image of a defenseless child touches even the most hard-hearted person. Without the marital bond between a husband and wife to provide a safe, defined space for children, they are adrift on the sea of life, buffeted by winds of chance and cruelty. Despite all our good intentions, despite our urge to rush in to save all "our" children, the absence of marriage means that the fundamental needs of children are at risk in what is quite often a cold, hostile, and unforgiving world.[14]

Safer from Poverty

In the 1960s, when liberal thinkers were pushing for expansion of the welfare state, their policy proposals would have been deemed unthinkable had the public known that fifty years later, 41 percent of today's children would live in single-mother homes. They would not, however, have been surprised by the fact that the poverty rate of single mothers with children is 5 times higher than the rate for married couples with children and, also, that the rate for single fathers is more than 2.5 times the married-couple rate. To understand the implications of the changes in household structure look at these facts:

- Children in single-parent families with no spouse present comprise three out of ten children (i.e., 21.8 million out of 72.8 million).
- The poor children in single-parent households constitute almost two-thirds of all poor children (i.e., nearly 8.5 million out of the 12.8 million poor children, or 66 percent).
- In contrast, in 1960, poor children in single-parent families comprised only 25 percent of all poor children.[15] Estimates by the Beverly La-Haye Institute indicate that, if the family structure of the population remained the same in 2007 as it was in the early 1970s, the poverty rate of all families, instead of increasing from 11.8 percent in 1972 to 15 percent in 2007, would have been lower (10.7 percent) in 2007 than it had been in 1972.
- In 1973, married-couple families with children under eighteen made up 84.7 percent of all families with children under eighteen, and single-parent families with children under eighteen were 15.3 percent.
- In 2007, the poverty rate of married-couple families with children was 6.7 percent and the poverty rate of single-parent families was 32.7 percent.[16]

The two problems, poverty and fatherless families, are inextricably linked; yet as a nation we continue, for the most part, to operate our antipoverty programs in a manner that disregards the connection to family structure. In fact, we have so-called authorities—particularly the theoreticians in academia far removed from the realities that anyone can plainly see just driving through the mean streets of the ghettos of our large cities—constantly peddling the myth that one kind of family structure is as good as another. Some experts go so far as to try and sell the idea, especially to impressionable young people who are the ones most likely to start a family, that we should celebrate the variety of family structures in America.[17] Such pernicious views ignore the plain fact that five out of every ten women who have a baby out of wedlock end up in poverty. Having second babies out of wedlock raises the odds of winding up in poverty to six out of ten.

The message from the data is very clear: nothing comes close to benefiting children as much as having a married mom and dad who work together to ensure their children's well-being. While many valiant single mothers are heroes in sacrificing for their children, in providing for their needs and ensuring their well-being, they are typically the first ones to declare the need for a father to share the joys and the responsibilities—including the expense—of raising children.

Safer from Exploitation and Abuse

One of the saddest ramifications of the decline in marriage is the way that it has increased the child sex exploitation industry and the child abuse problem. Child sexual exploitation has proliferated into a multibillion dollar industry that is expanding to every corner of our modern-day world through electronic media. These children are known to law enforcement officers as "throwaway kids"—they are kids "nobody wants"; kids who are "loners" or "runaways." They are easy prey for the predators who search for them at the typical hangouts—bus stations, run-down malls, and ghetto street corners. They are the victims of a culture where marriage has become optional.

Within the growing number of dysfunctional families in America today, there is a report of child abuse every ten seconds and at least three children (some researchers put the estimate at more than five) die every day as a result of abuse and neglect.[18] This should be a matter of national concern; an estimated 80 percent of abused children carry physical, psychological, behavioral, and societal consequences that last a lifetime.

We should all recoil when innocence is stolen—whether in one awful trauma so horrific that makes the news or through persistent, unrelenting acts of neglect, anger, sexual dominance, or vicious, sadistic physical abuse. It is painful to contemplate the many children who are living in situations where they are neglected and mistreated, rather than cherished and nurtured. Millions of children learn early that they rate a distant second or third in priority behind drugs and/or boyfriends. Sadly, over 6.6 million American children live in households where at least one parent is dependent on alcohol or drugs, whether prescription medications or illegal substances.[19] There is little wonder these children live in fear of what is in store for them next. Their family instability, lack of supervision, and miserable conditions keep them from having the happy childhood that we would wish for all children; worse, their childhood mistreatment threatens their future, indeed, their health and life.

Every year, more than two thousand children in the United States die of child abuse and neglect. Children under four years of age account for nearly 80 percent of those fatalities, mostly infants and toddlers.[20] Sadly, the mothers' boyfriends are most often the perpetrators of abuse deaths, and mothers are more often responsible for the neglect fatalities.[21] Whether or not the abusing adult—most often, a single mother or her boyfriend—is mean, controlling, selfish, mentally ill, drug addicted, or unable to cope, the abused child ends up emotionally scarred and psychologically damaged, often with feelings of self-loathing, fear, worthlessness, and guilt that can persist throughout the child's life.

Child Protective Services (CPS) agencies report that incidences of child abuse and neglect have increased dramatically—a 149 percent increase since 1980. Children of single parents are at a sickening 77 percent greater risk of physical abuse and an appalling 80 percent greater risk of serious injury or harm. They are three times more likely to be educationally neglected and more than two times more likely to suffer some type of child abuse than children living with both parents.[22] The correlation of abuse with nontraditional families is dismaying. According to a legal scholar:

- Abuse is six times higher in stepfamilies than in intact families.
- Abuse is fourteen times higher in a single-mother family than in intact families.
- Abuse is twenty times higher with parents who are cohabiting than in an intact family.
- Abuse is thirty-three times higher with mere partners who are cohabiting than in an intact family.[23]

All this abuse—primarily because someone thought they did not need that "piece of paper" called marriage—is costing taxpayers over $20 billion with related costs adding another $100 billion (crime, medical care, special education, etc.).[24] How many more children will be abused before we acknowledge that the investment America needs to make for the nation's children is to adopt policies to encourage rather than tax marriage? A married father–mother home is the safest and most nurturing place for the nation's children.

Marriage Can Provide Children with a Moral Foundation and a Value System

While children have a primary need for a married mother and father to provide protection and nurturing, they also need married parents to instill those character traits that will enable them to become ethical and productive citizens. American society—and its public policy—needs to support, rather than thwart, the family's efforts to provide a strong moral and spiritual foundation for children. Public opinion polls reveal that most Americans believe that the disintegration of our nation's moral standards and quality of life have contributed to the breakdown of marriage and family. Americans also believe that the negative effects of that downward spiral particularly influence children's well-being.[25]

Plato, in his *Laws*, cautioned centuries ago, "So long as the young generation is, and continues to be, well brought up, our ship of state will have a fair voyage; otherwise the consequences are better left unspoken." Current trends make it abundantly clear that if parents fail to teach their children basic morality, manners, and respect for the Judeo-Christian principles that are essential for harmonious social interaction, it will be impossible for that child to become a productive citizen. Instead, that child will grow up to be "a problem person," and when such problem people reach a "tipping point"—as is the case in many areas of the country and in many of the nation's classrooms, the community or classroom cannot be maintained, and, ultimately it disintegrates into chaos.

Many people have noted that Edward Gibbon's *The History of the Decline and Fall of the Roman Empire* documents the fact that the decline of the Roman empire was paralleled by a decline in the morality of its citizens. Others have noted that there is a similar parallel between the decline in morality and the decline in public manners—that when common decency disappears from the public square there is a similar disappearance of morality. Certainly, both are built on the foundation of the Golden Rule: doing unto others as you would have them do unto you—or unto your beloved sister (as is more relevant in the context of promiscuity and single motherhood).

The family is a child's training ground for becoming an ethical, moral, and empathetic person—one capable of being a contributor to a good and prosperous society. Most moral qualities—such as a sense of responsibility and self-control, caring and respect for others, delayed gratification, compassion, sense of fairness, generosity, empathy, and honesty, among others—are not just learned rationally through instruction. For the most part, they are absorbed—inculcated, if you will—through seeing them modeled in everyday family life. In order to learn those moral qualities, children need to see those characteristics acted out with consistency in the interactions, reactions, and relationships of the adults around them. Yet, too many children are growing up without ever seeing moral authority in an adult. Children too often miss out on critical moral development because they do not have the benefit of seeing essential moral qualities lived out in the efforts of a mother and father doing the hard work required to keep their commitments to each other and to their children.[26]

Many cultural critics today argue that family breakdown—the absence of married father–mother families—is producing a generation of children devoid of both morals and human decency and that many of them are becoming predators who threaten the safety of communities and neighborhoods. Their commentaries sound remarkably like a fulfillment of the warning that came from the Russian Marxist and communist, Vladimir Lenin: "The best revolutionary is a youth devoid of morals." Indeed, Judge Robert H. Bork, author of *Slouching towards Gomorrah*, sees the lack of moral instruction in the home as a "wake-up call" regarding cultural decline. He declared, "A nation's moral life is the foundation of its culture."[27]

Along with the decline of marriage has come the gradual decay of the social standards that emanate from a community populated by strong families; the preservation of these standards in the culture and community has, consequently, suffered substantially as the percentage of families headed by a married couple has steadily declined. Dozens of the problems plaguing our nation are rooted in the disappearance of essential, basic moral codes from everyday life. Their absence has been ruinous to vulnerable children who are the ones most devastated by the social engineers and "the armies of bureaucrats and theory-wielding experts" who "wreaked havoc on society."[28]

The family is a child's first society; thus, the family needs to be whole and healthy, because it is where children learn—for good or for ill—how to respect other people and how to live their lives productively and harmoniously. When the family disintegrates and marriage declines, the inevitable result is erosion in the quality of community life and a corresponding breakdown in social cohesion and morality.

Marriage Provides Children with Educational and Cultural Advantages

American education policy experts have tried everything to improve children's education in the United States, including the nationwide $15 billion a year "No Child Left Behind" program. We have spent more than $10,000 *per child* in the nation's public school programs (more than some top-quality private schools) and we continue to spend 7.4 percent of the national Gross Domestic Product to educate the nation's children. But evaluations consistently show that student achievement scores fail to measure up to what is needed to equip our students for the hi-tech future they face; in fact, in many areas, American children lag behind those of other nations in their scores. Many experts consider American public schools to be "in crisis" and Bill Gates, the founder of Microsoft, describes the school system as "obsolete"—with about one-third of students dropping out before graduation (one-half among minorities) and about 40 percent having to complete remedial work before being eligible for college admittance.[29]

It is long past time for everyone to realize that the nation's public schools—even with thousands of dedicated and excellent teachers—cannot compensate for the decline in marriage and the subsequent weakening of the influence of two-parent families in American culture. We continue to pour money into programs and policies that focus on the "four walls of the classroom," but it should be obvious to anyone not hindered by ideological blinders that money, computers, and standards of learning will inevitably fail unless we restore the "essential ingredient"—parents.

Increasingly, today's technologically advanced society requires well-trained, highly skilled workers; the complexity of the modern world demands clear thinkers, highly developed logical ability, wide knowledge, discernment, and good judgment. Yet it is obvious—and very well documented—that our public schools are failing many of the nation's children by not preparing them to meet even the most basic standards for being well-educated or to compete for good-paying jobs requiring skilled workers.[30]

It is no wonder that the number of home-schooled children increased by 77 percent from 1999 to 2007. Such rapid growth clearly speaks to a high level of parental dissatisfaction with the conditions of American schools.[31] Many parents are deeply disturbed by mediocre schools and ill-equipped teachers pushing radical ideologies—more concerned with condoms, abortion, and sexual orientation than with reading, writing, and arithmetic—that create an increasingly hostile environment for those holding traditional values. About one-third of the nations' students who have left public schools report having done so because of the negative "environment" and because of parental desire to "provide religious or moral instruction."

Further, the perennial complaint that quality education is not possible in the public schools because there are not enough teachers just does not square with the facts—there is an average of just over fifteen students per teacher, according to the Department of Education's National Center for Education Statistics (NCES).[32] The enormous challenges facing those nearly four million teachers engaged in classroom instruction across the nation include unmotivated and unmanageable students. These difficult students fall behind because they are ill-prepared to compete with those whose motivation stems from encouragement at home and who have learned discipline and self-control. Whether as dropouts or as graduates pushed out the door with marginal skills, those unmotivated and unmanageable students will not be ready to contribute to their own or the nation's prosperity.

Further, poor education produces uninvolved citizens and a society without the manpower necessary for efficient, effective functioning. There are fault lines in the nation's schools that are producing wide gaps in educational attainment between those whose school district is of good quality and those whose schools are not performing at acceptable levels.[33] By and large those fault lines divide according to family structure—when married couple families predominate, the schools do better; when single-mother families are the dominant home arrangements of the students—even though many mothers are exceptions to the rule, working extremely hard to care for their children—the student achievement levels go down. This is clearly evident in the numerous reports of many education experts who point to the "disproportionate influence of factors beyond the control of educators in the performance of students."[34]

While there are occasional exceptions, parents are the essential ingredients in transmitting cultural advantages to children. Though a great deal of factual information is conveyed primarily at school, all the measurements point to the fact that cultural knowledge is "most strongly transmitted within the home rather than the school."[35] Parents with high levels of cultural capital promote the development of academic ability in their children in many ways; participation in cultural activities is just one of these. Most importantly, children pick up vocabulary, styles of expression, ideas, information, and forms of argument from listening to their parents talk. Parents are instrumental in teaching their children reading and other skills, and pass on attitudes and beliefs. With rare exception parents are a more important key to cultural competence than is any other factor in a child's upbringing or education. Sociologists Pierre Bourdieu and Jean-Claude Passeron said, "By doing away with giving explicitly to everyone what it implicitly demands of everyone, the educational system demands of everyone alike that it has what it does not give. This consists mainly of linguistic and cultural competence and that relationship of familiarity with culture which can only be produced by family upbringing when it transmits the dominant culture."[36]

The idea that so much rides on parental involvement and influence is rather daunting in light of a study by England's prestigious 125-year-old Children's Society (published in 2010) that caused quite a stir. The media referred to the study—*A Good Childhood: Searching for Values in a Competitive Age*—as a "wake-up call for parents" because it revealed that childhood in England has become "toxic." The study condemned parents, saying, "Our children are desperate for love, for time and for affirmation of their fragile self-esteem. Yet we too often substitute toys, TV and Facebook."[37] *A Good Childhood* concluded that there were too many "working mothers and absent fathers." As a result, there has been an increase in emotional and behavioral problems among children who are materially spoiled, but ignored, and among children also deprived of moral instruction and left without a spiritual foundation.[38]

Here in America, we face a similar situation with "media clutter" and this "tsunami of media" often replaces parental guidance in cultural education. Even two-year-olds today can recognize "Big Bird" and, immediately know that the "Golden Arches" means McDonald's. Tweens—those who are no longer little children but are not yet teenagers—have become the target of advertisers who, increasingly, subvert the roles of too-busy mothers as gatekeepers for their children's innocence, and, thus, have virtually free rein in shaping tweens' attitudes about what is "cool."[39]

Advertisers invest billions of dollars in three thousand advertisements per day[40]—all targeted at children—to ensure that the culture becomes familiar with their logos. In the 1982 movie, *ET*, the producers were paid to place Reese's Pieces candy in a pivotal scene. The Russian space program even launched a rocket that displayed a thirty-foot Pizza Hut logo.

Experts explain, "Parents used to be the channel through which children learned about the outside world. "[41] The home lives of families used to be somewhat isolated from the public sphere—safe havens, where the parents determined the "whats," "whens, " and "ifs " concerning the types of experiences their child had beyond the home. With the invasion of a multitude of media—television, the Internet, video games, DVDs, cell phones, etc.—the family sphere now is permeable, and the outside world constantly pervades the living rooms, kitchens, and bedrooms of our homes. Parents face a bigger than ever challenge of shaping their children's values, attitudes, and beliefs rather than allowing today's media to be the major influences on their children's cultural knowledge and perceptions. This challenge is all the more difficult for the single-parent family, where the parent works outside the home and the children grow up in daycare before graduating to the status of "latch-key " kids.

It is not surprising that an Urban Institute study found that all household arrangements are inferior to those of married biological or adoptive parents in terms of outcomes for children. Less than 8 percent of the children living in a married biological/adoptive family are poor, as compared to poverty rates of nearly 20–43 percent for children who are in cohabiting or single-mother households. Children in families with married couples are read to more often than those in other household arrangements (20 percent who are read to versus more than 25 percent that are "seldom" read to). Less than 5 percent of children in married families have behavioral problems, but the percentage of children with behavioral problems in other household structures is at least double and, in some cases, multiplied by five.[42]

The Urban Institute researchers found that older children (six to eleven years of age) living in cohabiting-partner households exhibited the highest number of behavioral problems (16.4 percent); cohabiting-parent households were next highest at 14 percent, with single-parent households at 9 percent, as compared to only 3.5 percent among those living with married parents. For teens, the situation is similar—cohabiting and single-parent households produce several times more behavioral problems in teens than are exhibited in teens living with their married parents.[43]

Many studies show that a household structure not anchored by one's own biological parents constitutes a significant risk to the future of a child,[44] and that cohabitation and out-of-wedlock births are associated with increased risks of negative outcomes for the children involved and, thus, for society in general.[45] United Families International stressed:

> Stable, traditional marriages produce economic, physical, emotional and psychological benefits for men, women and children that alternative relationships cannot match. As marriage declines, the demand for government intervention and social programs rise. Taxpayers then increasingly foot the bill for the steep costs of poverty, drug addiction, court services, crime, remedial education services, crisis pregnancy, health problems, foster care, child support enforcement, mental health needs and more. Marriage is the vehicle in which every successful society works to channel human sexuality and provide children the attention, love and resources of a mother and a father.[46]

Conclusion

Popeye the Sailor is a 1930s comic strip character who is still popular through home video productions of the television cartoon series. What stand out in the old Popeye series are the "Popeye Moments"—the times when Popeye says, "I've had all I can stand! I can't stands no more!" He flexes his biceps, and off he goes to straighten things out.[47]

Those of us who study America's cultural and domestic situation know exactly how Popeye felt. There are moments when we just "can't stands no more!" America stands at a Popeye Moment regarding children living in fatherless families, and we need to do everything we can to "straighten things out." We have had plenty of warning about illegitimacy and the very real dangers of "father absence." Somehow, though, the ever-increasing trends have not really set off an alarm in the public square.

In the mid-1960s, the late Senator Daniel Patrick Moynihan[48] warned us about the dangers of fatherless families.[49] Yet, while the percentage of nonmartial births have steadily increased, it has been politically incorrect to warn against "illegitimacy." Little attention has been given when researchers and social science analysts have cited the predictable negative outcomes of an absent father in the family or when they compile the data showing that illegitimacy feeds on itself—the daughters of unwed mothers are more likely to have children out of wedlock. For years, nobody really noticed or cared when conservative thinkers and activists provided strong evidence that sex should be reserved for marriage and that married mothers and fathers provide the best place for raising children.

Yet, in recent years, our work has produced widespread promotion of increasingly sophisticated and effective abstinence-until-marriage programs. As a result, teen childbearing has dropped dramatically since the early 1990s. This decrease shows the positive impact of abstinence programs on the teen birth rate as well as the teen abortion rate, which has dropped even more than the teen birth rates.

Even so, the latest figures from the National Center for Health Statistics (NCHS) reveal that a little more than 40 percent of all American children (two out of five) are born out of wedlock. Illegitimate births total over 1.5 million a year. Many will be surprised to learn that it is not teenage hormones that are driving this disastrous increase. Instead, single adult women are the ones who are increasingly having the babies without marrying the fathers of these children. The trend of unwed births to mothers over age twenty has been steadily upward since 1975. Those who have not actually experienced father absence may have ill-founded notions that cause them to celebrate books like *Single by Chance, Mothers by Choice* or *Raising Boys Without Men*. Listening to those who have grown up living without a father is a totally different matter.

Ray Lewis[50] is an All-American football hero; he has twice been a National Football League Defensive Player of the Year and was Super Bowl XXXV's most valuable player. There are those who make a strong case that he is the greatest linebacker and best football player in NFL history. He grew up, though, in a single-mother home, and, while he is very close to his mother, his rage is palpable whenever he talks about his absent father.

In the television profile, "Beyond the Glory,"[51] it was painful to observe and listen as Lewis described the emotional toll the absence of his father had on his life. He recounted numerous attempts to reconcile with his father. He sobbed as he relived a recent attempt when his father agreed to meet with him, but, when the time came, did not show up. He said, "My father was always lying to me, telling me he was going to see me on this day or bring me something on that day, and he never did."

During high school, Ray was determined to outdo his father in athletics. He set a goal of breaking every single sports record his father had established. Ray said he succeeded in "replacing his name with mine." Following the typical pattern, Ray—himself a single father—does not want his children to go through what he went through without a dad. In spite of this, he has not married either of the mothers of his four children. Ray Lewis is a high-profile example of a common phenomenon: problem lifestyles being passed on from one generation to the next. His life illustrates the data, and his experiences characterize the impact that father absence has on the lives of literally millions of children in America. There are far too many children who never see their dads—even many who have no idea who their dad is. Those children are paying an exorbitant price in a nation where everybody, from politicians to corporate presidents, talks about the motivation to do things "for our children."

At this national "Popeye Moment," it is time to cry out, "Our culture has had all it can stand! It can't stands no more!" We have to move marriage to the top of our national policy and political priorities. Woodrow Wilson once described politics as a "war of causes." The result of the illegitimacy crisis on our nation's children is an ultimate cause. Unless we wage war on the root causes of out-of-wedlock births and the decline in marriage, and unless we do something about rebuilding America's families, we can forget about maintaining our place as a great nation and a world superpower.

The promise of the twenty-first century rests on whether America reverses the disintegration of marriage and family. The restoration of marriage and the family is no longer a nice luxury; it a necessity for the survival of American civil society. But the social indicators and warning signs have too long been ignored. Sometimes, it seems as if champions of the family and traditional values are akin to Chicken Little—the chicken who, according to an old fable, ran through town screaming, "The Sky is Falling! " so often that people paid no attention to the warning.[52]

But today's young people freely admit that their sky *is* falling. They have been the painful pawns of ugly divorce suits. They have experienced emptiness at the end of meaningless one-night stands. Their self-esteem has plummeted. Their cries for meaning have produced a web of social institutions that try to fill the void of family connections and reproduce the security and contentment that the family was meant to produce. The security, fulfillment, and love that young people seek, however, are found in the affectionate ties of close-knit families.[53]

It is past time for us to rebut and uproot the negative cultural perceptions about marriage. This will not happen unless we demonstrate by our own personal commitments the value of marriage, on both an individual level and at the community/societal/national level. We must trumpet the personal rewards of marriage and its community-wide social benefits. We must dispel the cynics' myth that a happy marriage is unattainable, and, in the process, we must give young people the tools to seek and build good marriages.

If we fail at these tasks—if the positive messages about marriage and its impact on children do not reach the culture in a transforming manner, the next generation will suffer even greater damage than those of the last half-century. If marriage is seen as merely one of many viable family structures, or as an unattainable ideal, the inherent aspiration for a good marriage will not have a revitalizing effect on the next generation of young people.

Democracy as a form of government depends on the moral character of its people. When we cease to be a moral people, the freedoms that are afforded by democracy will not long survive, nor will democracy itself. Already, our children cannot play outside without supervision. Most of them cannot walk to and from school alone. They cannot run down the street to play with a friend after dark. The freedoms that were commonplace for children short decades ago—when the nation had strong moral standards reinforced by religious convictions that made such freedoms possible—are increasingly rare.[54]

We need to raise up legions of ordinary men and women who will speak out about what it means to live and love within the safe and nurturing framework of the natural family. When family life again flourishes, children will be able to thrive from infancy to adolescence and on to adulthood as well-adjusted persons. Further, they will have the internal strength and confidence to become successful in their personal and professional lives as well as prepared and willing to contribute to their communities and their nation.

Notes

1. Janice Shaw Crouse, *Children at Risk: The Precarious State of Children's Well-Being in America* (New Brunswick, NJ and London: Transaction Publishers, 2010), 193, http://www.janiceshawcrouse.com (accessed October 3, 2011).
2. Paul Taylor and others, "Generation Gap in Values, Behaviors: As Marriage and Parenthood Drift Apart, Public is Concerned about Social Impact," *Pew Research Center Report*, July 1, 2007, 3, http://pewresearch.org/assets/social/pdf/Marriage.pdf (accessed October 3, 2011).
3. Ibid., 5.
4. Barbara Dafoe Whitehead and David Popenoe, "The Marrying Kind: Which Men Marry and Why," *The State of Our Unions: The Social Health of Marriage in America, 2004* (Rutgers University, The National Marriage Project, 2004), http://www.virginia.edu/marriageproject/pdfs/SOOU2004.pdf (accessed October 3, 2011).
5. Sally C. Clarke, "Advance Report of Final Marriage Statistics, 1989 and 1990," *Monthly Vital Statistics Report* 43, no. 12 Suppl. (July 14, 1995): 7, Table 1, http://www.cdc.gov/nchs/products/pubs/pubd/mvsr/mvsr.htm#vol44s (accessed October 3, 2011).
6. U.S. Bureau of the Census, Series A 160–171, "Marital Status of the Population, by Age and Sex: 1890 to 1970," in *Historical Statistics of the United States: Colonial Times to 1970, Part I* William Lerner, ed. (Washington, DC: GPO, 1975), 20–21.
7. U.S. Bureau of the Census, "Marital Status of the Population 15 Years Old and Over, by Sex and Race: 1950 to Present," *Families and Living Arrangements*, Historical Time Series: Marital Status, Table MS-1 (Internet release July 2008), http://www.census.gov/population/www/socdemo/hh-fam.html#history (accessed October 3, 2011).
8. Rose M. Kreider, "Living Arrangements of Children: 2004," *Current Population Reports*, Series P-70, no. 114 (Washington, DC: U.S. Bureau of the Census, 2008), 4, Table 1, http://www.census.gov/prod/2008pubs/p70-114.pdf (accessed October 3, 2011).
9. U.S. Bureau of the Census, "Unmarried-Couple Households, by Presence of Children: 1960 to Present," *Families and Living Arrangements*, Historical Time Series: Living Arrangements of Adults, Table UC-1 (Internet release July 2008), http://www.census.gov/population/www/socdemo/hh-fam.html#history (accessed October 3, 2011).
10. James Q. Wilson, *The Marriage Problem: How Culture has Weakened Families* (New York: HarperCollins Publishers, 2002).
11. Robert P. George, "What's Sex Got to Do with It: Marriage, Morality, and Rationality," in *The Meaning of Marriage*, ed. James Q. Wilson, Robert P. George, and Jean Bethke Elshtain (Dallas, TX: Spence Publishing, 2006), 142–43.
12. Ibid., 146.
13. http://www.childrensdefense.org (accessed October 3, 2011).
14. Crouse, *Children at Risk*, 26.
15. U.S. Bureau of the Census, "Related Children by Number of Working Family Members and Family Structure," *POV 13. Annual Social and Economic (ASEC) Supplement*, 2009. [These data come from the CPS 2010 Annual

Social and Economic Supplement, formerly called the March Supplement.] http://www.census.gov/hhes/www/cpstables/032010/pov/toc.htm (accessed October 3, 2011).

16. Computations by the author for this hypothetical comparison are as follows: If the distribution of families that existed in 1973 had existed in 2007, the poverty rate would have been 10.7 = 6.7 x 0.847 + 32.7 x 0.153. The data come from: U.S. Bureau of the Census, "Poverty Status of Families, by Type of Family, Presence of Related Children, Race, and Hispanic Origin: 1959 to 2007," Current Population Survey Reports: Historical Poverty Tables—Families, Table 4, http://www.census.gov/hhes/www/poverty/data/historical/families.html (accessed October 3, 2011).

17. Crouse, *Children at Risk*, 36.

18. "The Relationship between Parental Alcohol, Drug Use and Child Maltreatment," Study Number: 14, *ChildAbuse.com*: Prevention through Education and Awareness, http://www.childabuse.com/fs14.htm (accessed October 3, 2011).

19. Ibid.

20. Michael R. Petit, *Homeland Insecurity: Why New Investments in Children and Youth Must be a Priority in the Obama Administration and the 111th Congress* (Washington, DC: Every Child Matters Education Fund, January 2009), 6, http://www.everychildmatters.org/storage/documents/pdf/reports/homelandinsecurity3.pdf (accessed October 3, 2011).

21. National Center for Child Death Review Policy and Practice, "Fact Sheet," *Child Abuse and Neglect*, http://www.childdeathreview.org/causesCAN.htm (accessed October 3, 2011).

22. Andrea J. Sedlak and Diane D. Broadhurst, *U.S. Department of Health and Human Services, The Third National Incidence Study of Child Abuse and Neglect* (Washington, DC: GPA, 1996), Executive Summary.

23. Jan LaRue, "When Beauty is the Beast," *Human Events*, May 15, 2006, http://www.humanevents.com/article.php?id=14780 (accessed October 3, 2011).

24. Crouse, *Children at Risk*, 100.

25. Ibid., 193.

26. Ibid., 195.

27. Robert H. Bork, *Slouching towards Gomorrah* (New York: Regan Books/HarperCollins, 1996), Back Cover.

28. D. James Kennedy, Ph.D., "Breakdown of the Family," *Issues Tearing Our Nation's Fabric* (Ft. Lauderdale, FL: Coral Ridge Ministries [Updated July 13, 2002]), http://www.leaderu.com/issues/fabric/chap03.html (accessed April 19, 2011).

29. "The Oprah Winfrey Show," *Failing Grade*, April 11, 2006, Screen 1, http://www.oprah.com/world/Failing-Grade (accessed October 3, 2011).

30. Crouse, *Children at Risk*, 181.

31. Ibid., 183.

32. *Digest of Education Statistics*, 2007, 13, Table 2.

33. Ibid.

34. Walt Gardner, "Schools Alone can't Close Achievement Gap," *The Record* (Bergen County, NJ), July 19, 2008, found at *HighBeam Research*, http://www.highbeam.com/doc/1P1-154434715.html (accessed October 3, 2011).

35. P. Bourdieu and J. C. Passeron, *Reproduction in Education, Society and Culture* (London: Sage, 1990), 494. As quoted in Alice Sullivan, "Cultural Capitalism, Cultural Knowledge and Ability," *Sociological Research Online* 12, no. 6 (November 30, 2007): http://www.socresonline.org.uk/12/6/1.html (accessed October 3, 2011).

36. Ibid.

37. "This is a Wake-up Call for Parents," *The Gloucestershire Echo*, February 4, 2009, *HighBeam Research*, http://www.highbeam.com/doc/1P2-19839979.html (accessed October 3, 2011).

38. Ibid.

39. Media Awareness Network, "How Marketers Target Kids," under *For Parents: Marketing and Consumerism*, http://www.media-awareness.ca/english/parents/marketing/marketers_target_kids.cfm (accessed October 3, 2011).

40. American Academy of Pediatrics Committee on Communications, "Children, Adolescents and Advertising," *Pediatrics* 118, no. 6 (December 2006): 2563, http://www.wsu.edu/~eaustin/pdf/AAP_statement.pdf (accessed October 3, 2011).

41. Joshua Meyrowitz interviewed by Barbara Osborn, "Altered States: How Television Changes Childhood," *Center for Media Literacy*, http://www.medialit.org/reading_room/article59.html (accessed October 3, 2011).

42. Gregory Acs and Sandi Nelson, "The Kids are Alright? Children's Well-Being and the Rise in Cohabitation," *New Federalism: National Survey of America's Families* Series B, no. B-48 (July 2002): Table 1, http://www.urban.org/url.cfm?ID=310544 (accessed February 20, 2009).

43. Ibid.

44. Phyllis Bronstein and others, "Parenting Behavior and Children's Social, Psychological and Academic Adjustment in Diverse Family Structures," *Family Relations* 42, no. 3 (July 1993): 268–76.

45. Alan Booth and Ann C. Crouter, eds., *Just Living Together: Implications of Cohabitation on Families, Children, and Social Policy* (Mahwah, NJ: Lawrence Erlbaum Associates, 2002), 134–36, 142–43.

46. Marcia Barlow, United Families International, "A Guide to Family Issues: Cohabitation vs. Marriage: Part I," *Family Issues Guide* (May 2007): 9, http://unitedfamilies.org/downloads/Cohabitation_Part_I.pdf (accessed October 3, 2011).

47. Janice Shaw Crouse, "America Faces a Popeye Moment," *Townhall*, December 13, 2006, http://townhall.com/columnists/janiceshawcrouse/2006/12/13/america_faces_a_popeye_moment/page/full/ (accessed October 3, 2011).

48. Daniel Patrick Moynihan, "The Negro Family: The Case for National Action," *The Moynihan Report (1965)*, Office of Policy Planning and Research, United States Department of Labor, March 1965, In BlackPast.Org, http://www.blackpast.org/?q=primary/moynihan-report-1965 (accessed October 3, 2011).

49. Rich Lowry, "The Moynihan Report and Ongoing Family Breakdown, *National Review*, May 11, 2010, http://www.nationalreview.com/articles/229730/moynihan-report-and-ongoing-family-breakdown/rich-lowry (accessed October 3, 2011).

50. Ray Lewis Official Website, http://www.raylewis52.com/ (accessed October 3, 2011).

51. Fox Sports Net, "Ray Lewis Episode," *Beyond the Glory*, May 9, 2004, http://www.tvguide.com/detail/tv-show.aspx?tvobjectid=200020&more=ucepisodelist&episodeid=4162615 (accessed October 3, 2011).

52. Crouse, *Children at Risk*, 29–30.

53. Janice Shaw Crouse, "Seeing Marriage through the Trees," *Townhall*, 2009, http://townhall.com/columnists/janiceshawcrouse/2009/04/06/seeing_marriage_through_the_trees/page/full/ (accessed October 3, 2011).

54. Crouse, *Children at Risk*, 201.

Part IV

Marriage: The Impact on the Public Sector

8

The Ramifications of Same-Sex "Marriage"

Gays and Lesbians have a right to live as they choose, they don't have the right to redefine marriage for all of us.

—Maggie Gallagher

There are ideologues among our educational elites (credentialed but not intelligent in the sense of understanding reality) who believe and preach that any group of people can be a family. Alongside that attitude is the argument that a woman does not need a man and the concept that marriage is no more than a "piece of paper." Ironically, the disparagement of marriage and the attempt to redefine family coincides with the increase in social science data that demonstrates the necessity of a married-couple family—comprised of a mom and a dad—in producing the best outcomes for women and children. As I have noted, data are increasingly substantiating the desirability of marriage and family for men's well-being, too. For both children and adults, marriage—as the union of one man and one woman for life—is the ideal household arrangement. To this point, this book has focused on the private benefits of marriage—why marriage matters to individuals, both children and adults.

Now we turn to the public benefits of marriage and family and the rationale for marriage and family to be endorsed and supported in our nation's public policies, as well as in federal and/or state laws. Many people argue that the government should not be involved in promoting marriage and family. Probably in response to such attitudes, the U.S. Centers for Disease Control and Prevention (CDC) declared in 1988 that it could no longer "afford" to keep track of official marriage and divorce data.[1] The marriage reports volume of *Vital Statistics of the United States* used to contain detailed accounts (age of bride and groom, marriage rates according to previous marital status, remarriage, etc.) of what was happening across the spectrum of marriage issues. The divorce reports contained similarly thorough information about the number of divorces, as well as demographic data about those divorcing. Now we no longer have that basic demographic information that would enable us to more easily track societal trends regarding marriage formation and dissolution.

Since then, however, the CDC has somehow found the funds, as well as the time, to compile its lengthy and thorough National Health Statistics Reports (NHSR) on oral sex, anal sex, same-sex contact, and the correlations between sexual attraction and sexual behavior—including among teens only fifteen years old.[2] So the federal government deems it too expensive to track marriage and divorce data; instead, it turns its attention to tracking data about sexual activity, behavior, attraction, and identity of teens and adults. Obviously, the intent of the report is to document same-sex attraction, identification, behavior, and activity, rather than to report on sexually transmitted diseases (as the title would suggest). Is this a sign of the times, or a calculated effort to continue pushing the homosexual agenda? Or is it both? Is it in citizens' interest to track same-sex identification rather than document marriage trends?

In such a cultural climate, Linda J. Waite and Maggie Gallagher, authors of *The Case for Marriage*,[3] recognized that over the past thirty years, marriage—"the most basic and universal of human institutions"[4]—has become controversial. They set out to make a case for marriage as both a private and public institution. In a similar vein, David Blankenhorn, president of the Institute for American Values, in his book, *The Future of Marriage*,[5] bluntly laid out what is at stake if the institution of marriage is destroyed. He writes, "We do not build social institutions around purely private emotional connections that no third party can understand. If marriage does not have a valid, comprehensible public dimension, then marriage for all intents and purposes does not exist."[6]

Arthur Goldberg, author of *Light in the Closet*, warns that if "moral relativism continues to be the lodestar of western society, our children and grandchildren may find themselves living in a world where long-cherished values of objective morality will no longer be 'tolerated' by a society founded on a compulsory, acritical and indiscriminate 'tolerance.' Once we throw away the compass of right and wrong bequeathed to us by ancient wisdom, we find almost everything to be subjective opinion—usually the result of a little self-indulgence and a good deal of creative rationalization."[7]

Modern authors are not the first to view marriage as the foundation for communities and nations; Marcus Tullius Cicero (106–43 BC), a Roman orator, lawyer, politician, and philosopher, called marriage the "first bond of society." Nor are modern authors the first to see marriage as the place where children are nurtured to become citizens of character and integrity; Kahlil Gibran (1883–1930), a Lebanese poet and philosopher, referred to parents as the "bows from which children as living arrows are sent forth."

With the push today to redefine marriage to include so-called "same-sex marriage," arguments are typically about adults' desires rather than children's needs. As David Blankenhorn has pointed out, "Gay and lesbian leaders are not asking for marriage with an adjective in front of it, but marriage itself."[8] In other words, the same-sex "marriage" movement seeks to change the definition of marriage—to alter the meaning of marriage and to make the whole institution radically different from what it has been over centuries and across cultures.

In their powerful article, "What is Marriage?" Sherif Girgis, Robert P. George, and Ryan T. Anderson[9] argue that understanding the nature of marriage is essential in order to understand why society needs to protect the institution of marriage for the common good. The authors describe two competing views of marriage:

- The conjugal view sees marriage as the "union of a man and a woman who make a permanent and exclusive commitment to each other," and who "consummate and renew their union by conjugal acts." The authors declare that marriage is inherently valuable, but its value is enhanced by its "orientation to bearing and rearing children" and its "norms of monogamy and fidelity." They add: "This link to the welfare of children also helps explain why marriage is important to the common good and why the state should recognize and regulate it."[10]
- The revisionist view sees marriage as "the union of two people (whether of the same sex or of opposite sexes) who commit to romantically loving and caring for each other and to sharing the burdens and benefits of domestic life." The union is "of hearts and minds, enhanced by whatever forms of sexual intimacy both partners find agreeable." The state's interest—if, indeed, there even is one—is purely in the "romantic partnerships and in the concrete needs of spouses and any children they may choose to rear."[11]

Girgis, George, and Anderson declare that the "common good of our society crucially depends on legally enshrining the conjugal view of marriage and would be damaged by enshrining the revisionist view"[12].

They argue that "legally enshrining the conjugal view of marriage is both philosophically defensible and good for society, and that enshrining the revisionist view is neither."[13] The authors isolate the debate over marriage to a central question: "Is it possible for the kind of union that has marriage's essential features to exist between two people of the same sex?" To anyone who is in touch with reality, the question answers itself with a resounding "no." Thus, the goal of proponents of same-sex "marriage" is "to abolish the conjugal conception of marriage in our law and replace it with the revisionist conception."[14]

Such alterations in understanding the nature of marriage would become—to use Stanley Kurtz's description—a "culture-shifting event." Other scholars have said that same-sex "marriage" would "massively reshape the social landscape" without a single study being conducted and in spite of "mountains of empirical evidence showing the negative effects on society that occur when the family structure breaks down."[15]

According to Jeffrey Satinover, a Princeton psychiatrist, the negative impact would be especially severe for the nation's children. He assures the public that his assertion is not made for "sentimental reasons"; instead, he says, it is based on "sound science."[16] Satinover adds, "The evidence is overwhelming. Mountains of evidence, collected over decades, show that children need both mothers and fathers."[17]Henry Biller, a clinical psychologist trained at Duke University, explains that this is because the father and mother offer the child two different kinds of persons to learn about and provide the child with separate sources of love and support from two different perspectives. These differences, though obvious to the layman with common sense, had to be scientifically documented in order to debunk the feminist claim that men and women are interchangeable. Science has demonstrated that "there are hundreds of nuances about men and women that even newborn infants can readily distinguish and that make a difference in the way the child develops.[18]

The core concern that must remain our focus throughout the debate is whether or not the nurturing of our children and the desire to see them attain their best outcomes will remain a top priority for the nation. In terms of the public policy aspects of marriage, the question is whether or not the nation will encourage stable marriages as a safe haven for children and as the best place for children to be nurtured into adulthood in order to become involved, informed, and contributing citizens. Social science data are clear that family structure is a powerful influencer of the outcome of a child's development[19]; the nation, then, has a vital interest in producing children who will be well prepared to make a positive contribution to the survival and quality of society and to strengthen the foundations of the culture.

Author and journalist David Frum raised another issue that deserves consideration; he sees same-sex "marriage" as having the potential to turn children into commodities. He describes the surrogate father who donates to a sperm bank as one who—for a certain amount of money—signs a contract to relieve himself of his paternal responsibilities. Likewise, a surrogate mother, for a fee, agrees to stipulations that the state is obligated to enforce as a legal contract. Frum notes that every sperm bank in America could be out of business if the state announced that it would not enforce the contracts; it is all about the child being a commodity that is for sale.[20] It does not take much imagination to extrapolate from Frum's surrogacy example the problems that are inherent in same-sex "marriage" situations.

> What we are doing by creating this institution to be called 'gay marriage' is smashing marriage and replacing it with a whole new set of arrangements that apply to everybody, not just homosexuals, everybody, in which marriage is a unique contract between any two or more adults who want to enter into it and set by any rules. It makes marriage impermanent, and it turns children into commodities.[21]

The same-sex marriage issue is not really about adult's legal rights either. With all the writing about legal needs, there is an amazing lack of specificity about exactly what legal benefits would be accrued to homosexual couples that are not already available to them under their human rights as individuals living in America. Redefining marriage is, at its core, an attempt to change the traditional meaning of marriage from the union of a man and a woman in an attempt to make homosexuality as acceptable as heterosexuality. This special-interest agenda of a small minority of Americans is antithetical to children's needs and is a precursor to an onslaught of "unintended consequences" that are typical of such special-interest social engineering.

The need for children to have a married-couple family, comprised of a mother and a father, was addressed in an article in *The Journal of Communication and Religion* (JCR)[22]. It analyzed the importance of opposite-sex parent relationships. The common sense conclusions reported in the JCR are backed up with social science data and affirmed by a peer-reviewed scholarly article, titled "Girls Need a Dad and Boys Need a Mom."[23]

The study showed how communication is an essential building block for all family relationships; indeed, family interaction is the crucible for attitudes, values, priorities, and worldviews. Beyond the shaping and modeling of these essential personal characteristics, the family shapes an individual's interpersonal system and self-identity.

Further, stable homes include specific talk about religion (particularly, its role in addressing the meaning of life and in defining moral standards for our interactions, e.g., "the Golden Rule") and support for children's involvement in religious activities. These families create high-quality relationships through specific communicative attributes, such as openness, assurance, and dependency. Those same characteristics, not incidentally, are powerful predictors of marital success or failure.

G. L. Forward, Alison Sansom-Livolsi, and Jordanna McGovern—the authors of the JCR article, stress the fact that a family is more than merely a group of individuals who live under the same roof. The parents, both as a couple and individually as "Mom" and "Dad," play gender-specific roles, and each parent has a unique impact on the children—whether of the same or of the opposite gender. The authors cite numerous studies showing how each parent plays a crucial role in a child's personal and social development. In fact, a child's relationship with his or her parents is the single-most important factor in predicting that child's long-term happiness, adjustment, development, educational attainment, and success. Beyond that general information, studies indicate that girls get better support from the family than do boys. Girls feel closer to their parents, perhaps because parents converse with and express emotion more readily with daughters than with sons. In general, mothers spend far more time with daughters than with sons. Likewise, fathers spend more time with sons than with their daughters. Yet, paradoxically, father–daughter and mother–son relationships tend to have greater impact on a child's future intimate relationships than their relationship with the parent of the same sex.

All of this information has greater significance today then ever before because family and household arrangements are changing more rapidly now than at any previous time. The National Center for Health Statistics (NCHS) reported in 2006 that 48 percent of all marriages in the United States ended in divorce. Other studies indicate that cohabitation, delayed marriage, serial marriages, and numerous blended family structures are all affecting relationships and expectations between family members. Case in point, studies conclude that after a divorce, mothers are less affectionate and communicate less often with their children. Long-term erosion of family relationships is common, with the father–child relationship being the most endangered relationship following family turmoil and disruption.

The NCHS survey, given to students at two private church-related universities in Southern California, asked students to evaluate their family's relationship satisfaction, religiosity, and communicative behaviors with the opposite-sex parent. Specifically, the study looked at the openness, assurance, dependency, and religiosity between the student and his or her mother or father.

Dependency—The authors define dependency as the attachment and emotional bonding that provides a sense of security throughout a child's lifetime. Healthy dependence is essential for autonomy. Ironically, parent–child dependency provides the foundation that enables the child to separate from the parents as he or she matures and becomes an adult. Social and emotional growth stems from a secure attachment; having a safe haven with parents enables a child to move away from his or her secure base to explore autonomy and independence as an adolescent and emerging adult. In other words, the more secure the base, the easier it is for a child to leave the nest; he or she knows that the parents are there and feels secure enough to transition into a confident adult.

Openness—When parents and children openly and comfortably share their thoughts and emotions, the transition into healthy adulthood is easier. Such openness assists the child in decision-making. Greater interaction leads to fewer family problems. Parents who express love, offer frequent praise, and encourage "give-and-take" produce adolescents who are less likely to engage in dangerous behaviors when alone or with friends.

Assurance—A child's self-esteem is strongly linked to parental assurance of worth. A vote of confidence from parents is particularly significant to adolescents. In fact, the ability to communicate assurance to a child is identified as a key to parental success. Successful parents give a child a sense of worth and lovability; coercive parents imply untrustworthiness and incompetence. These communicative patterns especially affect girls; a father's open encouragement and supportive attitude makes a daughter feel confident and creates a greater sense of personal worth.

Religiosity—The authors cited numerous studies that link religious beliefs and practices to a strong family unit and noted the fact that the most noticeable impact of religiosity is during adolescence. The majority of studies found an inverse relationship between religiosity and high-risk adolescent behaviors (drinking, drug use, sexual activity, depression, etc.). Other studies indicate a strong relationship between the family's religious belief and practice and a teen's emotional health and family well-being. This is especially true of teenage boys.

While family communication and interaction is critical to high-quality relationships for children and adolescents, this study points to the fact that the opposite-sex parent is especially important in making children feel validated and encouraged. This is true of boys as well as girls, but it is especially true of daughters. Fathers have the greatest impact on their daughters' vitality as a teen entering college. Daughters who have strong relationships with their fathers are more self-confident, self-reliant, and are more successful in school and in career than those who have distant or absent fathers. Finally, the study validates the old adage, "The family that prays together, stays together"—even during those stressful adolescent and teen years.

This study, along with others that focus on the roles of opposite-sex parents, is especially relevant now that so-called same-sex "marriages" are legal in five states—Connecticut, Iowa, Massachusetts, New Hampshire, and Vermont, where the words "bride and groom" are replaced with the names of the individuals, who are each called "spouse" or "Person A" and "Person B" on their applications and marriage certificates. In 2010, the District of Columbia (D.C.) voted to allow legal marriage ceremonies for same-sex couples. Shortly afterward, more than one hundred couples—some coming from nearby states—came to D.C. for ceremonies. The same-sex "marriage" movement has gained such cachet that those who oppose same-sex "marriage" are branded by the liberal media with derogatory labels: "bigot," "narrow-minded," and "hate-filled," among the nicest. Such public relations campaigns and name-calling obscure the very real problems associated with watering down and denigrating traditional marriage.

Let us begin by examining the basic argument that people are "born gay." Activists may wish to believe this, but the science is not there to substantiate their oft-stated premise that homosexuality is genetic and immutable. The studies that purport to support the idea have not been replicated; instead, they have been repudiated or considered inconclusive. Activists are counting on the first principle of propaganda that if you say something often enough, people will believe it—even in the face of factual evidence that falsifies it.

The actual present state of knowledge is that some people may be predisposed to emotional vulnerabilities that can be exacerbated by external factors, such as parental approval, social acceptance, and gender affirmation. But the evidence is just not there to substantiate the claim that being "gay" is innate and immutable. In point of fact, a growing number of formerly homosexual individuals have chosen to reject the homosexual lifestyle. In addition, there is an acknowledgment, even among homosexuals, that persons can "choose" their sexuality (for example, the choice to be bisexual or not). Here, we have one of the major inconsistencies of the activists' pronouncements in their claim of both genetic immutability and "fluidity" in sexual orientation; they argue that persons should "experiment" along the spectrum of sexual desires, which implies choice in sexual orientation and, thus, the potential for seduction and recruitment as opposed to a genetically dictated destiny that would not be chosen.

In his classic article, "Born or Bred?"—which has never been successfully refuted, Robert Knight surveys the scientific literature and finds that "the science does not support the claim that homosexuality is genetic."[24] Knight's analysis is important because "immutability is a central tenet of demands for 'gay rights' and 'gay marriage.'"[25] He cites studies showing that people have changed their "sexual orientation" from homosexual to heterosexual, and he urges caution to those researchers and media personalities who want to promote the concept of being "born gay." Knight also notes the body of information about experimentation with various labels—those who switch from "straight" to "gay," from "bisexual" to "straight," and back again—with one study reporting that "almost two-thirds" of a group of teenage females had "changed labels" during the course of the study. Knight has carefully examined the various studies that seek to establish a biological cause, and he reports that they are "inconclusive at best." He says, "It is both more compassionate and truthful to give [those who question their sexual "orientation"] hope than to serve them up politically motivated, unproven creations like the 'gay gene.'"[26]

A report by the National Association for Research and Therapy of Homosexuality (NARTH), titled "What Research Shows," summarizes "over a century of experiential evidence, clinical reports, and research evidence to demonstrate that it is possible for both men and women to change from homosexuality to heterosexuality; that efforts to change are not generally harmful, and that homosexual men and women do indeed have greater risk factors for medical, psychological and relationship pathology than do the general population."[27]

The NARTH report concludes that homosexuality is not immutable or without significant risks to medical, psychological, and relational health. NARTH points out that the American Psychological Association's (APA) Code of Ethics supports every client's rights to autonomy and self-determination in therapy and mandates that therapists either respect a client's practice of religion and sexual orientation or refer the client to a professional who will offer such respect. The APA has two elements to its policy position. First, it states that clients who are "not distressed about their sexual orientation should not be directed to change by mental health professionals." Conversely, "clients who seek sexual reorientation deserve properly informed and competent psychological care from therapists who use interventions that have been scientifically demonstrated as helpful for achieving this goal."[28]

Let us look at five other myths associated with same-sex "marriage."[29]

Myth #1: Having Same-Sex Couples Celebrate Their Love Does Nothing to Harm Anybody Else's Marriage or Damage the Institution of Marriage

The proposition that "what I do is my business and doesn't hurt anybody but me" is an old argument that has been refuted in numerous ways. The institution of marriage that has existed throughout history in almost every culture to protect women and children is under relentless attack from a promiscuous, "me-centered" culture that derides the male who marries and, thus, "gives up" his independence; he is labeled a "powerless wimp." Women who "hold out" for marriage are called "prudes" and worse. These cultural changes are bad enough. Society pushes further down the road toward cultural destruction if the definition of marriage is broadened to the point that it becomes meaningless. Blankenhorn reports that he analyzed thirty-five nations from the 2002 International Social Survey Programme, "which found marriage is weakest in nations where support for gay marriage is strongest." Blankenhorn is not saying "one causes the other"; he does say that the two developments "go together." He adds, "If you do support marriage and want it to be this robust social institution, then you ought to think twice about saying you're for gay marriage."[30]

Counterfeits always devalue the real thing. Counterfeit marriage will lead to unions where "anything goes"; there will be no legal reason to deny any arrangement a place under the umbrella of "marriage." The age of those seeking unions will be irrelevant; blood relationships will not matter; the number of partners seeking the ceremony will not be an issue. Thus, arrangements of various characteristics could expand until the institution of marriage is rendered irrelevant and becomes a meaningless farce.

The potential harm to marriage is not mere speculation. We have only to look at what has happened in the Scandinavian countries. They legalized "same-sex marriage," and, now, cohabitation rather than marriage is the prevalent household arrangement.

An illuminating precursor to the same-sex marriage struggle with which we are contending can be seen in the life and career of an eminent sociologist who argued that embracing and supporting traditional marriage was essential for a strong society. Pitirim A. Sorokin, a Russian intellectual who came to America in 1923 not speaking English, later founded Harvard's department of sociology just seven years later and served as chairman for fourteen years (1930–1944). His conservative views and his intellectual arrogance caused problems for him among his colleagues. Even so, Sorokin developed a substantial body of research and work, and he was elected president of the American Sociological Association in 1963.

Sorokin was "controversial" because of his "social stratification" views and his prediction that Western civilization was doomed due to decadence.[31] He warned about the prevalent "sensate" culture and exhorted his students to return to "ideational" righteousness. He was described as having moved in the "direction of social prophecy and away from detached scholarly inquiry"; some colleagues called him a "prophet of doom and disaster."[32] Even his harshest critics acknowledged that many of those things that he warned against became reality—to the point that he seemed to have an "almost uncanny sense of things to come."[33] Certainly, if he were alive today, he would classify the same-sex "marriage" movement as evidence of a "sensate" culture that would, ultimately, undermine and destroy the foundations of America.

Myth #2: Same-Sex "Marriage" Is an "Equal Rights" Issue

Activists argue that same-sex "marriage" is like the civil rights issue of racial equality, and that homosexuals "deserve" the right to "marry" and have the same benefits and protections of marriage that heterosexuals enjoy. Any denial of that "right," they say, violates their "equal rights." The reality, however, is that the same-sex "marriage" effort is more about getting society's approval for behavior and the effort of homosexuals to gain the same standing in general society as they have, for instance, in Hollywood; it is *not* about benefits or protections. All American citizens have the right to marriage, and all the protections that homosexuals seek are already embedded in American law.

There is nothing in the Bill of Rights or any other federal or state law that would deny homosexuals the civil rights enjoyed by every American citizen. While there are laws specifying restrictions on marriage (children cannot marry, close blood relatives cannot marry, bigamy and polygamy are outlawed), these laws protect individuals and society—as well as the institution of marriage—and are universal prohibitions.

Further, there are already-existing contract law instruments by which people can legally designate beneficiaries and establish who can or cannot visit them in hospitals. Thus, the push for same-sex "marriage" is not really about rights denied, as it is being billed. Instead, it is a push for forced legitimization and approval, mainstreaming an aberrant set of values, and condoning certain behaviors. The claim that gay "marriage" is needed for establishing equal "rights" is simply false; equal rights already exist.

Marriage is more than a "legal" institution; it is an organic institution, legitimized and supported by the oldest customs and traditions of society as a haven for children, as the foundation of the family, and as the well-spring of civility and national strength. The homosexual activists are seeking a special right—one that denies the human truth that males and females are sexually complementary, designed to be "one," and are created as the natural means for propagating the human race.

At last, it seems that some judges may be beginning to understand the implications of same-sex "marriage" and its effects on children. In her provocative publication, "Do Fathers and Mothers Matter?" Elizabeth Marquardt describes a New Jersey schoolteacher who hired a surrogate through a brokerage agency to carry his child while the surrogate's husband was away on active duty with the military. The mother delivered twins, who needed neonatal intensive care. The "father's" behavior raised concerns among the nurses, who saw him with a live bird on his shirt and, later, with bird feces on his sleeve. They noted that he seemed appallingly unaware of the care the infants would require, that he had no provisions for their needs, and that he planned to drive them from the hospital in Indiana to New Jersey by himself. Marion Superior Court Judge Marilyn Ann Moores was outraged. She condemned the "brokerage of children" and wrote, "There seems to be no concern regarding the emotional impact on children who learn that they, in effect, were bought and paid for and that their mother gave birth as a means of obtaining money."[34]

Myth #3: Any Group of People—Including Homosexual Couples—Can Contribute to the Well-Being of Children and Form a Productive Unit of Society

It defies common sense and logic to confer marital status upon any group of people—giving them societal affirmation and establishing them as an essential element of society—when the research indicates that they are not capable of adequately performing certain crucial functions. Social science research sends a clear and unequivocal message: the married-couple family—made up of a mom and a dad—is not just good, but is best for children in comparison to any other household arrangement. Other households (headed by anyone other than the married mother and father) are far inferior and damaging to children's well-being and their futures. Already, our children are at risk from the increase in cohabitation and the decline in marriage. If we add same-sex "marriage" into the mix, we are blatantly disregarding the best interests of our nation's children. American children are at risk in carefully documented ways when they are raised in any household other than a married mom-and-dad family. They make worse grades, are more likely to drop out of school, are more prone to getting into trouble, have greater health problems, are more likely to experiment with drugs and/or alcohol, and will likely engage in early sexual activity and, thus, be more likely to contract a sexually transmitted disease, have one or more abortions, and/or get pregnant as a teen.

Reports from a wide variety of think tanks and research institutions—for example, Child Trends, Brookings Institution, Center for Law and Social Policy, The Institute for American Values, the Woodrow Wilson School of Public and International Affairs at Princeton University, and the Heritage Foundation—provide a large body of compelling evidence that demonstrates the essential need for married "mom-and-dad" parents to fully and adequately provide for all aspects of children's well-being.

In popular culture, the move toward "intentional" families is gaining momentum. Elizabeth Marquardt analyzes the theory that any group of adults can "intend" to form a family and that their serious intent will inevitably be good for children. Thus, single motherhood or single fatherhood is viewed in light of the adult's happiness and fulfillment rather than consideration for the impact of the decision on the child. Marquardt describes a homosexual Philadelphian man who, in order to have a child, "paid a 25-year-old, married doctoral student to donate her eggs and a gestational surrogate to carry the pregnancy."[35] The egg donor, who has contributed to two pregnancies for the man—a two-year-old girl and four-month-old twin boys, on seeing the children several years later, enthused, "I think it's really fantastic when children are born into situations where they're wanted that much." Marquardt comments, "While it is true the babies' father seems to want them very much, how will the children make sense of an egg donor and surrogate mother who did *not* want them?"[36]

Another fact that has received little attention is that same-sex relationships between women are distinctly different from those between men. "They have utterly different demographics, life spans, health and behavioral characteristics and sexual behaviors...If you were to create gay marriage, you end up with three totally different marital entities"—heterosexual marriages, female same-sex "marriages," and male same-sex "marriages." Satinover believes these various households would have different impacts on the children raised in those different environments. We would have three separate classes of children and three sets of negative effects on those children.[37]

Myth #4: Same-Sex "Marriage" Is a Matter of Freedom of Conscience and Freedom of Religion

This is one of the more insidious myths related to "same-sex marriage." There is no way to ignore the fact that same-sex "marriage" violates the deeply held beliefs of millions of Christian, Jewish, and Muslim citizens, whose opposition to same-sex "marriage" is founded on central tenets of their faith. Knowing this, homosexual activists are working through indoctrination programs to sway the minds of the nation's children. Our public schools are becoming the means through which activists plan to change public opinion, moral teaching, and the rule of law. Curriculum programs are instilling the idea that there is no legitimate opposition to homosexuality; instead, any opposition is "bigoted" and "hate-filled." Laws are being changed to force innkeepers, businesses, and our social services to accommodate homosexuality. The next step will be to follow the European and Canadian models, which make raising any objection—even a religiously based one—a hate crime subject to criminal prosecution.

Same-sex "marriage" is already used to bludgeon religious liberties and drive out Christian social services. For example, Massachusetts and the District of Columbia have both driven out Catholic adoption agencies, whose moral stand is unacceptable to the homosexual agenda. The radical politics of homosexuality requires orphans to remain without parents rather than to allow a Christian agency the religious liberty to find them a home.

The aforementioned article, "What is Marriage?"[38] devotes considerable attention to the question of whether or not marriage is an intrinsic right. The authors contend that there is no "right" to "have any type of relationship that you desire recognized as marriage."[39] The authors define and describe marriage as involving a comprehensive union of spouses, a special link to children and norms of permanence, monogamy, and exclusivity. All three of these elements, they emphasize, point to the conjugal understanding of marriage and not to the revisionist interpretation. Marriage, then, is unique to the union of a male and female, and, thus, the appeals to equality fail:

> The principle of equality requires treating cases alike. So the judgment that same-sex and opposite-sex unions are alike with respect to marriage, and should therefore be treated alike by marriage law, presupposes one of two things: Either *neither* relationship is a real marriage in the above sense, perhaps because there is no such thing, marriage being just a legal fiction (in which case, why not justify apparent inequities by social-utility considerations?) or both relationships are real marriages, *whatever* the law says about them. The latter presuppositions entails the belief, which most revisionists seem to share with advocates of the conjugal view, that marriage has a nature independent of legal conventions. In this way, the crucial question—the only one that can settle this debate—remains for both sides: What is marriage?[40]

Based on the three elements descriptive of marriage (comprehensive union—linked to children and having the norms of permanence, monogamy, and exclusivity), Girgis, George, and Anderson assert that same-sex relationships cannot be *marriages,* neither in reality nor in law. The authors, additionally, argue that "abolishing the conjugal conception of marriage would weaken the social institution of marriage, obscure the value of opposite-sex parenting as an ideal, and threaten moral and religious freedom."[41] In redefining marriage, the authors claim, the "law would teach that marriage is fundamentally about adults' emotional unions, not bodily unions, or children, with which marital norms are tightly intertwined."[42] The state cannot be value-neutral with respect to marriage; if by abuse of its sovereign authority, the state forcefully eradicates the singularity of the conjugal view of marriage, it would make other partnerships equivalent and, thus, falsely classify those who support the conjugal view with its exclusive claims as "bigots who make groundless and invidious distinctions."[43]

Myth #5: Same-Sex "Marriages" Are Just Like Heterosexual Marriages

This last myth is possibly the one furthest from the truth. In actuality, homosexual unions—by and large—have a very short lifespan (this is notoriously the case with gay men); many of the same-sex "marriages" in Massachusetts have already been dissolved. In Scandinavian countries, where same-sex "marriage" has been possible for over a decade, there is a "lack of movement toward marriage" as well as a lack of movement toward monogamy among homosexuals.[44] Further, the health risks associated with homosexual practice are very real and very much evidenced in the emergency rooms of hospitals. Experience shows very clearly that homosexual behavior often is dangerous and destructive to the human body. Both HIV and HPV are epidemics among homosexual men. In addition, domestic violence is a frequent problem—twice as prevalent among homosexual couples as it is among heterosexual ones.

Legally creating a union does not enable two men or two women to become "one flesh," nor does a legal ceremony give the union sanctity. Instead, the ceremony creates a sham that will devalue all marriages. The government establishes "standards" for measurement and value; to declare a sham union equal to marriage would devalue the "standard" and render all unions worthless and irrelevant. If the U.S. government establishes same-sex "marriages" under law, it will be artificially redefining marriage, and the consequences for society will be irrevocable. Such unfounded, unreasonable legislative action would contradict the prevailing social science research. There is an irreconcilable difference between (1) a family created and sanctioned by society—when a man and a woman commit to each other and, thus, form a cohesive unit, and (2) a couple or group of people who live together to form a household in defiance of the prevailing moral codes, thereby rendering meaningless an institution that has been the bulwark of the family and society throughout history.

The bottom line is that such ill-advised, harmful tampering with the traditional definition of marriage is social engineering of the most brazen and foolish sort; it is a defining moment for our society, and, given the dominant role of the United States in world affairs, it will not just affect this nation. Let us be very clear: what the homosexual activists are seeking is not a minor shift in the law, but a radical change in the fundamental institution that forms the basis for society. The question before us is if we will defend marriage as the primary institution protecting women and children, or if we will, instead, surrender to the forces that claim no one has obligations to others and that adults can do anything they want in their sexual lives, regardless of how those actions undermine society, children, and the public good.

The myths associated with same-sex "marriage" are linked to the negative impact that such unions would have on the broader culture. Businesses would feel the impact immediately. As Peter Sprigg, Senior Fellow for Policy Studies at the Family Research Council, explained in testimony before the Rhode Island House Judiciary Committee (as that state considered same-sex "marriages"):

> Currently, some employers already offer "domestic partner" benefits to same-sex couples as a matter of choice. But if homosexual couples are granted the full legal status of civil marriage, then employers who do not want to grant spousal benefits to homosexual partners—whether out of principle, or simply because of a prudent economic judgment—would be coerced by court orders to do so. You, as a taxpayer, consumer, or small business owner, would be forced to bear the expense of subsidizing homosexual relationships—including their higher health care costs.[45]

Public schools have already been forced to mainstream homosexual relationships for students as young as kindergarten, and private schools will be next—as will "churches, para-church ministries, religious educational and social service organizations and individual believers"[46]; Sprigg cites specific examples of instances where homosexual activism trumped religious liberty. Catholic Charities of Boston was told by state authorities that it could not provide adoption services unless it placed children for adoption with same-sex couples.[47] A faith-based camp was stripped of its tax exemptions when it refused to rent its facilities for a lesbian "civil union" ceremony.[48] Yeshiva University was forced to allow same-sex "partners" to live in married-student housing.[49]

Those impacts are just the obvious ones. Stanley Kurtz, in a *Weekly Standard* article, reported on the impact of same-sex "marriage" in Scandinavia.[50] Those countries, says Kurtz, have effectively separated marriage and parenthood to the point that "marriage itself is outdated." Three Danish sociologists described the outcome of the societal changes that followed same-sex "marriage," stating, "Marriage is no longer a precondition for settling a family—neither legally nor normatively...What defines and makes the foundation of the Danish family can be said to have moved from marriage to parenthood." Kurtz links the "deep decline" in traditional marriage to "gay marriage."[51]

David Popenoe, a Rutgers University sociologist who "documented the slow motion collapse of the Swedish family" links family decline to welfare policy, which generously supports single-parenting as well as nonmarital living arrangements. Other sociologists have documented the dismal outcomes for the Swedish children in those single-parent households.[52] But the major finding of Kurtz's research is that "rising out-of-wedlock birthrates disassociate heterosexual marriage from parenting"—thus, making gay "marriage" conceivable. Gay "marriages," then, "lock in and reinforce the very cultural separation between marriage and parenthood that makes gay marriage conceivable to begin with."[53] Further, Kurtz reported, "Gay marriage has served to validate the belief that individual choice trumps family form."[54]

Conservative activists question the recent polls that indicate that Americans are becoming more open to the idea of same-sex "marriage." These polls contradict the votes that people have cast in states where the issue has been on the ballot. A total of thirty-one states has had same-sex "marriage" on the ballot; voters in each of those states voted to ban same-sex "marriage." That is a remarkable outcome and is the only "poll" that really counts. Voters have repeatedly voted by turning up at the polls. Those votes are clear and unequivocal, unlike the wording on some polling questions. In addition, laws are being enacted in many states, reflecting the public's desires to protect marriage. To date, the constitutions of twenty-six states have prohibitions against same-sex "marriage," and nineteen states have enacted statutes prohibiting same-sex "marriage" in their states. Think about it—until recently, motherlessness and father absence were considered serious problems facing children, and the social sciences documented the negative outcomes that were risk factors for such children. Now, special interest groups are proposing a society-wide change that would make such family structures intentional and acceptable. As Elizabeth Marquardt explained, "The only reason this change has occurred is because—increasingly in the eyes of society's leaders—an adult's right to children outweighs children's hardwired need for their mother and their father."[55]

The results of usurping and unnaturally transforming the institution of marriage, as the activists are demanding, would be revolutionary, profound, and far-reaching. Make no mistake, the move toward same-sex "marriage" would fundamentally change the institution of marriage and leave it open for even more changes, such as polygamy or bisexual unions, incorporating three or more partners. "Among the likeliest effects of gay marriage is to take us down a slippery slope to legalize polygamy and polyamory (group marriage)," writes Stanley Kurtz, Senior Fellow at the Hoover Institute. "Marriage will be transformed into a variety of relationship contracts, linking two, three or more individuals...in every conceivable combination of male and female." All of this would fly in the face of what we know about the importance of family structure to children's well-being and to the strength and vitality of the nation.

Beyond the individual concerns, however, looms the possibility that "the establishment of same-sex marriage will contribute to the demise of political liberty."[56] Seana Sugrue, associate professor and chairman of the department of political science at Ave Maria University, argues that institutions of civil society—family, market, and religion—help to limit state power and sustain robust republican governance; thus, those institutions are supportive of political liberty. She elaborates by describing their roles to "socialize and to coordinate people within their distinctive yet overlapping spheres."[57] The state's role, properly understood, is a limited role, and, as the author specifies, it is to "maintain a measure of respectful distance and to uphold their core norms." Thus, when the sexual revolution—including the efforts toward same-sex "marriage"—tears down the buffer of social order between the citizen and the state, it ends up being destructive to political liberty.

Sugrue astutely points out that the outcome of the state overstepping its proper bounds by abusing its sovereign authority will lead to "human misery that the state is not equipped to put right."[58] She notes, "Marriage rooted in procreation and sexual difference is to be replaced by marriage for the gratification of two consenting adults." By dismantling the connection between marriage and family, that assault and its results will have "long-term and far-reaching consequences."[59] The advocates of the same-sex "marriage" movement view their tinkering as a "relatively novel" assault on marriage. It appears that they have no idea about the role of marriage as the central normative and coordinative institution of American culture. Or, perhaps, they do.

While the legal and societal consequences are deeply troubling, the consequences of the further erosion of true marriage will be disastrous—both in the present and the future—for the nation's children. It seems fitting to end this chapter with David Frum's warning: "There is no middle ground on this question. You're either having marriage as we've understood it as an institution, which people enter of their own free will, but are then bound by their choice, or you are having a variety of sequential cohabitations...based on the needs of adults, in which we permit children to be bought and sold."

Michael L. Brown's new book, *A Queer Thing Happened to America*, reports on the "massive societal shifts that have taken place in the last generation" and questions where America will go from here. I conclude this chapter with his advice: "In times like these, when it is easy to be discouraged, we do well to recall the words of Mahatma Gandhi: 'When I despair, I remember that all through history the ways of truth and love have always won.'"[60]

Notes

1. Janice Shaw Crouse, "Marriage doesn't Count; Feds Tabulate Same-Sex Behavior," *Townhall*, March 17, 2011, http://townhall.com/columnists/janiceshawcrouse/2011/03/17/marriage_doesnt_count (accessed October 3, 2011).

2. Anjani Chandra and others, "Sexual Behavior, Sexual Attraction, and Sexual Identity in the United Sates: Data from the 2006-2008 National Survey of Family Growth," *National Health Statistics Reports*, no. 36 (March 3, 2011): http://www.cdc.gov/nchs/data/nhsr/nhsr036.pdf (accessed October 3, 2011).

3. Linda J. Waite and Maggie Gallagher, *The Case for Marriage: Why Married People are Happier, Healthier, and Better Off Financially* (New York: Doubleday, 2000).

4. Ibid., 1.

5. David Blankenhorn, *The Future of Marriage* (New York: Encounter Books, 2009).

6. Ibid., 15.

7. Arthur Goldberg, *Light in the Closet: Torah, Homosexuality and the Power to Change* (Beverly Hills, CA: Red Heifer Press, 2008), 5.

8. Amazon.com, "The Future of Marriage," Editorial Reviews, Product Description, http://www.amazon.com/Future-Marriage-David-Blankenhorn/dp/1594032416/ref=sr_1_1?s=books&ie=UTF8&qid=1303084559&sr=1-1#_(accessed October 3, 2011).

9. Sherif Girgis and others, "What is Marriage?" *Harvard Journal of Law and Public Policy* 34, no. 1 (Winter 2010): 245–87, http://papers.ssrn.com/sol3/papers.cfm?abstract_id=1722155## (accessed October 3, 2011).

10. Ibid., 246.

11. Ibid., 246–47.

12. Ibid., 248.

13. Ibid.

14. Ibid., 249.

15. Susan Brinkmann, "Gay Marriage: Who's Minding the Children?" *Catholic Standard & Times*, May–June, 2004, http://catholiceducation.org/articles/sexuality/ho0090.html (accessed October 3, 2011).
16. Ibid.
17. Ibid.
18. Ibid.
19. Note the official report from NCHS that echoes the findings of numerous think tank and academic studies. Deborah L. Blackwell, "Family Structure and Children's Health in the United States: Findings from the National Health Interview Survey, 2001–2007," *Vital and Health Statistics Series 10*, no. 246 (December 2010): http://www.cdc.gov/nchs/data/series/sr_10/sr10_246.pdf (accessed October 3, 2011).
20. David Frum, "Modern Marriage, Modern Trouble," in *Marriage: Just a Piece of Paper?* ed. Katherine Anderson, Don Browning, and Brian Boyer (Grand Rapids, MI: William B. Eerdmans Publishing, 2002), 359–65.
21. Ibid., 364.
22. G. L. Forward and others, "The Religious Communication Association," *The Journal of Communication and Religion* 31, no. 2 (November 2008), 245–71.
23. Janice Shaw Crouse, "Girls Need a Dad and Boys Need a Mom," *Concerned Women for America*, January 9, 2009, http://www.beverlylahayeinstitute.org/articledisplay.asp?id=16223&department=BLI&categoryid=family&subcategoryid=blifam (accessed October 3, 2011).
24. Robert Knight, "Born or Bred? Science does not Support the Claim that Homosexuality is Genetic," *Concerned Women for America*, 2000, http://www.cwfa.org/images/content/bornorbred.pdf (accessed October 3, 2011).
25. Ibid., 2.
26. Ibid., 13.
27. Scientific Advisory Committee, "What the Research Shows," National Association for Research and Therapy of Homosexuality, *Journal of Human Sexuality* 1 (2009): 1–128.
28. Ibid.
29. Janice Shaw Crouse, "Five Myths about Same-Sex Marriage," *Concerned Women for America*, March 9, 2010, http://www.cwfa.org/articledisplay.asp?id=18578&department=BLI&categoryid=commentary&subcategoryid=blifam (accessed October 3, 2011).
30. Sharon Jayson, "Blankenhorn: A Family Guy with a Cause," *USA Today*, March 14, 2007, http://www.americanvalues.org/html/FUMA.htm (accessed October 3, 2011)
31. Larry R. Ridener, "Pitirim A. Sorokin –– 1889-1968," *Dead Sociologists' Society*, January 26, 2006, http://www.bolender.com/Sociological%20Theory/Sorokin,%20Pitirim%20A/sorokin,_pitirim_a_.htm (accessed October 3, 2011).
32. Ibid.
33. Ibid.
34. Elizabeth Marquardt, "Do Fathers and Mothers Matter?" *Propositions* 3 (April 2011): 7, http://centerforpublicconversation.org/propositions/2011-04.pdf (accessed October 3, 2011).
35. Ibid., 6.

36. Ibid.
37. Brinkmann, "Gay Marriage."
38. Girgis et al., "What is Marriage?"
39. Ibid., 251.
40. Ibid., 252.
41. Ibid., 260.
42. Ibid.
43. Ibid., 264.
44. Stanley Kurtz, "The End of Marriage in Scandinavia: The 'Conservative Case' for Same-Sex Marriage Collapses," *Weekly Standard* 9, no. 20, February 2, 2004, http://www.weeklystandard.com/Content/Public/Articles/000/000/003/660zypwj.asp (accessed October 3, 2011).
45. Peter Sprigg, "Testimony in Opposition to House Bill 5012," *Rhode Island House Judiciary Committee*, February 9, 2011, http://www.frc.org/testimony/peter-sprigg-testifies-before-rhode-island-house-judiciary-committee (accessed October 3, 2011).
46. Ibid.
47. Ibid.
48. Ibid.
49. Ibid.
50. Kurtz, "End of Marriage," 6.
51. Ibid., 2.
52. Ibid., 3.
53. Ibid.
54. Ibid. 6.
55. Marquardt, "Do Fathers and Mothers Matter?" 7.
56. Seana Sugrue, "Soft Despotism and Same-Sex Marriage," in *The Meaning of Marriage: Family, State, Market, & Morals*, ed. Robert P. George and Jean Bethke Elshtain (Dallas, TX: Spence Publishing, 2006), 172–96.
57. Ibid., 174.
58. Ibid.
59. Ibid., 175.
60. Michael L. Brown, *A Queer Thing Happened to America: And What a Long, Strange Trip It's been* (Concord, NC: EqualTime Books, 2011), 597.

9

Legislative and Public Policy Challenges to the Institution of Marriage

Skin color is a benign, nonbehavior characteristic.
Sexual orientation is perhaps the most profound
of human behavioral characteristics.
Comparison of the two is a convenient but invalid argument.
—General Colin Powell, former Secretary of State

Not only is there a war of words being waged in the public arena for the minds and attitudes of the citizenry toward what the definition of marriage should be, but there are also challenges in the courts over the constitutionality of the federal government's support of marriage, as it has traditionally been understood. Those challenges, if successful, would profoundly weaken the social fabric of America and her strength as a nation. Without strong marriages and families to foster moral character, democracy will degenerate, as the founders feared, and our neighborhoods and communities will not be the havens of freedom and liberty we have known. Chuck Donovan of the Washington-based think tank, The Heritage Foundation, put it this way: "Current challenges to the primacy of marriage and family as well-established civil institutions are often premised on the assumption that they will inflict little damage beyond that done by previous changes in law and culture. Those prior experiments, however, bear witness to the unintended consequences of ill-considered changes in public policy."[1]

In this final chapter, we will examine the legislative and policy issues that are most threatening to marriages and families in America.

Defense of Marriage Act (DOMA)

While the federal Defense of Marriage Act (H.R. 3396)—commonly referred to as DOMA—has been law for the past fifteen years and reflects the traditional cultural values America has followed since its founding, the beliefs of the majority regarding marriage are currently under attack by a small, determined, and powerful cadre of homosexual activists and their supporters. This attack has been ongoing for quite some time, and it is not a surprise to lawmakers who have long been walking the line between political correctness, modern culture, and core values.

DOMA was designed to define marriage as "a legal union between one man and one woman for purposes of all federal laws, and provide that states need not recognize a marriage from another state if it is between persons of the same sex."[2] The definition of marriage limits words like spouse, husband, and wife to apply in federal law to the marriage relationship between one man and one woman. Moreover, under DOMA, none of the individual states is required to give "full faith and credit" (acknowledgment) to the actions or laws of any other state that redefines marriage as anything other than the union of a man and a woman.

The attack on marriage via efforts to reverse DOMA reflects an attempt to produce a shift in culture in favor of what is still an alien minority view. The defense of marriage, specifically through the defense of DOMA, is an important effort for both individuals and the nation. The effort to redefine marriage is not simply about giving rights to others; rather, it is about taking rights away from the majority of Americans who are in a traditional marriage and who are mothers and fathers committed to bringing up their children—the next generation of Americans—in a fashion that preserves our Judeo-Christian heritage. What is deeply troubling is that there are many in government—as well as others—who help shape public opinion, yet are determined not to understand that the government has a vested interest in encouraging marriage and the establishment of families in a manner that is proven to best protect and nurture children and, thus, provide for the nation's future. Those who would change our society to suit their prejudices have provoked an intense and heated dispute over these facts. But the reality remains that government, as the instrument invested with the responsibility to preserve the common good, does not have a similarly vested interest in encouraging same-sex relationships, which are high-risk, dysfunctional, and entail consequences that ultimately drain both the national treasury and the nation's social infrastructure.

DOMA has two specific purposes. "The first is to defend the institution of traditional heterosexual marriage. The second is to protect the right of the States to formulate their own public policy regarding the legal recognition of same-sex unions, free from any federal constitutional implications that might attend the recognition by one State of the right for homosexual couples to acquire marriage licenses."[3] DOMA was enacted in 1996 because the state courts in Hawaii seemed on the verge of issuing marriage licenses to same-sex couples, and both lawmakers and citizens were rightly concerned about the negative consequences on federal law as well as on the laws of individual states.[4] It should be noted that the same-sex "marriage" issue did not arise from a groundswell of public support; instead, it came from two members of the Hawaii Supreme Court, who issued an opinion in May 1993 that agreed that there might be merit to the plaintiff's claim of discrimination and then remanded it back to the trial court. This opinion was one that Hawaiian state representative Terrance Tom, chairman of the House Judiciary Committee, declared was "unprecedented in the history of jurisprudence."[5] Since then, there have been numerous "unprecedented" instances of judicial activism for the special-interest homosexual movement that legislated from the bench to foist same-sex "marriage" onto the federal agenda ahead of numerous issues of more pressing concern to citizens.

Since 2009, no state has adopted same-sex "marriage." Currently, according to Chuck Donovan at The Heritage Foundation, "Forty-five states have retained their protections for traditional marriage (Thirty-one of them actually strengthening their laws via voter-approved constitutional amendments)." Maryland unexpectedly voted down a change in their law in March 2011. Illinois and Delaware have passed civil union legislation. Indiana, Iowa, and Minnesota have legislation pending.[6] Thirty-seven states have their own DOMAs, while two more states have strong language that defines marriage as one man and one woman. There are thirty-one states that have constitutional amendments protecting traditional marriage, including the three states (Arizona, California, and Florida) that passed constitutional amendments in November 2008.[7]

DOMA was not simply passed on the whim of a small interest group fighting for traditional marriage on the basis of hate or discrimination. Rather, its proponents were supporting the definition of marriage that has been tradition and practice across the world—the one-man-one-woman definition that has stood the test of time. The legislation passed Congress with a bipartisan majority that encompassed 85 percent of both houses, and joined by a Democratic president who had access to comprehensive reports that detailed the many grounds for DOMA.[8] Clearly, this was not a partisan stab at establishing a special-interest agenda; it was Americans standing for long-established moral teaching and truth, fully understanding the policy implications and the day-to-day ramifications of their strong stance. It was a time-tested policy with no surprising unintended consequences:

> Certainly no legislation can be supposed more wholesome and necessary in the founding of a free, self-governing commonwealth, fit to take rank as one of the coordinate States of the Union, than that which seeks to establish it on the basis of the idea of the family, as consisting in and springing from the union for life of one man and one woman in the holy state of matrimony; the sure foundation of all that is stable and noble in our civilization; the best guaranty of that reverent morality which is the source of all beneficent progress in social and political improvement.[9]

DOMA ensures protection of the traditional family structure, and, thus, the nation's children, civil society, reproduction, and the future of America. Within the legislation, there are four main supports for the government's defense of marriage. They include: (1) advancing the "government's interest in defending and nurturing the institution of traditional, heterosexual marriage," (2) "defending traditional notions of morality," (3) "protecting state sovereignty and democratic self-governance," and (4) "preserving scarce government resources."[10]

The government's "interest in defending and nurturing the institution of traditional, heterosexual marriage" stems from the fact that it has a deep and abiding interest in encouraging responsible procreation and child-rearing. Simply put, government has an interest in marriage because it has an interest in children."[11] Policymakers have judged that it was imperative to keep the institution of marriage in place for the sake of children. Throughout man's history, marriage has been "our most universal social institution found prominently in virtually every known society,"[12] and it has played an irreplaceable role in childbearing and in maintaining the continuity of society from generation to generation. Though many claims are made concerning homosexuals raising children and sperm donation as legitimate ways of family formation, both history and social science research validate traditional heterosexual marriage as the best family structure across cultures and socioeconomic strata.

The second provision of this legislation is the "defense of morality" wherein the law recognizes that heterosexual marriage reflects the sacred aspect of marriage considered imperative by a large majority of people. To overturn this as truth and morality for the sake of a small, select group of people would be a direct assault on the valid convictions of those who believe marriage is a sacrament, a key expression of their religious faith.

DOMA also seeks to protect state sovereignty and democratic self-governance in allowing elected officials to decide matters related to homosexuality as it pertains to the "will of the people" in their respective states. This federal law ensures that no one state can effectually "make decisions" for the remaining states. "It is surely a legitimate purpose of government to take steps to protect the right of the people, acting through their state legislatures, to retain democratic control over the manner in which the States will define the institution of marriage."[13] If this law were not in place, Hawaii would have essentially set a precedent that (by virtue of the principle of interstate comity) would determine law for other states.

Currently, homosexual activists and their wealthy supporters are backing state politicians in order to gain control of legislatures; they are campaigning under the guise of civil rights. We must understand that this discussion is not about discrimination; it is about defending the institution of marriage, which is the "birthplace of liberty" and the foundation of our free society and democratic government. Homosexual activists are not campaigning for the betterment of society, children, or culture; instead, they are determined to undermine traditional values and mainstream their cause. Though arguments and times have changed from decade to decade since the original arguments laid forth in Hawaii fifteen years ago, the facts remain the same. Opposition to traditional marriage, however, has strengthened—gaining intensity, visibility, and support from the media, and even the present occupant of the White House.

Pro-marriage and pro-family forces have also strengthened as the threats have become clearer. The battle lines are now deeply entrenched.

After President Obama's announcement that his administration would abandon the government's defense of DOMA (thereby arrogating to the executive branch the judiciary's role in deciding which laws are and are not constitutional), Rep. Vicky Hartzler (R-MO) introduced a resolution in the House (H.Con.Res.25) that opposes any effort to eliminate DOMA and its protections for state marriage laws and condemns the president's action, calling on him to reverse course.[14]

In addition, the Speaker of the House of Representatives, John Boehner, announced that former Solicitor General Paul Clement would serve as the lead outside counsel in the House's defense of DOMA. Speaker Boehner explained that Mr. Clement would be doing the job the administration refused to do—defending the law before the court. Further, Speaker Boehner endorsed the idea (first proposed by Rep. Steve King) that the Department of Justice budget should be cut by the amount needed to defend DOMA. He said, "I have directed House Counsel and House Administration Committee to assure that sufficient resources and associated expertise, including outside counsel, are available for appropriately defending the federal statute that the Attorney General refuses to defend."[15]

Attorneys for the Alliance Defense Fund (ADF), a Christian legal group, expressed optimism about Clement's appointment. "The American people deserve to have their laws defended," Brian Raum, an ADF attorney, said in a statement. "The House is demonstrating that it will not let a law that it overwhelmingly passed, that President Clinton signed, and that the American people support go undefended."[16] Liberty Counsel, too, praised Clement: "He is a skilled advocate who has argued many times before the United States Supreme Court." Mathew Staver, founder of Liberty Counsel and dean of Liberty University School of Law, commented, "The defense of DOMA is now in better hands than when the Department of Justice was on the case. Rather than weakening the defense of DOMA, President Obama's decision to not defend the law has opened up the opportunity for Paul Clement and his team to provide a real defense."[17]

As the dust was settling from the Clement appointment to represent the Bipartisan Legal Advisory Group of the House of Representatives in its defense of DOMA, his law firm, King & Spalding, came under pressure from homosexual activists and withdrew from their agreement to defend DOMA. Lawyers from both sides of the political divide affirmed Clement's subsequent decision to resign from King & Spalding by saying that he followed the highest professional and ethical tradition and that America's "adversary system depends on vigorous advocates being willing to take on even unpopular positions." Clement wrote:

> I resign out of the firmly held belief that a representation should not be abandoned because the client's legal position is extremely unpopular in certain quarters. Defending unpopular positions is what lawyers do. The adversary system of justice depends on it, especially in cases where the passions run high. Efforts to delegitimize any representation for one side of a legal controversy are a profound threat to the rule of law. Much has been said about being on the wrong side of history. But being on the right or wrong side of history on the merits is a question for the clients. When it comes to lawyers, the surest way to be on the wrong side of history is to abandon a client in the face of hostile criticism.

Afterward, Clement joined a smaller Washington law firm, Bancroft PLLC, and will continue to defend DOMA for the House of Representatives' Bipartisan Legal Advisory Group.

The battle to defend the institution of marriage is moving full speed ahead and gaining momentum rapidly.

Employment Non-Discrimination Act (ENDA)

The *Employment Non-Discrimination Act (ENDA)*—a bill that would prohibit discrimination against employees on the basis of sexual orientation or gender identity by civilian, nonreligious employers with at least fifteen employees—has been around since 1994 with little hope of passing until the Democrats gained control of Congress in 2006. After dropping the requirement in the bill that persons claiming to be transgender be treated as a protected class, the bill passed the House but never passed the Senate. In The Heritage Foundation's *Backgrounder*, Thomas M. Messner wrote, "Individuals who support marriage as the union of husband and wife have strong reasons to be concerned about nondiscrimination proposals like [ENDA]. ENDA would elevate sexual orientation to a protected status under workplace nondiscrimination laws."[18] But the true purpose of ENDA is that "intermediate measures like sexual orientation nondiscrimination laws can 'help bring marriage equality closer.'"[19] Indeed, as Messner points out, such laws have already been used to achieve legal recognition for homosexual unions in several states, even when supposed safeguards are included in the legislation. Gay rights advocates are quite open in declaring the passing of ENDA as an important incremental step in achieving a redefinition of marriage. Further, they argue that small changes will bring about greater public acceptance as a gradual adjustment period will make same-sex "marriage" more acceptable. In short, ENDA is a major milestone along the road toward the ultimate goal of legalizing same-sex "marriage."

With the Democrats still controlling the Senate, ENDA was reintroduced there in April 2011, apparently with the hope that debate on the bill will keep the issue alive and that more supporters will come on board. On the theory that persistently pushing on the issue will eventually cause positive movement, the activists continue to bring the bill forward again and again, keeping their arguments in the media and trying to claim the public's attention. Supporters have gained the endorsement of more than seventy-five Fortune 500 companies, including two huge ones, Nike and Sara Lee. Such corporate support is ironic in that ENDA, in essence, is an infringement on "their right to set their own standards for employment...most large secular employers do not make a practice of inquiring into the sexual practices of their employees in the first place."[20] Peter Sprigg of the Family Research Council points out that most employers are relatively indifferent toward the homosexual behavior of employees "due (apart from a few stereotypes) to an invisible characteristic, and the behavior that defines the class—men having sex with men or women having sex with women—that is something that takes place predominantly in private, not in the workplace or on work hours."[21]

In the last session of Congress, Senators Merkley (D-OR) and Collins (R-ME) introduced ENDA in the Senate, with Representatives Barney Frank (D-4th MA) and Ileana Ros-Lehtinen (R-18th FL) introducing it in the House. Neither bill came to a full floor vote. It has been introduced in every congressional term since 1994 except the 2005–2007 session.

While ENDA supposedly exempts religious organizations and other nonprofits from its strictures, it is obvious from their track record of bringing suit at every possible opportunity that gay activists would challenge those exemptions of ENDA in the courts. Targeted religious and nonprofit organizations would have to defend their exemption at significant costs as well as possible public harassment.

Currently, twenty-three states and the District of Columbia have legislative policies that are aligned in some aspect with ENDA. Five other states have mandated prohibitions about discrimination on the basis of sexual orientation and/or gender identity. Nine other states have such rulings for public employees only. Fifteen states have laws that "have been interpreted to protect transgender persons." Approximately 260 private companies/corporations have embraced "rights and benefits" measures for GLBT (gay, lesbian, bisexual, and transgender) employees. Currently, 85 percent of Fortune 500 companies have nondiscrimination protections covering sexual orientation. Only a third have the same protections regarding gender identity.[22] Gay activists are pushing relentlessly, with persistent force, on every front to achieve their goals.

Robert Knight calls ENDA a "gay quota bill" and describes it as "profoundly dangerous" because it turns "private sin into a public right and brings the force of government against morality itself."[23] Knight adds that ENDA "falsely equates a changeable condition (sexual desire) with race and ethnicity. Worse, it turns traditional values into a form of bigotry punishable under the law."[24]

Any decent person opposes unjust discrimination, but there is "no evidence that homosexuals have unusual difficulty in finding employment, nor that such laws on the local or state levels have improved their economic situation."[25]

Probably the most contentious aspect of this very controversial bill is the special protection that it provides not just for sexual orientation, but also for "gender identity," which means that employers would have to hire transgender persons, whether transvestites (cross dressers) or transsexuals, and would have to put up with whatever attire or behavior the employee chooses for the workplace. ENDA would ensure the "right" for the transgender activists to engage in dress and behavior that is the opposite to their sex as a man or a woman, including their right to use the bathrooms, locker rooms, or showers of the opposite sex.

We are already seeing a push for unisex bathrooms and the so-called "right" of transgender persons to use the restroom of their choice. The Office of Personnel Management (OPM) issued a new federal policy in 2010 that added sexual orientation and gender identity nondiscrimination wording to their employment policies for "potential employees,"[26] a term that is left vague and nonspecific so that anyone can have access to any restroom. Such policies are already in effect in a dozen states, allowing for the potential for predators and pedophiles—an explosive problem just waiting to happen.

Again, opposition to ENDA—legislation that even its supporters claim is a stepping stone to ending traditional marriage—is not about approving discrimination or restricting anyone's human rights or freedoms. Instead, it is in opposition to creating special classes of rights for a small minority and establishing public policies that undermine human rights and religious freedom for the vast majority. In the case of ENDA, opposition is also about the effect it would have in undermining the institution of marriage.

Don't Ask, Don't Tell (DADT)

Enacted in 1993 by the Clinton administration (after extensive hearings and exhaustive debates that included input from the public),[27] the legislation that is popularly called "Don't Ask, Don't Tell" (DADT) prohibited open homosexual activity by those serving in the U.S. military. Kept in place by the Bush Administration, DADT was widely seen as necessary in order to preserve unity, cohesion, and morale among servicemen and women. At the end of 2010 (December 22, 2010), President Obama signed the repeal that had passed both the House and Senate during the 111th Congress during a lame-duck session where opposing views were limited and amendments were not allowed. Many Americans view the repeal as a threat to those members of the military who hold traditional values regarding sexual behavior and marriage. Further, those who value religious liberty and free speech are concerned lest their views pose a risk to their careers and, even their daily life become adversely affected. Chuck Donovan at The Heritage Foundation summarized some of the concerns regarding the effects of the repeal of DADT:

> The freedoms of religion and speech, subject as they are to the special conditions of military service, are nonetheless the heritage and birthright of every American. They are among the unalienable rights our armed forces exist to defend. It would be the height of irony if, in deference to hurriedly adopted policy changes centered around one of the most controversial topics of our time, men and women in uniform were denied the ability to express their views to fellow service members, military leaders, the public, and lawmakers. Service to the nation should never be made contingent on an enforced code of silence about such profound matters of belief and behavior.[28]

There are numerous concerns about DADT in regard to the institution of marriage. The law affects all facets of everyday life for military personnel—from enlisted service members to the chaplains counseling the members, from the teachers on bases working with young children to those in military hospitals. Those individuals who make up the vast majority of service members face the risk of losing their right to express disapproval of homosexual behavior, and they could be cited for discrimination by those individuals whose behavior violates the majority's religious and moral standards. Chaplains could lose the right to perform marriage ceremonies or provide counseling for heterosexual couples unless they are willing to provide similar services for homosexual couples, regardless of the Biblical views held by the chaplain.

In addition to the aforementioned everyday concerns that undermine the principles and factors necessary for a strong military, the repeal of DADT also undermines marriage by setting a social precedent for approval of homosexual behavior within our nation's military. That precedent will allow for further expansions of the boundaries of what is deemed to be permissible and will allow more special-interest "rights" to redefine community standards and morality for the nation. If homosexual behavior is openly allowed in our military—and, thus, deemed acceptable, approvable, normal, and mainstream conduct— homosexual activists will certainly push to see that such behavior is recognized and further validated within our local, state and federal courts, including same-sex "marriage."

This direct onslaught against marriage and traditional gender roles is no sudden surprise in the military structure. Diana West of *The Washington Examiner* wrote, "As sex roles were rewritten to check male dominance and expand the female role, and as women, in effect, were used to destroy the ideal of 'officer and gentleman,' other lines were crossed and blurred."[29] These lines included the ones relating to traditional marriage and homosexuals within the military. As we have continually allowed the lines to blur and the distinctions to be lost, we have seen an erosion of morals and virtue. In allowing these lines to be further blurred with a repeal of DADT, we can expect to watch our nation's security weaken (following the European example) right alongside our nation's morality.

Abstinence versus "Safe Sex" Programs

One of the hottest current public policy issues is the question of whether or not "safe sex" (i.e., condom-based) sex education or abstinence education is best for young people. Many argue that students are going to be sexually active anyway, so it is best to teach them "safe sex." Proponents of "safe sex" have successfully made the case that federal funds should support their programs. As a result, funding for "safe sex" programs is twelve times higher than funding for abstinence programs. Yet, the trends indicate that abstinence programs are far more successful and, thus, are more deserving of federal support as the most effective means of protecting adolescents and young adults and preparing them for successful futures—both personally and professionally.

The data support the abstinence position as the very best for young people's well-being, future success, and later happiness in marriage.[30] The teen pregnancy rate dropped 37 percent over the last two decades and currently is at a seventy-year low. During approximately the same time frame, teen abortions have also declined significantly and are the lowest in more than thirty years, so the decrease in teen pregnancy is not from increased abortions. Research studies indicate that the drop cannot be attributed to increased contraceptive use, either, because teen sexual activity has dropped as well. Peer-reviewed research studies report that teens in abstinence education programs are significantly less likely to be sexually active than their peers.[31]

While "sex education" proponents and those who benefit financially from teen sexual activity would like to cite other reasons and downplay the influence of more widespread support for the benefits of abstinence and for the abstinence message among young people, the data clearly indicate that the abstinence message is getting through to many of today's youth. Our teens are more aware of the variety and prevalence of sexually transmitted diseases, the harms of promiscuity, and the disruption that an unplanned pregnancy brings to a teen's life—in spite of Planned Parenthood and MTV's attempts to normalize the consequences of and profit from increased teen sexual activity.

Parents overwhelmingly (over 90 percent) want their children to get a strong message from school and society that they should not have sex until they are at least out of high school. This message has been consistent in every survey conducted by the National Campaign to Prevent Teen Pregnancy since 1997. A Zogby International poll indicated that 79 percent of parents wanted their teens and young adults to be taught not to engage in sexual activity until they are married or in an adult relationship leading to marriage. About 68 percent of parents want their kids to be taught that those who wait till marriage to have sex have the best chance for stable and happy marriages.

The benefits of abstinence education are obvious, both for the adolescent and for society. Those benefits include higher educational attainment and stronger marriages, which, in turn, produce higher standards of living and convey greater levels of sexual satisfaction and increased lifespan. It just makes sense: delaying sexual activity until marriage has the potential to improve life, increase finances, and create more stable marriages. Supporting abstinence programs for young people is, simply stated, good public policy that results in greater individual and societal well-being.

Proposition 8—California

In 2008, citizens of California and other Americans who wanted to preserve the institution of marriage thought that the issue of same-sex "marriage" was settled. After a hard-fought battle, voters passed the Proposition 8 (Prop. 8) ballot initiative, by a comfortable margin; that measure mandated the use of the traditional definition of marriage in California. Then, in a surprising unilateral move in August 2010, U.S. District Judge Vaughn Walker—himself a homosexual—ruled that California's Prop. 8 ballot initiative was unconstitutional. So, one self-identified practicing homosexual judge declared by judicial fiat that Californians had a constitutional "right" to marry regardless of whether the intended marriage partner is of the same or opposite sex.

Now, Prop. 8 is tied up in court (the next steps are the Ninth Circuit Court and, likely, the Supreme Court) and the nation has a "textbook example of judicial activism."[32] Worse, Judge Walker repudiated the votes of millions of Californians who worked for months and then went to the polls to vote for traditional marriage. Like forty-five other states, California debated the issue and its citizens voted to preserve the institution of marriage as the union of one man and one woman. In this democratic nation, one judge cannot be allowed to overrule the results of an election.[33] The people spoke and the courts must back the voters' right to protect marriage. A small, special-interest group is determined to push every lever possible to impose its values on the rest of the nation, regardless of vote outcomes. Prop. 8 is another in a continuous series of assaults against traditional marriage, and it is one of countless attempts to impose the will of the minority (a very, very small sliver of the population) on the majority. Such actions cannot stand.

Taxpayer Funding for Abortion

The Centers for Disease Control and Prevention (CDC) reports that one in five of the U.S. women who obtain abortions are married[34]; their reasons vary from not wanting the adverse effects on their careers to the pregnancy being the result on an extramarital affair. One study found that in 44 percent of instances, the husband instigated the abortion[35] because of finances or wanting the wife's extra income for luxury items. Ironically, nearly half (46 percent) of abortive women report that the abortion precipitated a major crisis in the marriage, and that in a quarter of the cases, the couple attributed their breakup to the abortion.[36] Teri Reisser, director of services at the Right to Life League of Southern California, explained the relationship of abortion to marriage in this way:

> A family is an organized structure. Any event in any part of the system affects the rest of the system. Every experience within the system belongs to the system. When a woman is given the legal right to act independently in pregnancy resolution, the sacred concept of "we-ness" is negatively impacted in the most severe manner. When a husband coerces an abortion decision, the family cohesion is also seriously challenged. Instead of the family being a powerful and effective problem-solving unit, an individual now acts in an autonomous manner, jeopardizing the stability of the whole system. The roles of father, mother, husband, wife, and parent are summarily suspended as one person makes the unilateral life and death decision.[37]

Another factor linking abortion and marriage is the increasing number of men who are unwilling to make a commitment to a woman with whom they are having sex—which feeds into today's trend of decline in the number of marriages (with a parallel increase in cohabitation and promiscuity). Obviously, as more and more men are unwilling to actually father their children, it falls to taxpayers to "pick up the slack," which contributes to pressure from some quarters for taxpayers to fund abortions.

Some men, however, still see things from what might be called an "old-fashioned" perspective. Here is one young man's assessment of what is required for true manhood:

> This is why catch phrases such as "pro-choice" are heralded by many men with such ferocity because "pro-choice" to them doesn't just mean the woman's right...it also means they are "pro-choice" in regards to whether or not they have to stick around and care for the offspring they fathered. One of my friends who regularly pickets abortion clinics has informed me that we would be shocked to see how many sobbing girls are pushed into abortion clinics by their angry boyfriends and fathers. Perhaps more women would stop being "pro-choice"...if the fathers of these children would stop being "pro-choice" about actually shouldering their responsibilities, as has been the tradition of true manhood in the past.[38]

ObamaCare

The President's health care reform bill (commonly called "ObamaCare")—which the Democratic Party rammed through Congress in the most partisan fashion possible in total disregard for the opposition of the majority of Americans—has brought the public policy debate over taxpayer-funded abortions to the boiling point.

The House of Representatives voted overwhelmingly for an amendment to ObamaCare to ban funding abortion. With the capitulation of several formerly pro-life Democrats, the final bill (which ultimately passed) was stripped of the amendment banning taxpayer-funded abortions because President Obama promised that he would sign an executive order banning abortion funding. Shortly afterward, the Congressional Research Service confirmed that, indeed, as pro-lifers had confidently said was fact before the bill passed, the president's executive order *does not* prevent taxpayer-funded abortions. The outrage was led by 67 percent of all women and 50 percent of self-identified Democratic women who opposed taxpayer-funded abortions. Currently, only 35 percent of the American public supports the president's signature legislation.

Scrambling to take back the initiative and under political pressure to do something, President Obama issued a temporary ban that he declared would "neither expand nor scale back current restrictions on federal funding for abortion." Representatives Chris Smith (R-New Jersey) and Dan Lipinski (D-Illinois) offered a bipartisan amendment to make the ban permanent. The "No Taxpayer Funding for Abortion Act" solidifies existing, annual bans—including the Hyde amendment—and conscience protections for health care providers, and it bars taxpayer funding of abortions in other countries. The goal of the Smith-Lipinski bill is to uphold current laws and make the ban against taxpayer-funded abortion permanent. Obviously, this issue, which is closely linked to the preservation and strengthening of marriage, is very much alive.

Planned Parenthood

The debate over federal funding for Planned Parenthood,[39] the nation's largest abortion provider, remains heated. Planned Parenthood's latest annual report notes that they received a record $363 million from government grants and other taxpayer funds in 2008–2009. They set another record that year by performing over 324,000 abortions, giving Planned Parenthood the largest share in the abortion industry. As Congressman Mike Pence (R-Indiana) said, "The largest abortion provider in America should not also be the largest recipient of federal funding under Title X."

Planned Parenthood's carefully crafted (and perfidiously disingenuous) public relations campaigns—which emphasize their informational and educational programs as well as their "health services"—are intended to keep the public from focusing on the fact that Planned Parenthood is the nation's largest surgical abortion provider. Its annual report makes it quite clear to its supporters that, as previously stated, it performed 324,008 abortions during its 2008–2009 fiscal year. That number is its largest total number of abortions on record. It is instructive to observe what the record $363 million in government grants enables the organization to do. In 2006–2007, Planned Parenthood's annual report revealed that the group performed 289,570 abortions throughout its 860 locations, an *increase* that year of nearly 25,000 abortions—and 2008–2009, as we saw, is even worse. These dramatic increases have occurred at the same time that the number of abortions throughout the country decreased overall.

While Planned Parenthood claims that no federal money goes toward abortions, such claims are more than a bit disingenuous. While that statement may be true in some accounting sense, it hides the reality that the claim is nothing more than a bookkeeping allocation—federal funds applied to overhead costs, etc., free up other money to enable the organization to profit from the abortions that it performs. Mark Crutcher, of Life Dynamics, explained to One News Now, "[W]e're giving [Planned Parenthood] approximately $42,000 an hour, 24 hours a day, 7 days a week, 52 weeks a year." Crutcher added, "This is a cash cow for [Planned Parenthood]; they're lined up at the federal trough."

Welfare and Entitlement Reform

When Congress reformed the welfare system in 1996, it acknowledged the importance of married-couple families by stipulating that the Temporary Assistance for Needy Families (TANF) program would either directly or indirectly promote healthy marriages. Such redirection of our welfare policy is imperative because more than thirty years of experience in an "entitlement culture" had proven to be disastrous for marriage and families. The legislation that authorized the TANF program mandates that the Department of Health and Human Services (HHS) pursues the goal of "encouraging the formation and maintenance of two-parent families." To that end, HHS operates a "Healthy Marriage Initiative" in the Administration for Children and Families. HHS also funds programs that teach abstinence until marriage and emphasize its unique benefits in producing the best life outcomes.

After "welfare as we know it" (Aid to Families with Dependent Children—AFDC) was replaced by TANF, the number of welfare recipients declined by almost two-thirds (falling from 4.8 million families with 9.0 million children in 1995 to 1.7 million families with 3.0 million children in 2008). The decline was primarily due to two provisions: (1) recipients had to work, and (2) recipients had a time limit for receiving government support. In other words, the overarching philosophy became "welfare is a temporary safety net until you get back on your feet" instead of an entitlement where "government became the father of the family."

Gradually, recipients—with the encouragement and guidance of welfare advocates and sympathetic bureaucrats—found ways around the work and time limit requirements so that "government handouts now make up a record-breaking one third of the total amount of wages and salaries in the U.S."[40] Worse, while the rate of poverty declined for the first ten years after TANF was implemented, there are "more poor persons today than ever." What happened was that at the same time the economy was adding millions of jobs, cultural and demographic factors were at work to increase the number of poor people. First, the number of persons living in female-headed households rose by 2.6 million and, second, the number of unrelated individuals rose by 4.1 million from 2003 to 2007. It is precisely this demographic undertow that negated the effects of the recovery on the poverty rate.[41]

There are two numbers that really "frame the issue." In a roundtable discussion, "Back from the Brink: New Hope for Both Marriage and Divorce," Bruce Peterson said, "By the time their children are age five, 42 percent of unmarried parents have no contact with each other. That's after 82 percent were either cohabiting or romantically involved at the time of birth."[42] Peterson's point is that if couples miss the "magic moment" for marriage, the path toward single motherhood and, probably, poverty, is set. Given the financial difficulties that unmarried mothers face in trying to raise a family—their poverty rate is four to five times that of other families, it is no surprise that during the period from 2003 to 2007, three-quarters of the 1.4 million increase in the number of poor persons (that kept poverty from declining) are accounted for by the growth in the number of poor persons in those female-headed households and, the rest, by growth in poor unrelated individuals. It is worth noting that the poverty rate would have actually increased more had there not been a decrease of 240,000 in the number of poor persons living in all other types of families (i.e., those not having a female head of household).[43]

With the economy mired in recession since 2007, the number of unemployed—plus those who have left the labor force—has increased sharply, particularly among males. With the loss of over six million jobs from 2007 to 2009, plus the continuing cultural and demographic undertow, the number of poor persons has jumped dramatically in all categories. The economy will eventually recover, but cultural and demographic changes make the challenge of combating poverty daunting due to the continuing growth in the high-poverty sectors of the population (i.e., unmarried mothers and unrelated individuals).

The question, then, is: What accounts for growth in the segment of the population that remains unmarried and economically isolated? David Gelertner provides an answer in his review of Martin Amis' *The Pregnant Widow* in *The Weekly Standard*.[44] The change in women's attitudes about sex took their opening position from "no, unless I love you" to "yes, unless I don't like you." The conventional wisdom these days is: "Non-marital sexual relations are inevitable given that young people delay marriage in favor of getting an education and becoming established in a career. Besides, biology being what it is, men can hardly be expected to marry when female sexual partners are readily available without the accompanying responsibilities of marriage." Moreover, there is a never-ending stream of novels and movies these days celebrating the unmarried pregnant women who choose to go it alone, independent of the biological fathers. Hence, it is no surprise that nonmarital births now comprise 41 percent of all births, which feed the growth in the number of economically vulnerable single mothers.

Perhaps the nation's financial crisis will prompt reformations in extravagant welfare spending and cuts in the more than seventy means-tested wealth-distribution handouts. The formula the Republican Congress adopted in 1996 worked, but it was effectively repealed by President Obama's enormous increase in stimulus spending.

Many are still demanding that the economic safety net be strengthened. Critics, like me, contend that this is the wrong approach. Resources should be focused on jobs programs that will bring the poor to the point of self-sufficiency; making poverty more tolerable in the welfare hammock only increases the problem. Given the growing body of research—much of it summarized in my book, *Children at Risk*—showing the adverse effects on children of growing up in fatherless homes, plus the billions upon billions in taxpayer costs, the need for a more extensive economic safety net is debatable. However, the need to strengthen marriage and the moral safety net to protect women and children is indisputable.

No-Fault Divorce

In 2010, New York became the fiftieth state to adopt a no-fault divorce policy. Ironically, the no-fault divorce policy is more controversial now than ever before, even though it is also one of the rare issues where there is uniformity among state policies. Some experts claim that no-fault divorce has led to higher divorce rates; others claim that the partner filing for divorce "holds all the cards" with the one left behind at a disadvantage and, sometimes, not even initially informed about the split. Those supporting no-fault divorce argue that the old system was cut throat, leading to bitter confrontations and ugly divorce battles; some partners, they claim, even committed perjury in order to get the divorce. Even with no-fault divorce, however, there are often still very bitter court battles and heated arguments between the divorcing couple about the financial and custody settlement issues.

The first no-fault divorce state was California in 1969, and by 1985, all states except New York had passed some form of no-fault divorce law. Now, even New York has capitulated. Such laws simply mean that couples can get divorced without having to prove there was wrong doing or abuse. In New York before no-fault divorce, a couple wanting to dissolve the marriage without one or the other "at fault" had to live separately for at least a year. Now, a divorce is possible after only six months apart if a couple claims the marriage is "irretrievably" broken. While some lawyers chafe at the requirement for the couple to agree that the marriage is "irretrievable," others argue that the "innocent party" in a no-fault divorce is disadvantaged under the new system when he or she sometimes does not want the divorce but has no power to stop it or get fair treatment under the law. One critic asked, "How is no-fault divorce any different from saying, "I divorce you three times?"[45]

In an unusual development, The National Organization for Women joined with the New York State Catholic Conference to try to prevent no-fault divorce from passing in New York. They argued that no-fault divorce has proven to be harmful to women and children especially, but also harmed all of society. They were also concerned that no-fault divorce proceedings enabled judges to ignore any abuse within marriages and allowed husbands to hide their assets and cheat wives and children of their fair financial support. They did not mention a finding of a study from the University of Texas that only one-third of divorced couples agreed that the spouses had done enough to try to save their marriage.[46] Counselors have found that couples who learn how to work their way through their problems when they are on the verge of divorce end up with happier marriages five years later than they had before they faced their seemingly insurmountable problems.[47]

Furthermore, far too many divorces are the result of a life crisis the couple is going through, like unemployment, an illness, or an unfortunate affair during a midlife crisis. In fact, the majority of divorces of couples with minor children involve marriages that fell apart over a recently short period of time. Research shows that two-thirds of couples getting divorced were reasonably happy two years before the divorce and only one-third were in long-term, high-conflict situations.[48] There might be a connection to the fact that the couples driving the divorce rate are the less educated, which tends to be a self-perpetuating trend. Among women who married in 1990, only 16.5 percent of college-educated women were divorced ten years later, but 46 percent of the women who dropped out of high school were later divorced.[49] In a five-year counseling project with ninety-eight unmarried urban couples who wanted to stabilize their relationship, the counselor found that the couples had no role models for staying together and working through their relationship. For uneducated, low-income couples, "we have several generations that have not seen a functional, stable, lasting marriage."[50]

Plus, there really is such a thing as a divorce "epidemic." Social Norming Theory suggests that as divorce becomes more common in a social network, it gets to be the norm. Social network research suggests that an average person has a network of 20 people, and it is reciprocal. Thus, if 20 people each have a network of 20 people, an individual divorce will influence 400 people. Typically, they will be those with less education and less income, and, therefore, less able to handle the divorce and protect their children from the financial ramifications.[51]

Two renowned marriage experts, David Usher and Michael McManus, evaluated no-fault divorce laws and blamed them for many of the negative cultural trends of today: "No-fault divorce laws were a mistake that encouraged marital irresponsibility, resulting in a 50-percent divorce rate, a 51-percent decline in marriages since 1970, a sixteenfold hike in cohabitation and an 800-percent increase in out-of-wedlock births."[52]

Elizabeth Marquardt, an expert on divorce in America, does not believe there are any "good" divorces. Her book, *Between Two Worlds*— which reported her findings from surveys of 1,500 people ages eighteen to thirty-five who were among the one million American children every year who experience their parents divorce—describes the "inner lives" of children of divorce. While difficulties in the outer life of children of divorce are easily observable—"shuffling between two homes and having to adjust to step-parents and new siblings"—Marquardt argues that divorce "radically hurts" children in their inner lives much more, even when parents do all they can to make it easier.[53] Research backs up Marquardt's claims that children of divorce are more likely to suffer depression, have health problems, be victims of childhood sexual abuse, be arrested, and become addicted.

In her book, *The Unexpected Legacy of Divorce: A 25-Year Landmark Study*, Judith Wallerstein documents the long-term effects of divorce. Beginning in 1971, she periodically conducted in-depth interviews with 131 children and their parents from the time of divorce. "We've seriously underestimated the long-term impact of divorce on children, [and]...the numerous ways a child's experiences differ when growing up in a divorced family."[54]

The growing mountain of information about the negative impact of divorce hits hard at the increased ease of getting a divorce. The combination of falling marriage rates and rising divorce rates doubled the ratio of divorces to marriages from 1960 to 1979, raising the ratio to slightly over fifty divorces per one hundred marriages. Since marriage rates have declined parallel to the decline in the divorce rate since 1979, the trend in the ratio of divorces per one hundred marriages for the last twenty years remains at that fifty per one hundred figure.[55] Certainly, the social experiment of no-fault divorce and the elimination of waiting periods have helped to keep the divorce rates at such an unacceptable level.

As is evident from this chapter's brief overview of the various social issues confronting children and families in our nation, the institution of marriage is being battered by attacks from many different directions, which are undermining its strength and vitality as an institution of civil society. Clearly, marriage matters, but although it remains idealized to a degree in the culture (with most people expressing a desire to be married at some point), it is becoming less normative and more vulnerable as an institution. As one critic put it: "It's seen as a symbol of middle-class achievement and personal fulfillment rather than an instrument of social stability, and often comes without the familial and communal support offered past generations."[56]

Notes

1. Chuck Donovan, "Marriage, Parentage, and the Constitution of the Family," Heritage Foundation, *WebMemo*, no. 2783 (January 27, 2010): http://www.heritage.org/Research/Reports/2010/01/Marriage-Parentage-and-the-Constitution-of-the-Family (accessed October 4, 2011).
2. Comm. on the Judiciary, Defense of Marriage Act of 1996, H.R. Rep. No. 104-664, at 2 (1996), http://www.gpo.gov/fdsys/pkg/CRPT-104hrpt664/pdf/CRPT-104hrpt664.pdf (accessed October 4, 2011).
3. Ibid.
4. Ibid.
5. Defense of Marriage Act of 1996: Hearing on H.R. 3396, May 15, 1996, *Before the Subcommittee on the Constitution of the House Committee on the Judiciary*, 104th Cong., 2d sess. (1996): 53 (prepared statement of Terrance Tom, Member and Chairman of Judiciary Committee, Hawaii House of Representatives), http://www.access.gpo.gov/congress/house/pdf/104hrg/25728.pdf (accessed October 4, 2011).
6. Chuck Donovan, "Marriage Gets a Defense in Court," *The Foundry* (blog), The Heritage Foundation, April 19, 2011, http://blog.heritage.org/2011/04/19/marriage-gets-a-defense-in-court/ (accessed October 4, 2011).
7. "Doma Watch: Your Legal Source for Defense of Marriage Acts Information," *Alliance Defense Fund*, http://www.domawatch.org/index.php (accessed April 23, 2011).
8. Chuck Donovan, "Cinderella Congress: Marriage is Worth a Real Fight," *The Foundry* (blog), The Heritage Foundation, July 23, 2010, http://blog.heritage.org/2010/07/23/cinderella-congress-marriage-is-worth-a-real-fight/ (accessed October 4, 2011).
9. Comm. on the Judiciary, Defense of Marriage Act of 1996, H.R. Rep. No. 104-664, at 12.
10. Ibid., 2.
11. Ibid.
12. Ibid.
13. Ibid.
14. House Congressional Resolution 25, 112th Cong., 1st sess. (March 31, 2011): http://www.opencongress.org/bill/112-hc25/show (accessed October 4, 2011).
15. House Speaker John Boehner, "Boehner Says DOJ Funds should be Cut to Pay for DOMA Defense; Asks Leader Pelosi to Join in Supporting

Redirection of Funds," press release, Office of Speaker of the House, U.S. House of Representatives, April 18, 2011, http://www.speaker.gov/News/ DocumentSingle.aspx?DocumentID=237431 (accessed October 4, 2011).

16. Alliance Defense Fund, "Alliance Alert," April 20, 2011, http://www. alliancealert.org/2011/04/20/baptist-press-house-chooses-high-profile-attorney-to-defend-doma/ (accessed April 23, 2011).

17. Liberty Counsel, "Defense of Marriage Act Gets Boost from U.S. House Legal Counsel," press release, April 20, 2011, http://www.lc.org/index. cfm?PID=14100&PRID=1057 (accessed October 4, 2011).

18. Thomas M. Messner, "ENDA and the Path to Same-Sex Marriage," *Backgrounder*, no. 2317, The Heritage Foundation, September 18, 2009, http://www. heritage.org/Research/Reports/2009/09/ENDA-and-the-Path-to-Same-Sex-Marriage?query=ENDA+and+the+Path+to+Same-Sex+Marriage (accessed October 4, 2011).

19. Ibid.

20. Peter Sprigg, "ENDA Sanity?" *The Washington Times*, May 11, 2010, http:// www.washingtontimes.com/news/2010/may/11/enda-sanity/ (accessed October 4, 2011).

21. Ibid.

22. Michelle Garcia, "A Bipartisan Attempt at ENDA," *Advocate.Com*, April 15, 2011, http://www.advocate.com/News/Daily_News/2011/04/14/A_ Bipartisan_Attempt_at_ENDA/ (accessed April 19, 2011).

23. Robert Knight, "The Undeclared War to ENDA Our Liberty," *World Net Daily*, August 11, 2009, http://www.wnd.com/index.php?pageId=106530 (accessed October 4, 2011).

24. Ibid.

25. Sprigg, "ENDA Sanity?"

26. Donna Miller, "Social Security Shocker: Men in Women's Bathrooms?" *Concerned Women for America*, April 6, 2010, http://www.cwfa.org/content. asp?id=18712 (accessed October 4, 2011).

27. Elaine Donnelly, "Legislative History of the Law Regarding Homosexuals in the Military," *The Center for Military Readiness*, August 22, 2008, http:// www.cmrlink.org/HMilitary.asp?docID=336 (accessed October 4, 2011).

28. Charles A. Donovan, "A Clash of Integrities: Moral and Religious Liberty in the Armed Forces," *Backgrounder*, no. 2540, The Heritage Foundation, April 5, 2011, 2, http://thf_media.s3.amazonaws.com/2011/pdf/bg2540. pdf (accessed October 4, 2011).

29. Diana West, "Officers and Gentlemen No More Thanks to Activists," *The Washington Examiner*, January 2011, http://washingtonexaminer. com/opinion/columnists/2011/01/diana-west-officers-and-gentlemen-no-more-thanks-activists (accessed October 4, 2011).

30. Melissa Pardue, "More Evidence of the Effectiveness of Abstinence Education Programs," *WebMemo*, no. 738, The Heritage Foundation, May 5, 2005, http://www.heritage.org/Research/Welfare/wm738.cfm (accessed October 4, 2011).

31. Janice Shaw Crouse, "Teen Birth Rates Decrease: Are Real Consequences Having Read Effects?" *Concerned Women Blog, Concerned Women for America*, April 7, 2011, http://www.cwalac.org/cwblog/ (accessed October 4, 2011).

32. J. Matt Barber, "If the Judge ain't Straight You Must Vacate," *Christian Law Journal* (blog), April 15, 2011, http://www.christianlawjournal.com/blog/if-the-judge-aint-straight-you-must-vacate/ (accessed October 4, 2011).

33. The Heritage Foundation, "Prop 8 Reversal: Extreme Judicial Activism on Marriage," *Opposing Views: Issues, Experts, Answers*, August 4, 2010, http://www.opposingviews.com/i/prop-8-reversal-extreme-judicial-activism-on-marriage (accessed October 4, 2011).

34. "Abortion Surveillance: Preliminary Data United States 1991," *Morbidity and Mortality Weekly Report* 43, no. 3 (January 28, 1994): 42, http://www.ncbi.nlm.nih.gov/pubmed/8283964 (accessed October 4, 2011).

35. F. Lieh-Mak and others, "Husbands of Abortion Applicants: A Comparison with Husbands of Women who Complete Their Pregnancies," *Social Psychiatry* 14, no. 2 (1979): 59.

36. Teri Reisser, "The Effects of Abortion on Marriage and Other Committed Relationships," *Association for Interdisciplinary Research in Values and Social Change* 6, no. 4 (1994): found at LifeIssues.net, http://www.lifeissues.net/writers/air/air_vol6no4_1994.html (accessed October 4, 2011).

37. Ibid.

38. Jonathon Arie Van Maren, "Letters to the Editor: Where are all the Men?" *LifeSiteNews*, April 21, 2011, http://www.lifesitenews.com/news/letters-to-the-Editor45?utm_source=LifeSiteNews.com+Daily+Newsletter&utm_campaign=c6cd3ada2f-LifeSiteNews_com_Intl_Headlines04_21_2011&utm_medium=email (accessed October 4, 2011).

39. The information in this whole section comes from: Janice Shaw Crouse, "Cutting the Cord: The Case for Defunding Planned Parenthood," *Concerned Women for America*, February 2011, http://www.cwfa.org/images/content/cwfa_cuttingthecord_2011.pdf (accessed October 4, 2011).

40. David Gardner, "Welfare Nation: Government Handouts Make up One Third of America's Salaries and Wages," *Daily Mail* (UK), March 9, 2011, http://www.dailymail.co.uk/news/article-1364450/US-welfare-nation-Government-handouts-make-ONE-THIRD-salaries.html (accessed October 4, 2011).

41. Janice Shaw Crouse, "Sex, Poverty and Recession," *The Washington Times*, September 24, 2010, http://www.washingtontimes.com/news/2010/sep/24/sex-poverty-and-recession (accessed October 4, 2011).

42. William J. Doherty and others, "Back from the Brink: New Hope for Both Marriage and Divorce," *Center of the American Experiment*, April 2011, http://www.amexp.org/sites/default/files/article_pdf/Back%20from%20the%20Brink%20Web.pdf (accessed October 4, 2011).

43. Crouse, "Sex, Poverty and Recession."

44. David Gelernter, "Dead in the Water: The Age of Irony won't Grow up," *The Weekly Standard* 15, no. 44 (August 9, 2010): http://www.weeklystandard.com/articles/dead-water (accessed October 4, 2011).

45. Beverly Willett, "No Fault Divorce? Maybe Yogi was Right," *Huffington Post*, March 16, 2011, http://www.huffingtonpost.com/beverly-willett/post_1822_b_836052.html (accessed October 4, 2011).

46. Donovan, "Marriage, Parentage, and the Constitution of the Family."

47. For instance, Joshuas Coleman, *Imperfect Harmony: How to Stay Married for the Sake of Your Children and Still be Happy* (New York: St. Martin's Press, 2003).

48. Doherty et al., "Back from the Brink."

49. Stephen P. Martin, "Trends in Marital Dissolution by Women's Education in the United States," *Demographic Research* 15, no. 20 (2006): 546, Table 1, http://www.demographic-research.org/Volumes/Vol15/20/ (accessed February 16, 2009).

50. Doherty et al., "Back from the Brink."

51. Ibid.

52. David Usher and Michael McManus, "10 'Marriage Values' Policies to Rebuild America," *WorldNetDaily*, September 18, 2011, http://www.wnd.com/index.php?fa=PAGE.printable&pageId=165185 (accessed October 4, 2011).

53. Jane Eisner, "No 'Good Divorce:' A Review of Elizabeth Marquardt's *Between Two Worlds*," *Philadelphia Inquirer*, October 27, 2005, http://betweentwoworlds.org/comments/?page_id=46 (accessed October 4, 2011).

54. Judith Wallerstein and others, *The Unexpected Legacy of Divorce: A 25 Year Landmark Study* (New York: Hyperion Books, 2000), xxvii–xxviii.

55. Computations of the ratio are by the author from the number of marriages and estimated number of divorces. Marriage data are from: Eldridge and Sutton, "Births, Marriages, Divorces, and Deaths: Provisional Data for December 2006" and earlier reports, National Center for Health Statistics, http://www.cdc.gov/nchs/products/pubs/pubd/nvsr/nvsr/htm#TA (accessed February 16, 2009). Divorce data are from Tejada and Sutton, "Births, Marriages, Divorces, and Deaths: Provisional Data for 2007," and earlier reports, http://www.cdc.gov/nchs/data/nvsr/nvsr56/nvsr56_21.htm#56 (accessed February 16, 2009). Note: The last national estimate of the number of divorces by NCHS was for 1998; from that time forward, the author has estimated the number of divorces assuming the divorce rates NCHS has computed for those states, which continue reporting, is a reasonable estimate of the national rate, including the six nonreporting states.

56. Eisner, "No 'Good Divorce.'"

10

Conclusion

When we defend the family, we do not mean it is always a peaceful family; when we maintain the thesis of marriage we do not mean that it is always a happy marriage. We mean that it is the theatre of the spiritual drama, the place where things happen, especially the things that matter.

—G. K. Chesterton, The Home of the Unities

I wrote this book to provide perspectives on both the private and the public importance of marriage. To do that, this book examines the historic trends that are so troubling to those of us who are immersed in the social science research that tracks the decline of marriage and the breakdown of the family.

In Part I, this book lays out the groundwork necessary for strong marriages. I argue that so-called "sexual freedom" has usurped the appropriate role of love and romance in relationships between a special girl and her particular guy. I make the case for bringing back dating as the best way for couples to get to know each other in casual circumstances before taking steps to make the relationship more serious. I argue that dating provides excellent "practice" for mastering the social skills that are necessary as an adult for success in both private and professional circles.

Part II is a serious treatise of sex; first, its centrality in marriage, and then, the harms that are so often the consequence of casual, recreational sex—STDs and/or HIV/AIDS are the most obvious risks, but the breakdown of pair-bonding and the cheapening and coarsening of male–female relationships are equally disastrous results of uncommitted sexual hookups.

Part III examines the impact of marriage on the private sector, specifically the benefits for individual adults and, especially, for children.

Part IV analyzes the impact of marriage on the public sector by exposing the ramifications of same-sex "marriage" and summarizing the issues associated with the plethora of legislative and public policy initiatives that are linked inextricably to the marriage and family issues.

After several decades of changes that undermined marriage, there are public policymakers and opinion leaders who are taking courageous stands to promote stable marriages and discourage out-of-wedlock births. At the same time that numerous good things are happening in the public arena, other relationship and household structures are becoming more acceptable alternatives to marriage. While the trends can be dismaying, experience with "marriage lite" alternatives is caus-ing more and more young people to see the benefits of marriage—not just as a personal choice, but also as a solution for many of society's problems.

Surprisingly, one of the ramifications of the decline in marriage is widespread loneliness[1]; it seems that an environment of "carefree" sex leaves couples feeling pretty empty and alone. The National Sci-ence Foundation (NSF) reported in its General Social Survey (GSS) that unprecedented numbers of Americans are lonely.[2] Published in the *American Sociological Review* (ASR) and authored by Miller McPhearson, Lynn Smith-Lovin, and Matthew Brashears, sociologists at Duke and the University of Arizona, the study featured 1,500 face-to-face interviews, where more than a quarter of the respondents—one in four—said that they had no one with whom they could talk about their personal troubles or triumphs. If family members were not counted, the number doubled to more than half of Americans who had no one outside their immediate families with whom they could share confidences. Sadly, the researchers noted increases in "social isolation" and "a very significant decrease in social connection to close friends and family." Rarely has news from an academic paper struck such a responsive nerve with the general public.

These dramatic statistics from ASR parallel similar trends re-ported by the Beverly LaHaye Institute—that over the forty years from 1960 to 2000, the Census Bureau had expanded its analysis of what had been a minor category.[3] The Census Bureau categorizes the term "unrelated individuals" to designate someone who does not live in a "family group." Sadly, we have seen the percentage of persons living as "unrelated individuals" almost triple, increas-ing from 6 to 16 percent of all people during the last forty years. A huge majority of those classified as "unrelated individuals" (about 70 percent) lived alone.

Many single women have given up on the idea of lasting love, turning instead to impersonal, casual sex to satisfy their physical desires and depending on the "sisterhood" to meet their emotional needs. Many of them believe, as did the 2003 Golden Globe Award winner for best supporting actress in a television series, Kim Cattrall, who said, "Remember, women: Men come and go, but girlfriends last forever."[4] But even in the "sowing-your-wild-oats" scripts popularized by *Sex and the City, Friends,* and other arbiters of cultural chic, the freedom of casual sex frequently looks more like loneliness and alienation. Indeed, in the eyes of some, the shows reflect the hunger for intimacy more than the desire for independence.

The compelling findings about loneliness and isolation—and the ramifications for American society—prompted numerous publications and talk shows to focus on the prevalence of loneliness in America. It is no accident that the social interaction trend declined sharply in the mid-1960s, when "doing your own thing" became vogue and "sexual freedom" separated the physical act of sex from the embrace of an emotional attachment and/or a romantic relationship. Rabbi Daniel Lapin suggests that "we are raising a generation of children who are orphans in time."[5] He laments that today's generation of young people are "incapable of integrating their past and their future...[living] instinctively in an almost animal-like fashion only in the present." He notes that it is virtually impossible, then, to connect time and space in a way that enables them to build their "present." Thus, they wander aimlessly about without connections—physically, emotionally, or spiritually.

If you search deeply into the fine print in the GSS study, you can find the "actual scientific evidence" that certain qualities in a home made people happy.[6] A homebuilder used that information to construct a very appealing advertisement. They noted, of course, that surroundings are important and that certain design elements (theirs!) can improve health, well-being, and mood. But the one thing that the GSS study found—and that Rouse Chamberlin Homes used in its advertisement—is the capacity for social interaction, which "packs a big emotional wallop" in a home. Socializing is such a key factor in happiness that the NSF's study found that above wealth, work, or health, it is family relationships that make people happiest. With marriage declining and more people living alone—in cohabiting relationships or in single-parent situations, not much homemaking or "nest-building" is taking place. The declining willingness to make a marriage commitment increasingly strains the family, the "linchpin" that holds a society together. Is it any wonder that people are lonely and feel isolated when the opportunities for meaningful socialization are increasingly limited and unfulfilling?

Rather than acknowledging family breakdown, some commentators blame television for the increase in social isolation. In his book, *Bowling Alone*, Robert Putnam[7] cited a dramatic increase in television viewership—5 percent of American households had televisions in 1950 compared with 95 percent in 1970. The pervasiveness of television in family life is remarkable. Many homes have a TV in every room. Putnam provides further reasons for the fragmentation of the family circle and disintegration of family life since the 1960s, including the fact that families have 60 percent fewer family picnics and 40 percent fewer family dinners.

Other analysts see longer work days and longer commutes as sources of isolation. *The Washington Post* estimated that for every ten-minute increase in commuting time, there is a 10-percent decrease in time spent establishing and maintaining social ties.[8] The number of people who indicated that they had a neighbor in whom they could confide has dropped more than half since 1985—from around 19 percent to about 8 percent. As both the work week and commutes have extended, those who would ordinarily have taken the lead in developing and maintaining social structures—the well-educated and higher-earning people—are no longer available to mobilize efforts that build communities. Even the clergy are feeling the effects of social isolation in their personal lives. A Barna report reveals that 60 percent of pastors admit that they "have few close friends."[9]

In short, with the growth of two-career and single-parent families, people have lost connection with neighbors and have little time or energy for groups or volunteerism. With the growth in "bedroom communities," there are not enough moms available for field trips and community service projects that largely depend upon volunteerism. One of the most frequent complaints of home-schooling moms is that they are the only adults in their neighborhoods during the daytime.

In an era of instant communication via cell phone and e-mail, some would argue that it does not make sense that people are lonely.[10] Nevertheless, sharing—the antidote to loneliness—is not the same thing as talking. Chattering with another person can simply be a mask, a veil, a barrier, a poor substitute, and a distraction from loneliness, similar to having the television on in the background to keep the house from seeming empty and barren—or to make it less obvious that the people inside are not interacting with each other.

People from a faith perspective lament the loss of compassion in interpersonal interactions. Previous generations, they report, were steeped in Scriptural truths that compelled them to compassion: "Love thy neighbor as thyself." "Bear ye one another's burdens." These admonitions are opposite values to the predominant "me-centeredness" and self-sufficiency of today's culture. Those principles, of course, are both unknown and irrelevant to an increasingly unchurched population.

While sharing may be thought of as an event that takes place at a particular time, in a particular place, and in a particular manner, it springs forth from a set of attitudes and values rooted in the timeless Scriptures. The Scriptures provide a clear understanding of the big-picture issues that bear on our loneliness. They teach that human beings are driven by two distinct sets of impulses: our higher nature and our lower, sinful nature. Experience, as well, clearly illustrates that trustworthy friends are rare. Ask Caesar about his friend Brutus. Relatives, too, are not always reliable. Ask Abel about his brother Cain. While the technology available for communicating has changed, human propensities have not.

Sharing flourishes when those who are interacting are driven by their higher nature to trust each other and have the capacity for affection and empathy. But trust requires mutual respect and caring, as well as insight and understanding. Perhaps, more importantly, trust—and thereby, sharing—involves the indispensable ingredient of vulnerability, a quality sadly lacking when excessive self-reliance and self-sufficiency rule the day.

Indeed, a spirit of independence can be a barrier that impedes sharing. Aloofness is the opposite of all of the favorable ingredients necessary for camaraderie. Likewise, pride—the desire to be viewed as a "winner" and the determination to be "in control" at all costs—is a quality that isolates us from each other and keeps us from attaining interdependency with our families and friends.

Finally, the secular humanist view—namely, that human existence is disconnected from any higher power and from responsibility for anyone other than ourselves—gives a certain freedom to make one's own rules, but there is a price to pay for this freedom. Gone is human dignity. Gone is mankind's special connection to the Author of beauty, truth, and goodness. Ultimately, we are "free"; but autonomy is just another way to be alone. Autonomous individuals have no responsibility for others, just as others have no claim on them. There is no obligation to care about others' troubles, or even to listen when someone intrudes into another's priceless personal space in search of a sympathetic soul to whom they can voice their concerns and difficulties.

In the best of circumstances, sharing is not simple; it is a complex combination of conflicting factors. On the one hand, we have an innate need to be known and understood; the desire to be open and vulnerable with others is too strong in some and too weak in others. On the other hand, we need the freedom to control our lives and, particularly, our personal or emotional space. But, the self-centeredness that results from a culture dominated by the values of radical individualism is not a pretty thing; it does not contribute to the maturing of individuals, the strengthening of family, the growth of friendship, or the development of communities. As a song, "Let's Talk About Me" may be good for a laugh, but that attitude does not work as a way of life.

Those familiar with the creation story in Scripture know that when God viewed all that He had made, He pronounced it to be good[11]—except, of course, when He looked at Adam and said, "It is not good that man should be alone." Today's intelligentsia dismisses the story as a myth and regards the truth it expresses about the natural order of things as irrelevant. For many of them, traditional marriage is passé. From the academics in the university to the actors in Hollywood, those who are shaping popular culture today are pushing a self-destructive, "me-first" lifestyle. These opinion leaders gloss over the selfishness of the choices they promote and glamorize decisions about drugs and sex that ultimately scar the lives of those young people who follow their lead. "It's all good" is their mantra, except that marriage is not seen as "good."

Marriage, say the feminists, has always been about male domination of women, not about two people learning what it means to respect and value each other. According to the feminist view, marriage only degrades and oppresses women. But is that actually the case? What if the give and take of marriage—so necessary for two persons, usually opposite in many respects, to get along—is, in fact, a positive teacher? In the results of the current recession, we have a ready-made experiment by which to examine this question.

When the economy goes into recession, businesses (especially small ones) must make severe adjustments in order to survive. Among the things they do as sales decline is reduce their work force to lower production. Experienced personnel, however, are a valuable asset to a company, so managers try to hold on to their most productive workers where possible; often, this is done by giving them maintenance work to do that has been deferred during boom periods. And who gets the pink slip? Obviously, the least productive and/or the most difficult to manage get weeded out. The data for 2009 are very clear about which class of workers has the highest likelihood of ending up unemployed. Unmarried males—whether or not they have children—are twice as likely to become unemployed, and the same holds for unmarried females with children.

The unemployment rate for married men 25–54 years of age without children was 7.1 percent versus 14.5 percent for unmarried men of the same age group without children. If we look at this same age group for men with children, the comparison shows 6.7 percent unemployment for married men versus 14.8 percent for unmarried men. Clearly, marriage produces men who, on average, are more valued by businesses trying to survive during this recession.

But does marriage do anything for women in the business world? Although the current recession has been harder on men than women, the effects of marriage on women's employability are similar to those for men. The unemployment rate in 2009 for married women 25–54 without children was 5.4 percent, and for unmarried women without children it was 7.5 percent. In this same age group, the unemployment rate of married women with children was 5.2 percent, compared with an 11.8 percent rate for unmarried women with children.

It is unlikely that business managers looking to make it through tough times choose persons on the basis of whether or not they are married. So why do we see consistently higher unemployment rates for unmarried men and women alike (controlling for both age and presence of children)? There can be little doubt that managers choose to retain those who have a set of traits and attitudes—commitment, loyalty, perseverance, resilience, etc.—that marriage can help develop and that, in turn, help sustain a marriage.

Now, it goes without saying—there are good marriages and there are bad marriages, depending upon the values and virtues of the persons involved. But marriage does provide a framework with a tremendous potential and incentive for learning how to work together. Being unmarried may let you "have it your way," but a "my-way-or-the-highway" attitude does not pay off on the job, where the ability to compromise and get along are just as essential to smooth operations as they are to marriage. It appears as if the creation story may have had it right all along: "It is not good for man [or woman] to be alone."

At a very basic level, people know this; moreover, they have a pressing, inherent need for love and romance—in essence, they long for marriage. Commentators have been stymied by the popularity of television reality series like *The Bachelor, The Bachelorette*, and *Joe Millionaire*. Feminists claim that these programs degrade women. The problem is that they do not remember the story of Cinderella. These programs, however crass, are all about fairytales and the haunting echoes of romance. Those who have criticized the programs have not listened carefully to what participants say. Anticipating her "prize"—a single date, rather than a group date, with the bachelor—one woman said, "This is a magical moment." Another dreamily sighed, "I see the house, the white picket fence."

Kim Cattrall, of *Sex and the City*, played a character who embodied the quest of millions of single women today who are not finding an adequate substitute for a diamond ring and a wedding date—not from supposedly forever-loyal girlfriends or from hip, witty, gay male pals with exquisite taste in shoes. Tellingly, many of those women are searching for a soul mate with the intensity of the newly converted. *The Washington Post* recently reported that the latest "meet" market for upwardly mobile singles is the personal ad section of Harvard University's alumni magazine. Some women are paying up to $125 per hour for a professional writer to craft their personal description, hoping to catch the attention of Mr. Right.

Today's Cinderella, lured by "get mine, get yours" slogans, keeps waking up beside yet another fake prince, only to find she has not become a princess. She wonders about her "freedom" and what it is exactly that she gained, and at what cost. She feels merely sullied, with a distinct taste of ashes in her mouth. With her dreams a swirl of soot under her feet, she may come up with crude new slang to mask her pain and emptiness. But, driven by the imprint God placed in our nature, her heart longs to hear the age-old Song of Songs: *My beloved is mine, and I am his.*

Only if you close your eyes can you avoid seeing that there is a longing in the heart of virtually all of us for someone permanent who will accept us unconditionally and love us wholeheartedly, always and forever. And there is an emptiness in children that can only be filled by a mom and a dad who are absolutely crazy about them and are "there" for them consistently, always and forever. Furthermore, there is a desperate need in our communities—especially in our inner cities and minority areas—for the stabilizing influence of married-couple families as anchors that will hold the community's ship of state steady when it faces the howling winds of change, crisis, and unpredictable events. Marriage matters in all of those circumstances—it is both a personal relationship and a social institution of society. Both functions are essential for an individual's happiness and well-being—and for the effective functioning and stability of neighborhoods, communities, and the nation. This two-pronged vision of marriage is an ideal to be promoted and embodied in public policies.

As the conclusion to this book, I propose a conceptual ethic for public policy.

First, for marriage to continue to matter to the couples who make their vows and the families that they establish, public policies need to embrace the view that marriage is a sacred covenant that is rooted in Judeo-Christian moral principles and values of mutuality, respect, sacrifice for others and subordination of individual desires to the needs of the broader common good of the family, as especially "in the sight of God." Part of the disintegration of marriage and family can be explained by the acceptance of the view that marriage is solely a matter of personal fulfillment rather than seeing it in the broader context of its role in and contribution to social stability and obedience to divine purpose. Further, as the private sexual relationships of couples are disengaged from marital vows, the relationships lack the "blessing of God" and the family and community support that marriages typically sought in past generations.[12] Those seeking to strengthen and rebuild the institution of marriage need to approach the task recognizing the values-based dimension of marriage (See the sex pyramid in Chapter 4: The Centrality of Sex.) As marriage has been stripped of its moral foundations and dependence upon God's "unmerited favor," there has been no basis for defending the institution, nor is there a model for developing public policies friendly to its preservation.

Second, marriage needs to, once again, be viewed as a life-long, binding contract. The old joke about "murder, yes; divorce, no" has some merit, in the sense that couples feel an obligation to work together to build a relationship, continuing to care about each other during the difficult times knowing that they are building toward the future and that problems can and will be resolved if both partners are willing to give in, respect each other, and work together toward mutual goals. The concept of commitment and an attitude of "till death do us part" is a vision that couples need to embrace anew so that they will work toward interdependence and companionship as their love deepens.

No one, of course, should subject themselves or their children to brutality and abuse or possible fatal STD because of the unfaithfulness of a spouse; but otherwise, the marriage vow should be inviolate. If each knows that he or she can count on the other, they can face each day's challenges knowing that whatever trouble lies before them can be overcome if they work together.

Third, the benefits of marriage—financial stability, individual well-being, a haven for children's development and wellness, and its role in social stability—should be trumpeted loudly enough that professionals in the field of marriage and family, activists, social science researchers and academicians, as well as policymakers who work at legislative and executive levels, will have the "authority" that they need to promote marriage and family. There are numerous ways that outside forces can help strengthen marriage—both at the micro level of maintaining couples' relationships and at the macro level of helping couples and others understand the importance of marriages and families in strengthening communities and the nation. Training is important in life skills, communication, problem-solving skills, and conflict-resolution—as well as in practical matters like effective decision-making and establishing good habits, behavior modification, and evaluating options and choices.

Fourth, corporations, media moguls and others in positions of public influence need to be enlisted to help promote policies at the community and corporate levels that are marriage- and family-friendly. Corporations can also be encouraged to finance research and projects that will enhance and strengthen marriages and families. Companies should be encouraged to follow the example of corporations like Chick-fil-A that have a retreat center for employees as well as community and religious leaders, enabling them to spend time away from the daily grind to renew their own marriages and to learn and be inspired to be effective motivators in their spheres of influence. It will take an army of corporate, legislative, bureaucratic, academic, and religious "stakeholders" to turn society back toward a healthy attitude regarding marriage and family.

Those "in the know" recognize that promoting and strengthening marriage and the family are challenges that are in the national interest, and are, thus, appropriate and legitimate public policy issues. But the need for reform goes much deeper than either the personal or the public policy dimensions. Marriage is anchored in the spiritual dimension, and it is obvious that the institution has not fared well separated from the view of marriage as "a holy estate" that is "instituted by God."

Interestingly, I completed the first stage of the editing process for this book on the wedding eve of Prince William and Catherine "Kate" Middleton. More than two billion people around the globe watched the ceremony on April 29, 2011—whether live or via various media channels. Such a massive turnout was, perhaps, an indication that people still hold marriage in esteem and that the dream of love and romance culminating in a marriage of grand passion and lasting endurance still prevails in spite of the attacks that marriage has undergone in recent decades. This grand event, which came on the heels of my preoccupation for more than two years with the issues related to declining marriage and family breakdown, I was moved anew. I was moved by reading the words of the chosen hymns [*Guide me, O thou great redeemer and Love divine, all loves excelling*] and by the text of the traditional ceremony; by the solemnity and sacredness of the marriage ceremony and by the importance—no, the necessity—that such a ceremony marks for couples and those in their circle of family, friends, and associates; and, finally, by the threshold they cross when they give their bodies as well as their hearts into the keeping of one another. How fitting it was to be reminded that marriage—Holy Matrimony—takes place "in the sight of God" and that marriage is "adorned" by Christ and "beautified by His presence." How appropriate it was to hear that marriage is not to be entered into "unadvisedly, lightly or wantonly; but reverently, discreetly, soberly and in the fear of God, duly considering the causes for which Matrimony was ordained."

The historical wedding ceremony gives three unambiguous reasons for marriage: First, so that children can be "brought up in the fear and nurture of the Lord"; second, so that the "natural instincts and affections, implanted by God, should be allowed and directed aright...in pureness of living"; third, so that it will benefit the "mutual society" in that the couple will have each other for "help and comfort" in both "prosperity and adversity." While there is no mention of the community and national involvement in a couple's wedding, the fact that it is a public ceremony makes it clear that a wedding is more than just a private affair. As this book makes clear, it is not only those who personally know and love the couple that have a vested interest in the success of such marriages. It is also, collectively, *all of us.*

If this book helps in any way to bring back a right and proper perspective on marriage, it will have fulfilled my vision, goals, and hopes in writing it.

Notes

1. Note: In response to critics who tried to disprove the original findings, the authors published an update in 2009 that did not substantially change the original study's conclusions. This paragraph reflects their updated findings.
2. "Sociologists Debate: Are Americans Really Isolated?" press release, *American Sociological Review* (ASR), August 4, 2009, http://www.asanet.org/press/20090804.cfm (accessed October 3, 2011).
3. Janice Shaw Crouse, "Who Says Marriage is Obsolete?" *The American Spectator*, October 1, 2010, http://spectator.org/archives/2010/10/01/who-says-marriage-is-obsolete/ (accessed October 3, 2011).
4. Janice Shaw Crouse, "Get Mine, Get Yours," *Christianity Today*, May 1, 2003, http://www.christianitytoday.com/ct/2003/may/32.67.html (accessed October 3, 2011).
5. Rabbi Daniel Lapin, "The Role of Marriage in Transmitting Values between Generations," *The Family in the New Millennium, Vol. 2*, ed. A. Scott Loveless and Thomas B. Holman (Westport, CT: Praeger Perspectives, 2007), 127.
6. "Is Your Home a Happy Home?" *Rouse Chamberlin Homes* (advertisement), May 10, 2010, http://rousechamberlinblog.com/tag/national-science-foundation-general-social-survey/ (accessed October 3, 2011).
7. Robert D. Putnam, *Bowling Alone: The Collapse and Revival of American Community* (New York: Simon and Shuster, 2000), 221.
8. "Why You should Live in a Walkable Neighborhood," *SmartMove.org*, August 16, 2009, http://www.movesmart.org/guides/title/why-you-should-live-walkable-neighborhood (accessed October 3, 2011).
9. George Barna, "Pastors Feel Confident in Ministry, but Many Struggle in their Interaction with Others," *The Barna Report*, July 10, 2006, http://www.barna.org/leadership-articles/150-pastors-feel-confident-in-ministry-but-many-struggle-in-their-interaction-with-others (accessed October 3, 2011).
10. This section is from an article by Janice Shaw Crouse, "Why are More Americans Lonely Today?" *Human Events*, July 13, 2006, http://www.humanevents.com/article.php?print=yes&id=15987 (accessed October 3, 2011).
11. Crouse, "Who Says Marriage is Obsolete?"
12. Jane Eisner, Review of Elizabeth Marquardt's *Between Two Worlds: No Good Divorce*, *Philadelphia Inquirer*, October 27, 2005.

Appendix

Articles by Janice Shaw Crouse on Marriage

3/15/2011 "Marriage Doesn't Count; Feds Tabulate Same-Sex Behavior" http://www.cwfa.org/articledisplay.asp?id=20037&department=BLI &categoryid=dotcommentary&subcategoryid=blifam

3/17/2011 Townhall: http://townhall.com/columnists/janiceshawcrouse/ 2011/03/17/marriage_doesnt_count

2/25/2011 "President Obama Won't Protect Marriage" http://www.cwfa. org/articledisplay.asp?id=19964&department=BLI&categoryid= dotcommentary&subcategoryid=blifam

2/25/2011 American Spectator: "Obama Abandons Marriage" http:// spectator.org/archives/2011/02/25/obama-abandons-marriage

1/4/2011 "The 'Bad' Bachelor: A Cautionary Tale for Today's Young Adults" http://www.cwfa.org/articledisplay.asp?id=19785&department=BLI &categoryid=commentary&subcategoryid=blifam

1/4/2011 Townhall: http://townhall.com/columnists/janiceshawcrouse/ 2011/01/04/the_bad_bachelor_a_cautionary_tale_for_todays_ young_adults

11/19/2010 "Popping the New Question: 'Will You Live With Me?'" http://www.cwfa.org/articledisplay.asp?id=19680&department=BLI &categoryid=dotcommentary&subcategoryid=blifam

11/22/2010 Townhall: "Is Cohabitation the Modern Version of Marriage?" http://townhall.com/columnists/janiceshawcrouse/2010/11/22/ is_cohabitation_the_modern_version_of_marriage

11/17/2010 "Can Marriage Recover from the Assault of Radical Individualism?" http://www.cwfa.org/articledisplay.asp?id=19657& department=BLI&categoryid=datadigest&subcategoryid=blifam

11/17/2010 American Thinker blog Graph of the Day: http://www.amer-icanthinker.com/blog/2010/11/graph_for_the_day_for_november_ 2.html

10/19/2010 "Welfare Reform: The Argument" American Thinker's Graph of the Day: http://www.americanthinker.com/blog/2010/10/graph_ for_the_day_october_19_2.html

8/17/2010 "Who Needs Torrid?" http://www.cwfa.org/articledisplay. asp?id=19336&department=BLI&categoryid=dotcommentary&subc ategoryid=blifam

8/16/2010 Townhall: http://townhall.com/columnists/janiceshawcrouse/2010/08/16/who_needs_torrid

7/29/2010 "Clinton Wedding Raises Questions of Interfaith Marriage" http://www.cwfa.org/articledisplay.asp?id=19229&department=BLI&categoryid=dotcommentary&subcategoryid=blifam

7/28/2010 Townhall: http://townhall.com/columnists/janiceshawcrouse/2010/07/28/clinton_wedding_raises_questions_of_interfaith_marriage

6/11/2010 "'Put a ring on it': Marriage beats cohabitation in quest for happiness" http://www.cwfa.org/articledisplay.asp?id=19050&department=BLI&categoryid=reports&subcategoryid=blifam

6/10/2010 The Washington Times: http://www.washingtontimes.com/news/2010/jun/10/put-a-ring-on-it/

5/21/2010 "Obamacare: Payback Time for All the Single Ladies" http://www.cwfa.org/articledisplay.asp?id=18949&department=BLI&categoryid=commentary&subcategoryid=blifam

5/21/2010 Townhall: http://townhall.com/columnists/janiceshawcrouse/2010/05/21/obamacare_payback_time_for_all_the_single_ladies

3/9/2010 "Five Myths About Same Sex Marriage" http://www.cwfa.org/articledisplay.asp?id=18578&department=BLI&categoryid=commentary&subcategoryid=blifam

3/9/2010 Townhall: http://townhall.com/columnists/janiceshawcrouse/2010/03/09/five_myths_about_same_sex_marriage

2/3/2010 "Now, Pew Says, Marriage is a Better Deal for Men than Women" http://www.cwfa.org/articledisplay.asp?id=18385&department=BLI&categoryid=reports&subcategoryid=blifam

1/30/2010 American Thinker: http://www.americanthinker.com/2010/01/now_pew_says_marriage_is_a_bet.html

1/4/2010 "Stress and Marital Happiness" http://www.cwfa.org/article-display.asp?id=18222&department=BLI&categoryid=dotcommentary&subcategoryid=blifam

12/19/2009 American Thinker: http://www.americanthinker.com/2009/12/stress_and_marital_happiness.html

12/8/2009 "Of Marathons and Marriages" http://www.cwfa.org/article-display.asp?id=18092&department=BLI&categoryid=commentary&subcategoryid=blifam

12/5/2009 American Thinker: http://www.americanthinker.com/2009/12/of_marathons_and_marriage.html

11/20/2009 American Thinker: "Marriage Versus the Obama/Pelosi Nanny State" http://www.americanthinker.com/2009/11/marriage_versus_the_obamapelos.html

12/4/2009 Townhall: "Marriage vs. The Nanny State" http://townhall.com/columnists/janiceshawcrouse/2009/12/04/marriage_vs_the_nanny_state

11/15/2009 American Thinker: "The Differences Between Marriage and Cohabitation" http://www.americanthinker.com/2009/11/the_differences_between_marria.html

9/15/2009 "Being Sexually Deprived in a Sex-Saturated Culture" http://www.cwfa.org/articledisplay.asp?id=17719&department=BLI&categoryid=dotcommentary&subcategoryid=blifam

9/12/2009 American Thinker: http://www.americanthinker.com/2009/09/being_sexually_deprived_in_a_s.html

7/2/2009 Townhall: "Who Cares About a Politician's Affair?" http://townhall.com/columnists/janiceshawcrouse/2009/07/02/who_cares_about_a_politician%E2%80%99s_affair

6/19/2009 "Being a Daddy's Girl" http://www.cwfa.org/articledisplay.asp?id=17189&department=BLI&categoryid=commentary&subcategoryid=blifam

6/21/2009 Townhall: http://townhall.com/columnists/janiceshawcrouse/2009/06/21/being_a_daddy%E2%80%99s_girl

4/6/2009 "Reflections on Marriage" http://www.cwfa.org/articledisplay.asp?id=16784&department=BLI&categoryid=dotcommentary&subcategoryid=blifam

4/6/2009 Townhall: "Seeing Marriage Through the Trees" http://townhall.com/columnists/janiceshawcrouse/2009/04/06/seeing_marriage_through_the_trees

4/5/2008 American Thinker: http://www.americanthinker.com/2008/04/reflections_on_marriage.html

3/6/2009 "California Supreme Court Considers Proposition 8" http://www.cwfa.org/articledisplay.asp?id=16546&department=BLI&categoryid=commentary&subcategoryid=blifam

1/9/2009 "Girls Need a Dad and Boys Need a Mom" http://www.cwfa.org/articledisplay.asp?id=16223&department=BLI&categoryid=family&subcategoryid=blifam

1/5/2009 Townhall: http://townhall.com/columnists/janiceshawcrouse/2009/01/05/girls_need_a_dad_and_boys_need_a_mom

11/7/2008 "Marriage Unites as Politics Divides the Nation" http://www.cwfa.org/articledisplay.asp?id=15996&department=BLI&categoryid=dotcommentary&subcategoryid=blifam

11/7/2008 Townhall: http://townhall.com/columnists/janiceshawcrouse/2008/11/07/marriage_unites_as_politics_divides_the_nation

10/17/2008 Townhall: "Will Californians Reject the Sacredness of Marriage?" http://townhall.com/columnists/janiceshawcrouse/2008/10/ 17/will_californians_reject_the_sacredness_of_marriage

9/26/2007 "Married Today, Gone Tomorrow" http://www.cwfa.org/articledisplay.asp?id=13896&department=BLI&categoryid=dotcommentary&subcategoryid=blifam

9/27/2007 Townhall: http://townhall.com/columnists/janiceshawcrouse/2007/09/27/married_today,_gone_tomorrow

8/2/2007 "How To Make Your Honeymoon A Success" http://www.cwfa.org/articledisplay.asp?id=13546&department=BLI&categoryid=dotcommentary&subcategoryid=blifam

8/1/2007 Townhall: http://townhall.com/columnists/janiceshawcrouse/2007/08/01/how_to_make_your_honeymoon_a_success

7/3/2007 "Kids and Marriage No Longer Inseparable" http://www.cwfa.
org/articledisplay.asp?id=13384&department=BLI&categoryid=dot
commentary&subcategoryid=blifam

7/3/2007 Townhall: http://townhall.com/columnists/janiceshawcrouse/
2007/07/03/kids_and_marriage_no_longer_inseparable

6/20/2007 "Marriage Lessons from Ruth Graham" http://www.cwfa.org/
articledisplay.asp?id=13214&department=BLI&categoryid=dotcom
mentary&subcategoryid=blifam

6/20/2007 Townhall: http://townhall.com/columnists/janiceshawcrouse/
2007/06/20/marriage_lessons_from_ruth_graham

6/19/2007 "With All the Lamps Still Blazing" http://www.cwfa.org/
articledisplay.asp?id=13205&department=BLI&categoryid=dotcom
mentary&subcategoryid=blifam

6/19/2007 Townhall: http://townhall.com/columnists/janiceshawcrouse/
2007/06/19/with_all_the_lamps_still_blazing

6/7/2007 "The Problems of Pre-Term and Low Birth Weight Babies"
http://www.cwfa.org/articledisplay.asp?id=13087&department=BLI
&categoryid=dotcommentary&subcategoryid=blifem

2/6/2007 "Hanging on to Hubby" http://www.cwfa.org/articledisplay.
asp?id=12300&department=BLI&categoryid=dotcommentary&sub
categoryid=blifam

2/7/2007 Townhall: http://townhall.com/columnists/janiceshawcrouse/
2007/02/07/hangin%E2%80%99_on_to_hubby

4/3/2007 "Washington's Working Women" http://www.cwfa.org/
articledisplay.asp?id=12712&department=BLI&categoryid=dotcom
mentary&subcategoryid=blifem

4/12/2007 Townhall: http://townhall.com/columnists/janiceshawcrouse/
2007/04/03/washington%E2%80%99s_working_women

3/6/2007 "The Child Bride: Assaulting the Innocent" http://www.cwfa.
org/articledisplay.asp?id=12498&department=BLI&categoryid=
reports&subcategoryid=bliun

3/7/2007 Townhall: http://townhall.com/columnists/janiceshawcrouse/
2007/03/07/the_child_bride_assaulting_the_innocent

2/15/2007 "In Praise of Virginity" http://www.cwfa.org/articledisplay.
asp?id=12348&department=BLI&categoryid=dotcommentary&sub
categoryid=blicul

2/15/2007 Townhall: http://townhall.com/columnists/janiceshawcrouse/
2007/02/15/in_praise_of_virginity

12/14/2006 "America Faces a Popeye Moment" http://www.cwfa.org/
articledisplay.asp?id=12005&department=BLI&categoryid=dotcom
mentary&subcategoryid=blifam

12/13/2006 Townhall: http://townhall.com/columnists/janiceshaw-
crouse/2006/12/13/america_faces_a_popeye_moment

12/7/2006 "Mary Cheney's pregnancy affects us all" (Townhall) http://
townhall.com/columnists/janiceshawcrouse/2006/12/07/mary_
cheneys_pregnancy_affects_us_all

11/1/2006 "The Girls Who Loved the Greatest Generation Guys" http:// www.cwfa.org/articledisplay.asp?id=11725&department=BLI&categ oryid=dotcommentary&subcategoryid=blifam

11/1/2006 Townhall: http://townhall.com/columnists/janiceshaw-crouse/2006/11/01/the_girls_who_loved_the_greatest_generation_ guys

10/19/2006 "Marriage Is Not Dead: With a Little TLC, It Will Be Fine!" http://www.cwfa.org/articledisplay.asp?id=11657&department=BLI &categoryid=dotcommentary&subcategoryid=blifam

8/30/2006 "Belonging to the Beloved" http://www.cwfa.org/articledis-play.asp?id=11433&department=BLI&categoryid=dotcommentary& subcategoryid=blifam

7/24/2006 "The Inherent Vulnerability of Motherhood" http://www. beverlylahayeinstitute.org/images/content/inherentvulnerability.pdf

Index

ABC, 5

Abortion, 47–48, 52, 55–56, 58, 78, 99, 109, 147, 151, 173, 194–198
  "pro-choice," 196
  "pro-life," 197

Abuse, 83, 95–96, 120, 175, 201–202
  of Children, 142–144, 203, 218
  Domestic, 119
  Drug and alcohol abuse, 5, 105, 123, 127, 129
  Sexual, 136, 203
  Verbal, 47

Adams, Abigail, 46

Adams, John, 7, 46

Addiction, 50, 70–71, 96, 103–105, 143, 150, 203

Administration for Children and Families, 199

Adolescence, 3, 55–56, 80, 101, 153, 167–168, 194

Adoption, 52, 149, 174, 177

Advertisements, 1, 94, 100, 149, 211

Affection, 213

Aggression, 120, 127

AIDS, 99–100, 103–105, 209

Aid to Families with Dependent Children (AFDC), *see welfare*, 199

Allen, Charlotte, 46–47

Alliance Defense Fund (ADF), 188

Amato, Paul, 5

Americans, 5, 9–10, 25, 33, 65, 70, 99, 125, 131, 139–140, 144, 165, 178, 184, 186, 192, 195, 197, 210

American Dilemma Revisited, An: Race Relations in a Changing World, 126

American Idol, 59

American Journal of Preventive Medicine, 47

American Psychological Association (APA), 169–170

American Sociological Association (ASA), 171

American Sociological Review (ASR), 210

Amis, Martin, 200

Amsterdam, 10

Anderson, Ryan T., 163, 175

Androgyny, 78, 98

Aniston, Jennifer, 40

ANP news agency, 65

Anxiety, 50, 71–72, 95

Aristotle, 53

Arizona, 185, 210

Arlington National Cemetery, 115

Assurance, 27, 83, 91, 109, 117, 166–167

Atlantic, The, 65, 69

Attitude, 10, 22, 33, 40, 48–49, 56, 70, 73, 81–83, 89–90, 92, 94, 96, 105, 120–121, 124, 140, 148–149, 161, 166–167, 183, 200, 213–215, 217–218

Attraction, 3, 22, 35, 68, 74, 101, 162

Ave Maria University, 179

Baby Boomers, 53, 129

Bachelor, The, see TV shows

Bachelorette, The, see TV shows

"Back from the Brink: New Hope for Both Marriage and Divorce," 199

Backgrounder, 189

PLLC, Bancroft, 189

Barna, 212

Becker, Gary, 5, 10

Beltway, 74

Bennett, Jessica, 89

Bergalis, Kimberly, 103

Berne, Eric, 77

Betrayal, 35, 76, 106–107
Between Two Worlds, 203
Beverly LaHaye Institute, 141, 210
"Beyond the Glory," 151
Bible, 27
    Adam, 214
    Abel, 213
    Cain, 213
    Genesis, 27
    Isaac, 27, 29
    Jacob, 26, 29
    John 3:16, 75
    Joseph, 29
    New Testament, 75
    Rachael, 29
    Rahab, 29
    Rebekah, 27, 29
    Ruth, 29
    Sarah, 29
    Scriptures, 19, 21, 32, 35, 51, 75,
        213–214
    Song of Songs, 216
    Tamar, 29
Bigamy, 172
"Big Bird," 148
Biller, Henry, 164
Bill of Rights, 172
Biology, 81, 200
    Biological clock, 109
Bipartisan Legal Advisory Group,
    188–189
"Birds and bees," 81
Birth, 28–29, 49, 55–56, 66, 78, 93, 101,
    122, 140, 150–152, 172, 178, 199–200,
    203, 210
    Birth control, see contraception
    Teen Birth, 47–48, 55–56, 102, 151
"Birthplace of liberty," 187
Bishop, Jim, 41
Blankenhorn, David, 162–163, 170
Boehner, John, 188
Bogle, Kathleen, 58
Bonner, Dr. Florence B., 126
Bork, Judge Robert H., 145
"born gay," 168–169
    "Born or Bred?," 169
Boston Globe, The, 9
Bourdieu, Pierre, 148
Bowling Alone, 212
Boyfriend, 24, 39, 59, 77, 108–109, 120,
    143, 196

Brain, 49–51, 71–72, 95
Brando, Marlon, 97
Brashears, Matthew, 210
Breakup, 96–97, 196
Breakdown, 5, 8, 10–11, 43, 144–146,
    209, 212, 219
Brookings Institution, 173
Brokeback Mountain, 97
Brown, David, 46
Brown, Helen Gurley, 7, 44–46
Brown, Michael L., 180
Browning, Robert and Elizabeth
    Barret, 26
Brutus, 213
Bush, Freda McKissic, 58
Butterhorn Bakery and Café,
    108–109

Caesar, 213
California, 9, 50, 95, 167, 185, 195–196,
    201
Canadian, 174
Cancer, 99–100, 104, 122, 125
Capital, 11, 73, 115, 148
Capitol, 74
Career, 2, 29, 43–45, 58, 66–67, 73, 76,
    83, 92–93, 119, 126, 168, 171, 192, 195,
    200, 212
Case Against Divorce, The, 127
"Case Against Marriage, The," 89
Case for Marriage, The, 162
Cassidy, Eva, 20
"Catalog of Risks, A," 132
Catholic Charities of Boston, 177
Cattrall, Kim, 211, 216
CBS, 130
Celibacy, 82
Census Bureau, 3, 10, 210
Centers for Disease Control and Preven-
    tion (CDC), 8, 54–55, 57, 100, 104,
    161–162, 195
Center for Law and Social Policy, 173
Chaplains, 192–193
Chesterton, G.K., 209
Chicken Little, 152
Chick-fil-A, 218
Children, 1–7, 9–12, 22–23, 28–29, 52,
    54, 58, 67, 71, 73, 76, 78–79, 81, 83,
    92–93, 97, 102, 106–107, 109, 115–118,
    121, 124, 128–129, 131, 139–153,
    161–168, 170, 172–175, 177–180, 184,

Index

186–187,192, 194, 196, 199, 201–203, 209, 211, 215–216, 218–219
"Brokerage of children," 172
Child Protective Services (CPS), 143
Children at *Risk*, 131, 201
Children's Defense Fund, 141
Children's Society, 148
Child Trends, 173
Chlamydia, *see sexually transmitted diseases (STDs)*
Christianity, 6–7, 53–54, 81, 109, 121, 144, 174–175, 184, 188, 217
Chronicle of Higher Education, *The*, 48
Church, 3, 39–40, 93, 122, 167, 177, 213
Cicero, Marcus Tullius, 163
Cinderella, 216
Cinnamon Pass, 108
Civil union, 177, 185
Clarkson, Kelly, 59
Clayton, Dr. Obie, 126, 129
Cleaver, June, 5
Clement, Paul, 188–189
Clinton, Bill, 188, 192
CNN, 1, 19, 119
Cohabitation, 3, 24, 40, 79, 117–123, 128–129, 131–132, 140, 143, 149–150, 166, 171, 173, 180, 196, 199, 203, 211
Cohen, Bernard, 132
College, 4, 24, 40–44, 46–48, 54–55, 57–58, 71, 79, 89, 92, 98–100, 102–103, 108–109, 118, 126–127, 146, 168, 202
Collins, Senator Susan M., 190
Colorado, 108
Commitment, 1, 17–19, 23, 30–31, 35–36, 45, 48, 50, 53, 68, 79, 90, 92, 107–109, 121–123, 130, 145, 153, 163, 196, 212, 215, 217
Communication, 21–22, 41, 43, 72, 123, 165–166, 168, 212, 218
Community, 2, 22–23, 26, 79, 82, 118, 127, 130, 144–146, 153, 193, 212, 217–219
Companionship, 44, 131, 217
Concerned Women for America, 11, 100
Condom, *see contraception*
Conflict, 18, 26, 29, 31, 68, 79, 83–84, 202, 214, 218
Confusion, 10, 78, 95
Congress, 6, 10, 74, 186, 189–190, 192, 197–198, 200

Congressional Research Service, 197
Conjugal view (of marriage), 76, 163–164, 175–176
Connecticut, 168
Consequences, 4, 8, 11, 25, 28, 32, 44, 51–54, 57–58, 68, 78–81, 95, 98, 100, 118, 142, 144, 165, 176, 179, 183–186, 194, 209
Conservative, 3, 9, 74, 90, 127, 151, 171, 178
Contraception, 46, 51, 57, 101–102
Birth control, 46, 57
Condom, 90, 95, 99, 102, 147, 193
Cortisol, 67
Cosmopolitan, 45, 93
Courtship, 35, 46, 60, 68
Crime, 5, 11, 120, 123, 127, 129, 144, 150, 174
"Crocodile Hunter, The," 103
Crouse, Janice Shaw, 206, 220–224
Crucifixion, 75
Cruise, Tom, 18, 128
Crutcher, Mark, 198
Culture, 4, 8, 10, 25, 33, 39–40, 46–48, 53, 55–58, 65, 71, 75, 78, 81–82, 90, 94–95, 97, 101–102, 106, 117, 124–125, 140, 142, 145–146, 148–149, 152–153, 163–165, 170–171, 173, 177, 179, 183–184, 187, 198, 204, 213–214
Currie, Dr. Dave, 73

Dark Knight, The, 97
Dating, 10, 35, 39–44, 46–47, 55, 58–60, 81, 209
"Bring Dating Back" Facebook group, 59
Davis, Michele Weiner, 66, 72
Dean, James, 97
"Dear Abby," 94
Death, 18, 28–31, 75, 77, 84, 89, 96–97, 103, 109, 123, 143, 196, 217
Declaration of Independence, 6–7
Defense of Marriage Act (DOMA), 183–189
"Defining Deviancy Down," 8
Delaware, 185
Democracy, 5, 11, 153, 183
Department of Education, *see education*
Department of Health and Human Services, *see United States Department of Health and Human Services*

Department of Justice, 120, 127, 188
Dependency, 166–167
Depression, 47, 57, 67, 91, 95, 97–98, 121, 125, 167, 203
Detroit, 94
Diaz, Cameron, 18
Dickenson, Emily, 17, 26
Dines, Gail, 70
DINS (Double Income, No Sex) Syndrome, 67
Divorce, 3, 5, 24–25, 30, 46, 66–67, 76, 97, 106, 109, 118, 122, 125–129, 131–132, 152, 161–162, 166, 199, 202–203, 207, 217
    "No-fault," 92, 124, 201–203
DNA, 77
"Do Fathers and Mothers Matter?", 172
Donnelly, Denise A., 72
Donovan, Chuck 117, 183, 185, 192
"Don't Ask, Don't Tell" (DADT), 192–193
Drinking, 42, 53, 89–90, 127, 167
Dr. Phil, 65
Du jour, 74
Duke University, 164

Eating disorders, 95
Eat, Pray, Love, 119
Eberstadt, Mary, 69
Economy, 56, 199–200, 214
Education, 5, 48, 90, 118, 120, 125–126, 143–144, 148, 150, 161, 166, 177, 198, 200, 202
    Department of Education, 147
    National Center for Education Statistics (NCES), 147
    Public education, 1, 147
    Educational benefits of marriage, 4, 146
    Abstinence education, 57, 193–194
    Sex education, 57, 81, 90, 102, 193–194
Ellison, Jesse, 89
Employment Non-Discrimination Act (ENDA), 189–192
Eminem, 25–26
Emotions, 8, 17–18, 22, 25–26, 31–32, 43, 48, 50–54, 56, 58, 66, 69–72, 74–75, 77–82, 91–92, 94–98, 107–109, 116–117, 119, 121–123, 125, 128–131, 139, 143, 148, 150–151, 162, 166–168, 172, 175, 211, 214

Employment, 9, 125, 129–130, 189–191, 202, 215
Engineer Pass, 108
Entertainment, 40–41, 52, 70, 97, 120
Equality, 77–78, 99, 171, 175, 189,
    "Equal rights", 171–172
Epidemic: How Teen Sex is Killing Our Kids, 90
Eucharist, 116
ET, 149
European, 28, 174, 193
Evangelicals, 39
Expectations, 18, 67, 81, 84, 119, 166
Experimentation, 11, 49, 53–54, 77–78, 90, 93, 98, 102, 169, 173, 183, 203, 214
Exploitation, 70, 106, 142

Facebook, 59, 148
Faith, 9, 74, 122, 132, 174, 177, 187, 213
Family, 1–2, 4–6, 8–11, 18, 20, 24, 26, 28–29, 39, 47, 49, 56, 71, 74, 77, 79–80, 84, 92–93, 109, 115, 117–118, 124, 127, 129, 131–132, 139–149, 151–153, 161, 164–168, 172–173, 176, 178–179, 183, 186–187, 196, 199, 203, 209–212, 214, 217–219
Family Research Council, 177, 190
Family Violence Research Program, 120
Fatherhood, 2, 4, 6, 46, 73, 78–79, 97, 107, 109, 128, 139–140, 142, 144–145, 148, 150–151, 165–168, 173–174, 178, 184, 196, 201
Fear, 17, 26, 30–32, 36, 53–54, 71–72, 105, 107, 143, 183, 219
Feminism, 7, 26, 28, 34, 40, 46, 49, 52, 78, 90, 94, 164, 214, 216
Fertility, 92–93, 99–100
Fidelity, 27, 58, 73, 79, 82, 218
Fiennes, Ralph, 34
"Fifteen" 59
Finances, 1, 5, 9, 11, 19, 57, 119–120, 125, 128–131, 194–196, 199–202, 218
"First bond of society," 163
First Things, 65, 69
Flanagan, Caitlin, 1–2, 7, 82–83
Flapper, 90
Flirting, 31, 73, 75
Florida, 8, 91–93, 185
"Food Pyramid," 79
Forgiveness, 22–23, 40, 54, 82–84, 141
Fortune, 11, 84, 190–191
Forward, G.L., 166

Foster care, 5, 150
France, 102
Frank, Rep. Barney, 190
"Friends with benefits," 90
Frisco, 108
Frum, David, 165, 180
Fulfillment, 17–18, 23–24, 26, 30, 32, 73, 76, 79, 82–83, 145, 153, 173, 204, 212, 217, 220
"Full faith and credit," 184
Future of Marriage, The, 162
Fry, Richard, 126

Gallagher, Maggie, 13, 133–136, 161–162, 180
Gandhi, Mahatma, 180
Garden of Eden, 76
Gates, Bill, 146
Gay, *see GLBT*
Gay, Lesbian, Bisexual, Transgender (GLBT), 191
    Gay, 5, 46, 101, 161, 163, 165, 168–170, 172, 174, 176, 178–179, 181–182, 189–191, 216
    Homosexual, 101, 103–104, 136, 162, 165, 168–169, 171–177, 180–181, 184–193, 195, 205
    Lesbian, 101, 161, 163, 177, 191
    Bisexual, 104, 169, 179, 191
    Transgender, 189, 191
"Gay quota bill," 191
Gelertner, David, 200
Gender, 48, 69, 78, 98–99, 119–120, 122, 136, 166, 168, 189–191, 193
    Gender identity, 189–191
    Gender neutrality, 69
General Social Survey (GSS), 65, 85, 210–211, 220
Generation, 2, 8, 11, 27–28, 30, 39, 41, 45, 51, 58–60, 78, 81, 93–94, 124, 144–145, 152–154, 180, 184, 186, 202, 204, 211, 213, 217, 220
Geneva, 10
George, Robert P., 59, 140, 154, 163, 175, 182
Georgia State University, 72
Germany, 102
Gibbon, Edward, 144
Gibran, Kahlil, 163
Gilbert, Elizabeth, 119, 133
Gilder, George, 127, 135

Girgis, Sherif, 163, 175, 180, 182
Girlfriend, 48, 83, 211, 216
"Girls Need a Dad and Boys Need a Mom," 165, 181, 223
"Give-and-take," 167
Glamour, 59–61
Gnostic, 75
God, 6, 18–19, 21, 31–32, 39, 49–50, 54, 61, 68, 75–76, 80, 84–85, 89, 99, 109–110, 214, 216–217, 219
    Creator, 21–22, 54, 75–76, 105
    Christ, 76, 219
    Heavenly Father, 75
    Image Deo, 22
    Son, 75
Goethe, Johann Wolfgang von, 95, 139
Golden Globe Award, 211
Goldberg, Arthur, 162, 180
"Golden Arches," *see McDonald's*
Golden Rule, 145, 166
Gonorrhea, *see sexually transmitted diseases (STDs)*
Good Childhood, A: Searching for Values in a Competitive Age, 148
Good Girl Revolution, The: Young Rebels with Self-Esteem and High Standards, 58
Google, 86, 106, 135
Government, 3, 9, 13, 57, 124, 139, 150, 153, 161–162, 176, 183–184, 186–187, 191, 197–199, 206
Graham, Billy, 30, 32–33, 37, 224
Graham, Ruth, 32–33, 224
Grassroots, 66
Great Recession, 130–131, 137
Green, Eddie, 89
Grief, 96, 115
Grisham, John, 28
Gross Domestic Product, 146
Grossman, Dr. Miriam, 58, 95, 98–100, 103–105, 111
Guilt, 52, 66, 74, 78, 99, 143

Hair, 4
Happiness, 1–2, 5, 7, 19, 21, 24, 27, 31, 33, 45, 47–48, 51, 54, 66, 68–69, 73, 82–83, 91, 93, 96, 109, 115, 121–122, 125, 128, 130, 132, 139, 143, 153, 166, 173, 194, 202, 209, 211, 217
"Happy Mother," 139
Harris, Joshua, 40, 60
Hartzler, Rep. Vicky, 188

Harvard Gazette, 123
Harvard University, 13, 134, 216
Hawaii, 185, 187, 204
Health, 2–3, 8, 12, 76, 95, 98–101, 105, 118, 130, 136, 143, 146, 151, 162, 166–167, 169, 174, 181, 197–199, 207, 211
   Health benefits of marriage, 4, 117–119, 122–125, 128–129, 139
   Health consequences, risks, concerns, 53, 67, 90, 100, 107, 109, 128, 150, 173, 176–177, 203
   "Healthy Marriage Initiative," 199
   In sickness and in health, 19, 23
   Massachusetts Youth Health Survey,
   Mental health, 2, 4, 34, 95–96, 124, 150, 170
   National Health Statistics Reports (NHSR), 100, 162
   Public health, 103–104
Heart, 7, 12, 20, 23, 28–31, 36, 46, 51, 58, 82, 97, 106–107, 109, 111, 115–116, 125, 141, 163, 216, 219
   Heartache, 95
   Heartbreak, 77–79, 96, 108
   Heart Sense for Women, 72
   Heartrending, 103
Herbert Humphrey Building, 139
Heritage Foundation, The, 6, 12, 111, 117, 132, 173, 183, 185, 189, 192, 204–206
Herpes, *see sexually transmitted diseases (STDs)*
High school, 40–44, 55, 59, 89, 101, 109, 152, 194, 202
History of the Decline and Fall of the Roman Empire, The, 144
HIV, 99, 101, 103–105, 134, 176–177, 209, 220–221
Hollywood, 4, 17, 30, 40, 49, 70, 102, 171, 214
"Holy estate, a," 219
Holy Matrimony, 219
Home of the Unities, The, 209
Homosexual, see GLBT
Hookup, 3, 10, 30, 41, 46–48, 51, 55, 57–59, 95, 209
   Hooking Up: Sex, Dating, and Relationships on Campus, 58
   "I Don't Hook Up," 59
Hoover Institute, 179
Hormones, 55, 81, 151

House Administration Committee, 188
House Counsel, 188
Households
   Married-couple family, 4, 6, 139–141, 161, 165, 173, 198, 216
   Unmarried-Couple Households, 154
   Single-parent households, 2, 52, 117–118, 121, 124, 129, 131, 140–143, 145, 147, 149–152, 173, 178, 199–200, 211–212
House Judiciary Committee, 177, 182, 185
Howard Center, 11
Howard University, 126
Human papillomavirus (HPV), see *sexually transmitted diseases*
Hugo, Victor, 115
Hugs, 77
Hyde amendment, 197

I Don't Care about Your Band, 58
I Kissed Dating Goodbye, 40, 60
Illegitimacy, 150–152
Illinois, 185, 197
Image, 6, 22–23, 34, 54, 61, 65, 69, 75, 110–111, 115–116, 141, 181, 206, 225
   Image Deo, 22
Income, 9, 13, 57, 67, 125–126, 129–130, 196, 202
Indiana, 5, 172, 185, 197
Indiana University, 5
In loco parentis, 4
Institute for American Values, 130–131, 135, 137, 162, 173
Institute on Religion and Democracy, 11
International Social Survey Programme, 170
Internet, 39, 60, 70–71, 149, 154
Intimacy, 18, 31–32, 36, 42, 49–54, 66–69, 71–72, 75–78, 81–83, 94–95, 98, 105, 107, 130, 163, 211
Iowa, 131, 168, 185
Irwin, Steve, 103

Jerry Maguire, 128
Jewish, 174
Joe Millionaire, see TV shows
Journal of Communication and Religion (JCR), 165–166, 181

Joy, Dr. Donald, 51, 94
Judeo-Christian, 7, 53–54, 81, 144, 184, 217

King, Larry, 19, 30, 37
King & Spalding, 188
Kissing, 40, 75
Klausner, Julie, 58
Knight, Robert, 110, 169, 181, 191, 205
Kurtz, Stanley, 164, 177–179, 182

Lady Gaga, 59
Lake City, 108
Lapin, Rabbi Daniel, 211, 220
"Latch-key" kids, 149
Lawler, Peter, 6, 13
Laws (Plato), 144
Layden, Mary Ann, 70–71
Ledger, Heath, 96
Lee, I-Sing, 132, 135
Leman, Kevin, 73, 86
Lenin, Vladimir, 145
Lesbian, *see Gay, Lesbian, Bisexual, Transgender (GLBT)*
"Let's call the whole thing off," 69
"Let's Talk About Me," 214
Lewis, Ray, 151–152, 157
Liberty Counsel, 188, 205
Liberty University School of Law, 188
Liebau, Carol Platt, 25, 36, 58
Life Dynamics, 198
Light in the Closet, 162, 180
"Linchpin," 212
Lipinski, Dan, 197
Locke, John, 6
Loh, Sandra Tsing, 69, 86
Los Angeles Times, 99
Love and Fidelity Network, 58
Love Potion Number Nine, 49
"Lower nature," 75

McManus, Michael, 203
Madrid, 10
Magic, 77–78, 105, 199, 216
  "Magic moment," 199, 216
Manipulation, 44, 106
Mantra, 77, 93, 98, 103, 214
Marquardt, Elizabeth, 172–174, 178, 203
"Marriage premium," 129
Marriage Problem, The, 140

Maryland, 8, 185
Masefield, John, 39, 41
Massachusetts, 168, 174, 176
  Massachusetts Youth Health Survey, 8
Mathewes-Green, Frederica, 31
McDonald's, 8, 148
  "Golden Arches," 148
McGovern, Jordanna, 166
McIlhaney, Joe Jr., 58
McPhearson, Miller, 210
Mea culpa, 74
Media, 1, 4, 10, 21, 40, 55, 59, 74, 89–90, 93, 97, 100, 120, 122, 142, 148–149, 168–169, 187, 190, 218–219
Medved, Diane, 127
Meeker, Dr. Meg, 58, 90, 98, 100
Men and Marriage, 127
Merkley, Senator Jeff, 190
Messner, Thomas M., 189
Mexico City, 10
Michigan, 90
Microsoft, 146
Middleton, Catherine "Kate," 219
Minnesota, 185
Miscarriage, 93
Mistreatment, 21, 76, 106, 143
Mohler, Dr. Al, 89
Money, 9, 84, 121, 125, 129, 131, 146, 165, 172, 198
  "Money and Marriage," 131
  MoneyWatch, 130
Monogamy, 9, 27, 50, 163, 175–176
Moores, Marilyn Ann, 172
Morality, 3, 7, 13, 18, 26, 39–40, 53–54, 60, 78–79, 82, 93, 102, 107, 118, 139, 144–148, 153, 162, 166, 174–176, 183, 186–187, 191, 193, 201, 217
Morehouse College, 126
Morse, Dr. Jennifer Roback, 59
Moscow, 10
Moynihan, Senator Daniel Patrick, 8, 150
"Mr. Big," 91–92, 110
"Mr. Right," 30, 92, 216
MTV, 57, 78, 194
Muslim, 174
Mystery, 28, 30, 77–78, 83, 105
Myth, 51, 75, 78, 90, 93, 97, 99, 102–103, 119, 124, 126, 139, 142, 153, 170–171, 173–174, 176–177, 214, 222

National Association for Research and Therapy of Homosexuality (NARTH), 169
National Bureau of Economic Research, 69
National Campaign to Prevent Teen Pregnancy, 194
National Center for Education Statistics (NCES), *see education*
National Center for Health Statistics (NCHS), 101, 151, 166–167, 181, 207
National Football League (NFL), 151
National Health and Social Life Survey (NHSLS), 12, 128, 133, 136
National Health Statistics Reports (NHSR), 100–101, 162
National Marriage Project, 9, 130–131
National Longitudinal Study of Adolescent Health, 3
National Opinion Research Center (University of Chicago), 66
National Organization for Women, 201
National Press Club, 70
National Science Foundation (NSF), 210–211
National Survey of Family Growth, 101
NBC, 90
Netherlands, 65, 71
New Hampshire, 120
New Jersey, 172, 197
Newlywed, 75
New Science on How Casual Sex is Affecting Our Children, 58
Newsweek, 65–66, 89, 93, 109
New York, 201–202
New York State Catholic Conference, 201
New York Times, 102, 117, 119
Nike, 190
"No Child Left Behind," 146
Nock, Steven L., 121–122
Norweigan, 125
"No Taxpayer Funding for Abortion Act," 197
Notre Dame, 55, 59
Novak, Michael, 117
Nutrition, 76, 79

Obama, Barack, 8, 187–188, 192, 197, 200, 221–222
ObamaCare, 197, 222

Office of Personnel Management (OPM), 191
Olympic, 33
One News Now, 198
Ophir Pass, 108
Outb, Sayyid, 34
Out-of-wedlock pregnancies and births, 30, 55, 91, 120, 140, 142, 150–152, 178, 203, 210
Oxytocin, 49–51, 72, 94–96

Painted House, A, 28
Pas de deux, 92
Passeron, Jean-Claude, 148
Passion, 1, 13, 18, 26, 31–32, 36, 67, 72–73, 75–76, 83–84, 95, 98, 105, 107, 120, 189, 219
Patterson, Robert W., 5
Paul, Pamela, 70–71
Pearsall, Paul, 52
Pedophiles, 191
Pence, Congressman Mike, 197
Pennsylvania State University, 5
People, 90
Personal Responsibility and Work Opportunity Reconciliation Act of 1996, 6
"Person A," 168
"Person B," 168
Peterson, Bruce, 199
PET scans, 71–72
Pew Research Center, 5, 56, 126, 130–131
Philadelphia, 173
Philosophy, 3, 45, 53, 82, 93, 95, 117, 163–164, 199
"Piece of paper" (marriage), 92, 120, 144, 161
Pizza Hut, 149
Planned Parenthood, 57, 90, 101, 194, 197–198, 206
Plato, 65, 95, 144
Playboy, 4, 70, 93
Political correctness, 95, 99, 103–105, 121, 126, 132, 151, 184
Polygamy, 172, 179
Popenoe, David, 9, 119, 123, 133, 178
Popeye the Sailor, 150
"Popeye Moments," 152
Population, 5, 17, 41, 55, 127, 136, 141, 155, 169, 195, 200, 213
Population Association conference, 132

Pornography, 69–71, 73
Pornified: How Pornography is Damaging Our Lives, Our Relationships and Our Families, 70
Pornland: How Porn has Hijacked our Sexuality, 70
Wired for Intimacy: How Pornography Hijacks the Male Brain, 71
Poverty, 3, 5, 118, 120, 124, 130, 141–142, 149–150, 199–201
Powell, Brian, 5
Powell, General Colin, 183
Prague, 10
Prairie vole, 50
Pregnant, 39, 58, 77, 90–91, 93, 101–102, 109, 120, 173, 200
Pregnant Widow, The, 200
16 and Pregnant, see TV shows
Prince Charming, 27
Princeton University, 59, 70, 164, 173
Prince William, 219
"pro-choice," *see abortion*
"pro-life," *see abortion*
Professional Psychology, 57
Promiscuity, 4, 21, 27, 30, 39–40, 45–47, 51–53, 56–58, 60, 69, 79, 82, 89, 95, 98, 102, 105, 123, 145, 170, 194, 196
Proposition 8 (Prop. 8), 9, 195
Prostitution, 105
Prude: How the Sex-Obsessed Culture Damages Girls, 25, 58
Psychology Today, 65, 72
Public policy, 11, 48, 144, 164, 183, 185, 193, 195, 197, 210, 217–218
Public schools, 90, 146–147, 174, 177
Pulitzer Prize, 102
Putnam, Robert, 212

Queer Thing Happened To America, A, 180
Quindlen, Anna, 102

Raising Boys Without Men, 151
Rape, 34, 36, 107
Raum, Brian, 188
Regnerus, Mark, 55
Reisser, Teri, 196
Religiosity, 3, 6–7, 9, 11, 13, 39–40, 54, 74, 82, 99, 132, 147, 153, 165–167, 170, 174–175, 177, 179, 187, 189–190, 192–193, 218

Reproduction, 5, 50, 186
"Reproductive alliance," 140
Return to Modesty, A: Discovering the Lost Virtue, 58
Revisionist view (of marriage), 163–164, 175
Rhoades, Steven E., 48
Rhode Island House Judiciary Committee, 177
Right to Life League, 196
Rihanna, 25
Roberts, Alex, 130–131
Robertson, Lisa, 34
Rocky Mountains/Rockies, 107–108
Romance, 10, 17, 19, 24–25, 27, 29–31, 33–35, 48, 60, 69, 75, 84, 95–96, 209, 216, 219
Romeo and Juliet, 26, 75
Ros-Lehtinen, Rep. Ileana, 190
Rouse Chamberlin Homes, 211
Rutgers University, 9, 50, 178
Ruth Institute, The, 59

Safety, 4, 8, 12, 28, 41, 43, 49, 54, 72, 76, 107, 109, 119–122, 130, 140–142, 144–145, 149, 153, 164, 167, 193, 199–201
Salon, 59, 65
San Diego State University, 48
Sansom-Livolsi, Alison, 166
Sara Lee, 190
Satinover, Jeffrey, 164, 174
Scandinavia, 171, 176–177
Schmitz, Charles, 72
Schmitz, Elizabeth, 72
Schwartz, Dr. Pepper, 67
"Searchers," 49
Self-esteem, 34, 42, 51, 58, 148, 153, 167
Selfish, 73, 76, 106, 127, 143, 214
Senate Committee on Health, Education, Labor and Pensions, 118
"Settle down," 124, 130
Sex
  Casual, 3–4, 10, 40–42, 48–49, 51–53, 58, 65, 72, 78, 82, 89, 91, 93–95, 97–98, 100–101, 103, 105, 107, 123, 209, 211
  "Making love," 34–36, 68, 77, 107
  Oral sex, 91, 101, 162
  "Safe sex," 193
  Sex and the City, 40, 91, 94, 211, 216
  Sex and the Single Girl, 44
  "Sex Pyramid," 79, 81–82, 217

Sex (*continued*)
  Same-sex "marriage," 3, 7, 11, 101,
    161–179, 184–185, 190, 193, 195,
    209, 221
  Sex-Starved Marriage, The, 66
  Sexual freedom, 11, 52, 77, 90, 92,
    209, 211
  Sexual innocence, 69, 91, 143
  Sexual intercourse, 25, 31, 34–35,
    39, 42, 54, 57, 77, 82, 94, 105–106
  Sexuality Information and Education
    Council of the United States
    (SIECUS), 90
  Sexually repressed, 47, 53
  Sexual orientation, 99, 147, 169–170,
    183, 189–191
  Sexual revolution, 4, 39, 46, 48, 53,
    65, 82, 100, 102, 179
  Sexually transmitted diseases (STDs),
    52, 57–58, 78, 81, 90–91, 98–102,
    123, 129, 162, 194, 209, 218
    Chlamydia, 58, 99–100
    Herpes, 58, 91, 100
  Human papillomavirus (HPV), 58,
    99, 176
    Gonorrhea, 58, 91, 100
  Sexually transmitted infections
    (STIs), 99–101
Shalit, Wendy, 58
Silver Star, 115
Silverton, 108
Simon, Robin, 96
Sinatra, Frank, 25, 36
Sinatra, Jan, 36, 72
Single by Chance, Mothers by Choice,
  151
Sisterhood, 106, 211
Slippery slope, 179
Slouching towards Gomorrah, 145
Slut, 40, 52, 60
  Slut Walk, 52
Smith, Adam, 5
Smith, Rep. Chris, 197
Smith-Lovin, Lynn, 210
Smoking, 53, 78, 89–90, 95
Social Norming Theory, 202
Social science research, 2, 12, 67, 79, 117,
  121, 125, 139, 151, 161, 164–165, 173,
  176, 178, 187, 209, 218
Society, 1–11, 19, 22, 44, 79, 85, 93, 95,
  139–140, 144–148, 150, 152, 162–165,
  170–173, 176–179, 184, 186–187, 194,
  202, 204, 210–212, 217–219
Sorokin, Pitirim A., 171
South Carolina, 108
Spalding, Matthew, 6
Sperm bank, 165, 186
Spinoza, 74
SportsCenter, 83
Sprigg, Peter, 177, 190
Stanton, Elizabeth Cady, 1
Stanton, Glenn T., 10
Starbucks, 66
Staver, Mathew, 188
Steinem, Gloria, 7
Steinhauer, Jennifer, 117, 132–133
Stepp, Laura Sessions, 58
Stets, Dr. Jan, 120
Steyn, Mark, 65
Stress, 50–52, 67–68, 73, 83–84, 96, 98,
  119, 123, 125, 168, 170
Struthers, William, 71
Subcommittee on Children and
  Families, 118
Sugrue, Seana, 179
Surrogate, 124, 165, 172, 174
Suicide, 91, 98–99, 118, 121, 123,
  129
Sunum bonum, 107
Super Bowl, 151
Super-Marital Sex: Loving for Life, 52
Sweden, 102, 178
Swift, Taylor, 59

Tada, Joni Eareckson, 19
Taxpayers, 5, 144, 150, 177, 195–197,
  201
Telluride, 108
Temporary Assistance for Needy Families
  (TANF), *see welfare*
Temptation, 52–53, 74–76, 121
"Ten Principles," 119, 121
"THE TALK," 79
Think tank, 11, 117, 173, 181, 183
"Throwaway kids," 142
"Till death do us part," 18, 31, 84, 109,
  217
Time magazine, 1, 7, 65, 89, 129
Title X, 198
"Tolerance," 162
Tom, Terrance, 185
"Torrid," 73–76